TIFFANY!

WHAT A PLEASURE

TO SHARE THIS

Modern Greek
Cooking

BOOK WITH YOU!

KEEP UP THE

GREAT COOKING!

[signature]

Modern Greek Cooking

100 Recipes for
Meze,
Entrées,
and
Desserts

PANO KARATASSOS

WRITTEN WITH **JANE SIGAL**

PHOTOGRAPHS BY **FRANCESCO TONELLI**

FOREWORD BY **THOMAS KELLER**

RIZZOLI
NEW YORK

New York · Paris · London · Milan

I want to dedicate this book to my precious children Pano Alexander, Lucas, and Sophia, for their undying support of my hopes and dreams and for understanding that no matter how hard I work, they always come first.

First published in the United States of
America in 2018
by Rizzoli International Publications, Inc.
300 Park Avenue South
New York, NY 10010
www.rizzoliusa.com

© 2018 Pano Karatassos

Photography © 2018 Francesco Tonelli

Written with Jane Sigal
Project editor: Tricia Levi
Copyeditor: Lisa Leventer
Design by Jan Derevjanik

2018 2019 2020 2021 / 10 9 8 7 6 5 4 3 2 1

Distributed in the U.S. trade by
Random House, New York

Printed in China

ISBN-13: 978-0-8478-6144-6

Library of Congress Catalog Control Number:
2018943334

COOKING THE RECIPES

The recipes in *Modern Greek Cooking* represent the way I cook at Kyma. The focus is on a core collection of Greek-inspired recipes you can prepare at home. I stayed away from anything too complicated and recipes that require professional equipment. I adapted some of the recipes for the ease of the home cook.

For anyone who wants to go beyond the safe and familiar, there's a whole chapter of octopus recipes. I give instructions for exactly how to replicate the octopus preparations you'd experience at my restaurant. Other recipes are ambitious from an ingredient standpoint. You may need to search beyond your local supermarket, visiting markets and online vendors that specialize in Greek ingredients, but I'll guide you. I include notes about each recipe, explain the ingredients and techniques in detail, and provide serving suggestions.

In this cookbook, I made the choice to emphasize meze, small dishes that are a way of life as much as a food category. These little appetizers are meant to be shared. Each meze recipe makes two plates and serves four people. I suggest that you prepare three recipes of meze followed by one entrée recipe for four guests. This way, you and your guests can share the meze family style before settling down to enjoy your entrée and dessert. At Kyma we have at least 25 meze revolving on the menu at all times, and I have devoted

half of this cookbook to them. If one of the more complex meze recipe seems too time consuming to prepare as an appetizer, you can always double that recipe to create four entrée servings. As written, each of these meze would also work perfectly as an entrée for two. You'll find that these recipes are wonderfully versatile.

To give you a sense of how to compose an irresistible modern Greek meal, I offer suggestions for how to pair the recipes throughout. But these recipes will also fit seamlessly into a meal that's not exclusively Greek. For instance, try one of the spreads or vegetarian meze alongside a simple roast pork loin or grilled sausages. Or experiment: stuff Braised Red Wine Meatballs with Tomato Compote (page 103) into a baguette; tuck them into pasta; or use them as the meat in a hearty stew.

Greek dining is about sharing with family and friends, drinking excellent wine, listening to great music, and eating healthy, tasty and beautiful food! I hope you enjoy my story and I invite you to cook and share these recipes!

CONTENTS

FOREWORD

Pano Karatassos's sense memories of cooking with his grandmother Athanasia Tissura as a young child, his aunts in Athens, Greece, and his restaurateur father Ignatius Pano Karatassos at their restaurant Kyma, became the inspiration for *Modern Greek Cooking*. For Pano, cooking is about making memories and connecting with the past. With his family. With his Greek heritage. And now he's sharing those memories with us.

Awareness makes good chefs into great chefs. It's a strength I noticed in Pano at The French Laundry. He went about his work with an awareness of food's broader context—with a respect for the techniques he had learned from other great chefs like Eric Ripert and Jean-Georges Vongerichten and with an appreciation for the provenance of ingredients. He joined the line with great humility and curiosity and showed a deep appreciation for the stories of our purveyors. He often shared memories of his own culinary upbringing at festive family gatherings around shared plates of classic Greek salad, grilled eggplant spread, stuffed grape leaves with cumin yogurt, and grilled octopus.

Through the senses, the recipes in *Modern Greek Cooking* open our minds to a new level of awareness. An awareness of Greek food and of Pano as a chef rooted in both tradition and technique. He pays attention to the authenticity, the flavors, and relevance of his heritage, while using modern techniques and an instinct to, as he describes, "take Greek food to the next level."

Pano calls food "Greek Inspiration"—and you'll certainly be inspired to dine as the book encourages you to do so—with lots of shared plates (reaching is encouraged). You might start with meze and move on to entrées. Zucchini and feta fritters followed by Mussels Diane with Sour Pasta Pearls and Lamb Phyllo Spirals. But he's not dogmatic in his approach. Rather, there's a warm invitation to make his book your own. My favorites include two dishes I tried at Kyma—the Roasted Beet Salad with Manouri Cream and Buttered Walnuts, where the various temperatures of the beets in different preparations are sure to delight, and the Braised Whole Fish with Tomatoes, Garlic, and Onions. Or you can focus on a meal crafted around an assortment of meze from spreads to salads, such as the Yellow Split Pea Spread or the Lemony Quinoa Salad. And don't forget Homemade Pita, a recipe that is approachable rather than intimidating. Each recipe, moreover, includes an education on Greek grapes by Pano's cousin Sofia Perpera and is followed by a detailed wine pairing and a list of suggested Greek wineries. You'll soon recognize that *Modern Greek Cooking* is more of a memoir, mixing recipes with stories of Pano's childhood and reminders of his grandmother's influence.

When I asked Pano of his plans after his time in Yountville (as I do with all young culinarians who join us), he explained that although he would eventually return to work for his father, he wanted to be hired for his skill rather than because of nepotism. I would like to think he has earned his laurels.

Pano's strong sense of family and reverence for his cultural heritage shine through every page. The sense memories we form through a heightened awareness of the world around us are those that stay with us the longest. And these memories, which bring us back to the people with whom we've shared a meal, a moment, an experience, are the most important of all. Cooks cook to nurture. Pano is nurturing in a way that make both is father and his yia yia proud.

—THOMAS KELLER,
chef/proprietor,
The French Laundry

INTRODUCTION

The smell of sweet garlic and onion simmering in olive oil captures me. The sound of green beans and chunky potatoes bubbling in tomato sauce brings me to a halt. I close my eyes in these moments, remembering, as I listen for my yia yia's words, "What does it need? More seasoning? More salt? More lemon? The sensory memories of cooking with her are why I'm a chef; they are the source of the true joy cooking offers me and, if it wasn't for my grandmother Athanasia, I might not have written this cookbook.

I was born in Savannah, Georgia, and lived in Lake Ozarks, Missouri, until I was eight. I guess you could say my younger brother Niko and I were like Tom Sawyer and Tarzan, spending all day in the woods, swinging on vines, and not coming home till nightfall. My father, Ignatius Pano Karatassos, worked seven days a week at the Lodge of Four Seasons, as chef, food and beverage manager, and assistant hotel manager. Raised by our unselfish, loving mother, Georgia, we had plenty of time to mess around, especially with my older sister Anne, who dressed us up and fed us mud pies—boy did they look real!

Between the line dances, neckerchiefs, and barbecue ribs, I had no idea what my Greek heritage meant until we moved back to Atlanta, Georgia, when I was eight years old. My maternal grandmother Athanasia Tissura moved in with us, one mile south of the Greek Orthodox Cathedral. Between spending time with my yia yia every day and going to Greek church on Sundays, I learned I was a Greek American with roots in former Asia Minor, now Western Turkey. Both my paternal and maternal grandparents left Asia Minor after the Greco-Turkish War in the early 1920s and settled on the islands of Lesvos and Skiathos. Soon after, my grandparents sailed to the United States, and Savannah, Georgia, became their new home.

Sharing our home with my grandmother while my father grew a restaurant empire and my mother was busy raising three kids was always a culinary adventure. Whether watching her fuss at the grocery store clerk about the five-cent increase on zucchini or sitting at the table stuffing tomatoes while a stew of cow's tongue was simmering away, there was never a dull moment. My mother was and is an incredible cook, but my yia yia ran the house like a chef, finishing braises and sauces prepped the day before and setting herself up for the next day. Even my father, a graduate of the Culinary Institute of America (CIA), valedictorian of his apprenticeship at The Greenbrier, and eventual chef-owner-creator of 20 critically acclaimed and successful restaurants in Atlanta and South Florida, would come home between shifts to eat her cooking. For him, it was like returning to his childhood home, as his mother, my other yia yia, Theone, was an incredible cook too. Hence, my life revolved around cooking; my yia yia's and mother's home-cooked meals and my father's restaurants each filled my body and soul with beautiful foods, especially those from Greece.

I joined the restaurant business at age 15. Dad called me into his office and, with a stern look, demanded, "Summer is almost here, and I'm giving you one week to tell me what you want to do for a job." One week later, I laid out my plan to work the counter at TCBY, pumping out yogurt for the girls. Dad disagreed: "To hell you're not! Until you know what you want to do in life, you're working for me!" I followed his orders and worked at Pano's and Paul's, a restaurant that raised the stature of Atlanta's dining scene to a national level.

I'll never forget my first day at Pano's and Paul's. Dad walked me into the kitchen and gave chef Bill Jackson strict orders, "Do not treat Pano any different than anyone else—no special treatment!" In that first week, I burned the tips of my fingers prepping chocolate crepes and stabbed my hand with an oyster knife. But what didn't kill me made me stronger, and my addiction to professional cooking began.

Back then, every night at Pano's and Paul's was a Saturday night, and my dad was like a general in the kitchen. Once he arrived on the premises, everyone would start looking around and wiping their stations clean. From cook to cook, station to station, a whisper would circulate around the kitchen, "Pano's here, Pano's here, um . . . your dad's here." He'd walk in, inspect our stations, and if something was not up to his standards, it was thrown away. Even to this day, when he enters a kitchen, he reverts back to being that demanding-of-perfection chef.

"Running a restaurant is not one big thing; it's a thousand little things," he always says. My dad has the highest standards and if they are not met, he fights to get them there. In 1992, when the volume required by his Atlanta restaurants outweighed the quality that local purveyors could provide, Dad created Boutique Seafood. Now with his own seafood company that adheres to the highest of standards, the seafood at our restaurants is on the table within 18 to 36 hours of being taken from the water! Dad also wanted to have artisan breads, so he created the Buckhead Bread Company, a state-of-the-art bakery that services our family's restaurants and numerous outside accounts.

Little did I know that 30 years later I would be living in Atlanta with three beautiful kids, Pano Alexander, Lucas, and Sophia, working in the family business, and running one of the top Greek-inspired seafood restaurants in the country. I'm blessed to have a mother who takes care of our family with her never-ending unconditional love; my yia yia, whose love for cooking inspired me to cook; and my father, who gave me that push to cook during high school, earn a hospitality management degree from Florida International University, and graduate from the Culinary Institute of America, not to mention support me while I cooked for three of the top five chefs in the world, starting with chef Eric Ripert, the master of the revered French seafood restaurant Le Bernardin.

LE BERNARDIN

Crisp, clean chef coats, pressed white pants, and aprons to the ground. Servers in tuxedos carrying silver trays with silver cloches under the watchful eye of Maguy Le Coze. I was standing in Le Bernardin, the most highly acclaimed seafood restaurant in the world, my nerves were turned up, and chef de cuisine, and now close friend, Chris Muller, didn't do much to calm them down. He didn't even say hello.

"Have you ever cooked lobsters?" "Yes" I replied. "Have you ever cooked artichokes?"

"Yes" I replied again. Chris looked me in the eyes and said, "I'm starting you out on the monkfish station. Chef Ripert is out of town, so if you screw up, you'll be cleaning squid for the rest of your externship." It was August 1995, Le Bernardin had managed to retain its four-star rating from the *New York Times* after chef Gilbert Le Coze had passed away, and I had just arrived for my CIA externship. Suddenly, I was all alone and without a soul to talk to. I walked to my apartment, called my dad, and discussed every method of cooking lobsters and artichokes! Needless to say, I earned my spot on entrées and spent my externship cooking at the monkfish station.

Every night, chef Eric Ripert stood at the chef's counter (the "pass"), judging every plate as they went into the dining room with zero tolerance for mistakes. Chef Eric was very intense and his palate was amazing. With the tip of a plastic spoon or metal skewer, he'd send plates back for the tiniest imperfections. To bring my plates to the pass, I had to weave through a brigade of cooks then journey back to my station, praying not to get called out. "Who cooked the monk! There's not enough lemon in the sauce! Come back and get the plate!" I had to return, take off the components, fix the sauce, replace each element on a new hot plate, then weave back to the pass.

Le Bernardin had an amazing brigade system with twelve or so positions that increased in range and difficulty. Chefs Eric and Chris pushed us cooks to master each position and, within two years, we learned everything there was to know about how to handle and prepare raw and cooked seafood. At Kyma, my Greek seafood restaurant in Atlanta, I implemented the same style of brigade and have promoted 31 sous chefs in 17 years for Buckhead Life Restaurant Group.

My favorite position was saucier and chef Eric spared no expense when it came to making his stocks and sauces. On a daily basis, we kept up with about 10 stocks ranging from vegetable (nage), mushroom, fish, mussel, shrimp, squid, lobster, chicken, pork, and veal, along with about 25 sauces and vinai-grettes made from these stocks.

I learned how to infuse these stocks to make broths with fresh aromatics, like lemongrass, kaffir lime leaf, or saffron. We also turned them into emulsions by blending them with oil and creating foam. I use these techniques in my recipes such as Olive Oil–Poached Cod with Clams and Melted Leeks (page 126).

Once the stocks and sauces were made, we would assess them as if we were all back in my yia yia's kitchen. Was anything missing? Was the texture correct? Had it simmered properly, been skimmed assiduously? Was it under- or overcooked? Was it too sharp or too sweet?

I am so thankful for the lessons I learned and the friendships I made at Le Bernardin. Chef Eric became a mentor and a friend to me, advising me along my path at Le Bernardin and beyond. I can always count on him to give me good, sound, and honest advice.

JEAN-GEORGES

Time to take a breath, time to change the movie, time for chefs Jean-Georges Vongerichten, Wylie Dufresne, and Gabriel Kreuther—all-stars in the industry and super successful. Jean-Georges wore his Prada shoes to work, Wylie had his signature hair, and Gabriel stood poised, ready to grab 15 saucepots out of thin air and pull us out of the weeds.

It was March 1998, and I was cooking at Jean-Georges's four-star restaurant on Central Park West. Everyone worked with a smile on their face and a confidence that we were cooking food like no one else in the city because our chef was super cool and a genius.

After the seafood immersion at Le Bernardin, I had come to Jean-Georges for lessons in meat cookery. The restaurant served squab, duck, capon, rabbit, lamb, venison, and veal. Jean-Georges had a different technique for cooking each protein, ensuring the best flavor. I learned to sauté beef on high heat in grapeseed oil and gently cook venison medallions in melted butter to enhance their flavor, texture, and overall moistness. Game birds, such as pheasant and partridge, arrived at the restaurant with their feathers on. I mastered plucking them, waving them over a fire to singe any remaining feathers, and storing them upside down so the blood would run through the breast. To keep the flesh of lean pheasant moist, I learned to swaddle it in barding fat for the rotisserie, and baste it continuously with the juices and French butter infused with rosemary, thyme, and garlic from the trough below—"liquid gold"—Jean-Georges would call it.

The preparation of each jus was as individual as the animal it came from and Wylie Dufresne was an incredible teacher of Jean-Georges's methods. Venison roasted in 12 x 18-inch copper pans with red wine and spice; rabbit, cut into ¾-inch (2 cm) pieces in a medium cocotte with a lid to capture the aromatic vapors; duck roasted in large stainless steal pans deglazed with a gastrique of orange and molasses. In the end, each jus tasted just like the protein it came from.

With his embrace of other cultures, Jean-Georges was ahead of elite chefs in incorporating spices and aromatics like long pepper, mace, lemongrass, turmeric, tamarind, licorice root, kombu, and bonito.

After a year, I was able to switch to the fish station. Jean-Georges's fish cookery was totally different from Le Bernardin. Instead of mixing lobster bodies with a paddle for stock and roasting them in the oven, we were cutting the bodies into 1-inch squares and cooking them in a Swiss braiser. Instead of making fish stock from whole skeletons producing a crystal clear stock, Jean-Georges had us chop the skeletons in 2-inch pieces and sear them hard in olive oil, creating a stock with an inch of rich fish oil on top—the perfect flavor for his whole roasted sea bass.

There's so much of Jean-Georges at Kyma, from the way I season with salt, pepper, spice, and acid to cooking everything à la minute and cultivating a style that is exciting and flavorful. I am so thankful for the lessons I learned from Jean-Georges and for his generosity.

THE FRENCH LAUNDRY

"Timing is everything; it's the way life works," chef Thomas Keller explained in my interview. We sat in The French Laundry courtyard on a sunny day in Yountville, California. We spoke for 30 minutes, and then Chef gave me a tour of his restaurant. It was a chance meeting really; a friend of mine was getting married in Sonoma Valley the next day, so I had arranged an interview with Thomas, as we all call him, the day before.

At the time, Thomas may have been one of the most imaginative and impressive chefs in America. In my interview he was polite, serious, and patient. His nothing-but-you-matters-in-this-moment style was enough to make me move to the West Coast, and Thomas asked me to stage (view the kitchen) the following weekend.

My stage was like going to the symphony. The presentations were exquisite, consistency amazing, and timing on point. Cooks moved about with grace; their movements the same for each technique. Every pickup and every course was flawless.

"Come on, Pano," said Eric Ziebold, the chef de cuisine. "Let's go out to the garden." A vegetarian request had been made. Eric leisurely carried on a conversation with me and by the time the conversation timed out, we had harvested baby squash, roasted it with a drop of honey, butter, and star anise, and sent it into the dining room. I was sold. Thomas hired me to be his meat saucier.

My days started at 4:30 a.m. toasting brioche with my fellow chefs and drinking coffee in the courtyard while gazing at the stars. As a saucier, I had spent so much time making stocks and sauces with worldly influences that I was longing for the classics. Of course with Thomas's finesse, the classics were respected, flavors right on, but innovative and new again.

Fourteen hours later, Thomas, Eric, and chef Grant Achatz led us to create the following day's tasting menus. The rules were simple: know what produce, proteins, and products were available, and when it was your turn, avoid repeating any garnishes, pastas, or grains. The next rule was to contribute something new or yield to a French Laundry classic. The last rule was to write the verbiage accurately on the menu, French included. With chefs Eric and Grant assisting and challenging us to use our minds, I had a lot of fun creating for the first time and at the highest level of my life.

Thomas is the master of empowerment and I have never worked with anyone so confident in his expression, outreach, and vision that he would trust his cooks to conceptualize a recipe, write it on the menu, and execute it the next day.

After a 15-hour day, we would take home the menus as souvenirs, and nothing made me more proud than knowing one of my creations had made the menu. It was in those moments that I learned the true genius of Thomas Keller: by entrusting us cooks to create, collectively, we elevated the cuisine to another plane all together.

The French Laundry is where I became a chef and where my chef became more than just my mentor; he became a role model on how to live life to the fullest while remaining humble and true to yourself. Words cannot describe how thankful I am to have made the journey out to Napa Valley to work at the French Laundry and how grateful I am for the bond and influence that Thomas and I share to this day.

KYMA

As a young chef in training, I wanted to become the best chef I could be, a chef that my father would want to hire instead of a son he felt obligated to employ. One day, before heading into work at the French Laundry, I got that call and I will never forget my father's words: "How long are you gonna keep doing this? Haven't you done enough? I need you back in Atlanta. It's time!" My father had just signed a lease on the property that would become Kyma. At first I was taken aback. I thought, "My father needs me?" I had to remind myself those were the words I had wanted and been waiting to hear.

I had always thought that I would come home to Pano's and Paul's, where I could display all my French training, or open a new restaurant with my father that defined who I was. I was thankful to my father for this opportunity, but I wasn't sure how long I would last as the chef of a Greek seafood restaurant. But gradually I realized that this is who I am; I was coming full circle to the Greek foods of my ancestors, my yia yias, and my mother.

I asked myself, how can I take all my French training and make a Greek restaurant one of the best in the country? How can I apply what Thomas did for French cuisine to Kyma? How can I take the foods of my yia yias and represent them, authenticate them, but also produce them at the highest level? The more focused I became on these ambitions, the more I dug into my memories . . . but I needed a deeper understanding of Greek history and culture.

So, as he often did when developing a new concept, my father arranged a culinary trip so we could explore and find inspiration. We traveled to Greece and teamed up with my cousin Sofia Perpera, who I would get to know better as a culinarian and top wine authority during our time in Greece. We dined at the best meze (small appetizer) spots known as *mezethopolians*, casual restaurants or tavernas, and sophisticated seafood restaurants called *psarotavernas*. Galvinized by this trip and the family's passion for seafood, we decided to open a Greek-inspired seafood restaurant. We set our sights on flying the best seafood, fresh out of the water, from Greece to Atlanta, courtesy of Dad's Boutique Seafood Company, and pairing it with the highest-quality meze, Greek wines, and desserts.

I returned to Greece three months later after my son, Pano Alexander, was born. During our first trip, it became apparent that the finest Greek food was being cooked in private homes, so I stayed with three of my aunts, all amazing cooks who were living in Athens: Thea (Aunt) Stella—a perfectionist in the kitchen, Thea Maria—a fearless cook, and Thea Rena—an expert in bold flavors with a rustic nature. We would start our mornings with coffee, melons, and cheese and then hit the markets for some of the freshest produce and seafood I had ever seen. Between the three of them, we cooked morning, noon, and night for a total of six weeks. As much fun as we had, I think they were happy to see me go—I had worn them out!

On my way back home from Greece, I went over my notes and recalled everything about my yia yia's cooking and the techniques and methods of my chef mentors. I started to divide my recollections into three categories: heritage recipes like Maria's Braised Octopus with Pasta and Tomato Sauce (page 59), combination recipes like Sautéed Scallops with Yellow Split Pea Puree (page 63), and Greek-inspired recipes such as Poached Halibut with Tomato Broth (page 134).

As soon as I landed, I was inspired to immediately start cooking with my sous chef Stratos Lambos and chef Piero Premoli. Within a few weeks, my father and I had laid out a menu. For pastry, we called on a super-young talent, Frank Kaltsounis. For the wines, my father selected my cousin Sofia, our traveling companion in Greece and a Bordeaux-educated enologist, who came to Atlanta to put together one of the best all-Greek wine programs in the United States. This team came together to execute a vision of a highly intense Greek-inspired seafood restaurant in the United States.

All my training had added up since my first days at Pano's and Paul's, and I opened Kyma as executive chef on December 15, 2001, the day after my birthday. Needless to say, the self-applied pressure was enormous. I did not want to let my father, my mentors, and all of Buckhead Life Restaurant Group down. Kyma opened to a huge success and restaurant critic John Kessler awarded the restaurant with the *Atlanta-Journal Constitution*'s top star rating.

I am so thankful for and appreciative of my father for supporting me through all of my adventures, and for the gift of Kyma. He taught me to be successful in the restaurant business and how to be an entrepreneur. In addition to Kyma, my father, brother Niko, and I have opened six restaurants together, from Atlanta to South Florida, and I could not be more proud of the entire Buckhead Life Restaurant Group family.

So, "What are we going to cook today? What do you want to cook this week?" These are the questions that bind a Greek household together, a family narrative that continues to this day—and a thread connecting me to an incredible culture that I carry on, through my life and my work.

—PANO KARATASSOS

MEZE

SPREADS

Cucumber Yogurt Spread | 20

Spicy Red Pepper–Feta Spread | 21

Grilled Eggplant Spread | 22

Garlicky Potato Spread | 23

Potato-Caper Spread | 24

Coriander-Spiced Chickpea Spread | 25

Yellow Split Pea Spread | 26

Red Caviar and Brioche Spread | 27

VEGETARIAN

Stuffed Grape Leaves
with Cumin Yogurt | 30

Braised Giant White Beans
with Tomato Sauce | 34

Lemony Quinoa Salad | 35

Eggplant-Stew with Onions
and Tomato Sauce | 36

Roasted Beet Salad with Manouri
Cream and Buttered Walnuts | 38

Wild Mushrooms "a la Grecque" | 40

Shirred Eggs with Wild Mushrooms | 42

Zucchini and Feta Fritters | 44

Watermelon and Feta Salad | 47

Warm Potato-Tomato Salad | 48

Classic Greek Salad | 49

OCTOPUS

Pickled White Octopus in a Jar | 52

Pickled Red Octopus in a Jar | 53

Pickled Orange Octopus in a Jar | 54

Grilled Octopus Salad with Orange,
Almonds, and Arugula | 55

Grilled Octopus with Olives, Capers,
and Marinated Red Onions | 56

Braised Octopus with Pasta
and Tomato Sauce | 59

SEAFOOD

Tuna Tartare with Wild Mushrooms
and Shredded Phyllo | 62

Sautéed Scallops with
Yellow Split Pea Puree | 63

Oven-Roasted Oysters with
Champagne Avgolemono | 64

Mussels Diane with Sour Pasta Pearls | 66

Steamed Mussels with Feta Sauce | 67

Garlic-Cured Cod Fritters | 70

Baked Pasta with Lobster
and Cauliflower | 72

Seafood and Tomato Stew | 73

Calamari "Pasta" with Saffron Yogurt | 75

Tuna Meatballs with Chickpea Stew | 76

PHYLLO PASTRIES

Spinach-and-Feta Phyllo Triangles | 80

Cheese Phyllo Cigars | 82

Cheese and Wild Mushroom
Shredded-Phyllo Pies | 83

Lamb Phyllo Spirals | 84

Salmon-and-Leek Phyllo Spirals
with Tarama Mousse | 86

MEAT

Spiced Red Wine–Braised Rabbit | 90

Drunk Man's Stew | 92

Chicken with Yogurt Barley
and English Peas | 93

Mini Moussaka | 98

Lamb Meatballs with White Bean Stew
and Preserved Lemon Yogurt | 101

Braised Red Wine Meatballs
with Tomato Compote | 103

Grilled Spiced Pork Ribs
with Coriander Yogurt | 104

SPREADS

Cucumber Yogurt Spread

This variation on creamy tzatziki plays up the fine shreds of refreshing cucumber, but it doesn't water out the way some versions do. That's because the cucumber's seedy core is not used, and top-quality, thick, full-fat Greek yogurt absorbs all the ingredients.

• **MAKES ABOUT 2 CUPS (500 ML)**

⅔ European cucumber, peeled

1 cup (250 ml) Greek yogurt, preferably homemade (page 223)

2 tablespoons extra virgin olive oil, plus more for drizzling

1 tablespoon fresh lemon juice

1 tablespoon chopped dill

1 teaspoon Garlic Puree (page 219)

Kosher salt and freshly ground white pepper

Olives, for garnish, optional

1. Cut the cucumber in half crosswise. Using a mandoline (see Note), cut each half lengthwise ⅛ inch (3 mm) thick, working around the seedy core to get 4 sides. Discard the core. Stack the planks of cucumber and cut them lengthwise in half, then crosswise into shreds ⅛ inch (3 mm) wide.

2. In a medium bowl, combine the cucumber with the yogurt, oil, lemon juice, dill, and Garlic Puree and stir until smooth. Season with salt and pepper. Transfer to a serving bowl. Drizzle with oil, garnish with olives, if desired, and serve.

NOTE If you don't have a mandoline with safety guard, shred the cucumber lengthwise on the largest holes of a box grater, working around the seedy core.

VARIATIONS
You can change up this recipe in endless ways—for instance, by replacing the plain Greek yogurt with Cumin Yogurt (page 31), Preserved Lemon Yogurt (page 101), Saffron Yogurt (page 44), or Coriander Yogurt (page 104).

MAKE AHEAD The spread can be refrigerated for up to 3 days.

WINE Tsipouro.

PRECEDING SPREAD, CLOCKWISE FROM TOP LEFT:
Garlicky Potato Spread (page 23); Red Caviar and Brioche Spread (page 27); Coriander-Spiced Chickpea Spread (page 25); Potato-Caper Spread (page 24); Spicy Red Pepper–Feta Spread (page 21); Yellow Split Pea Spread (page 26); Cucumber Yogurt Spread (page 20); Grilled Eggplant Spread (page 22)

Spicy Red Pepper–Feta Spread

When I was fifteen and working at my father's restaurant, Pano's and Paul's in Atlanta, peeling bell peppers was one of my first jobs. Magically, if I slow-roasted the peppers, then sealed them tight, the skin slipped right off. This method produces fleshier peppers compared to grilling or broiling them until the skin turns black. It's the first step in making htipiti, this chunky puree of sweet peppers and tangy feta with a chile bite. My patrons, being Southerners, call it the "Greek pimento cheese."

• **MAKES ABOUT 2 CUPS (500 ML)**

4 red bell peppers, halved lengthwise and cored

2 tablespoons canola oil

4 ounces (125 g) feta cheese (see page 163), cut into 1-inch (2.5 cm) cubes

1 tablespoon extra virgin olive oil

1 teaspoon minced seeded jalapeño

¼ teaspoon cayenne pepper

Kosher salt and freshly ground white pepper

1. Heat the oven to 300°F (150°C). Line a rimmed baking sheet with parchment paper. Spread the bell peppers skin side up on the prepared sheet, drizzle with the canola oil, and rub to coat the skin with the oil. Cover the peppers with parchment paper and a second baking sheet. Transfer to the oven and roast the peppers, turning them skin side down halfway through and then replacing the top parchment and baking sheet, until the skin peels off easily, 1 to 1½ hours. Remove the sheet from the oven, transfer the peppers to a medium airtight container, and cover tightly for 20 minutes. Peel the peppers and discard the skin.

2. Set a colander over a medium bowl. Transfer the peppers to the colander and let drain in the refrigerator overnight.

3. In a food processor, pulse the peppers with the cheese, olive oil, jalapeño, and cayenne until coarsely smooth. Season with salt and white pepper. Transfer to a serving bowl and serve.

NOTES The roasted bell peppers need to drain overnight, so plan accordingly.

To better drain the roasted peppers, which makes for an even more ethereal spread, I tie them in cheesecloth in Step 2, instead of draining them in a colander, and let them hang over a bowl in the refrigerator overnight.

MAKE AHEAD The bell peppers can be prepared through Step 2 and refrigerated for up to 2 days. The finished recipe can be refrigerated for up to 5 days.

SERVE WITH I especially like to pair this spread with Garlic-Cured Cod Fritters (page 70).

WINE Crisp, floral Moschofilero from Mantinia.

Grilled Eggplant Spread

In Athens, my thea Maria showed me how to cook eggplant for melitzanosalata by wrapping it in foil and cooking it on her electric stovetop until the flesh caves in. Then, when I was cooking at the French Laundry in Napa Valley, chef Thomas Keller taught me the additional refinement of draining the soft flesh in cheesecloth to remove any bitterness. For this recipe, I've taken inspiration from both teachers and added my own stamp—grilling the eggplants to soften the flesh and stirring in yogurt and red wine vinegar. It's smoky, tangy, and velvety. • **MAKES ABOUT 2 CUPS (500 ML)**

Three 1-pound (500 g) eggplants

½ cup (125 ml) plus 1 teaspoon extra virgin olive oil, plus more for drizzling

Kosher salt

½ small red onion, finely chopped

2 tablespoons red wine vinegar

¼ cup (30 g) shelled walnuts, finely chopped, optional

1½ tablespoons Greek yogurt, preferably homemade (page 223)

1¼ teaspoons Garlic Puree (page 219)

Freshly ground white pepper

1. Heat a grill or a grill pan. Arrange the eggplants in a large baking pan. Stab each in 12 places with a fork. Drizzle with ¼ cup (60 ml) of the oil and rub to coat. Season generously with salt. Grill the eggplants over medium-high heat, turning them occasionally, until the skin blackens and the flesh collapses, 25 to 35 minutes. Return them to the pan and let cool slightly.

2. Set a colander over a medium bowl. Cut the eggplants in half, peel them, and scoop the flesh into the colander. Let drain overnight in the refrigerator; discard the bitter liquid that accumulates. Transfer the eggplant to a food mill and pass into the same bowl; discard the seeds (see Notes).

3. In a small skillet, warm 1 teaspoon of the oil. Add the onion and a pinch of salt and cook over medium-low heat, stirring occasionally, until softened but not browned, about 5 minutes. Stir in 1 teaspoon of the vinegar, remove from the heat, and let cool.

4. Stir the onion into the eggplant. One ingredient at a time, stir in the walnuts, if desired, the yogurt, Garlic Puree, and remaining 1 tablespoon plus 2 teaspoons of vinegar and ¼ cup (60 ml) of oil. Season with salt and pepper. Transfer to a serving bowl, drizzle with oil, and serve.

NOTES The grilled eggplant needs to drain overnight, so plan accordingly.

For a more refined version, tie the eggplant flesh in cheesecloth in Step 2, instead of draining it in a colander, and let it hang over a bowl in the refrigerator overnight. This drains the eggplant better, making it less watery.

For a more rustic spread, instead of using a food mill, puree the grilled eggplant in a food processor until smooth, then pulse in the remaining ingredients.

MAKE AHEAD The spread can be refrigerated for up to 5 days.

WINE Greek rosé with crisp acidity. Or fresh Assyrtiko from Santorini, Crete, or the mainland.

Garlicky Potato Spread

I'm addicted to the smell of garlic-charged skordalia coming off the bowl as it's whipped. And it's super easy. You boil baking potatoes, but instead of mashing in butter and cream, you add olive oil, vinegar, and garlic to get a puree that tastes like salt-and-vinegar potato chips. My grandmother Athanasia prepared both American mashed potatoes and skordalia. Since they look similar, my brother, Niko, used to play a trick on our non-Greek friends: He'd offer them the Greek version, then fall over laughing when they got a mouthful of garlic and freaked out. This recipe is tame by comparison; if you made it like my yia yia, you'd have to triple the garlic.

- **MAKES ABOUT 2 CUPS (500 ML)**

2 small (8-ounce/250 g) russet (baking) potatoes, peeled and cut into equal chunks

½ cup (125 ml) extra virgin olive oil, plus more for drizzling

¼ cup (60 ml) white wine vinegar

1 tablespoon Garlic Puree (page 219)

Kosher salt and freshly ground white pepper

Thinly sliced chives, for garnish, optional

1. In a medium saucepan of cold water, bring the potatoes to a boil and cook until tender, about 15 minutes; drain (see Notes).

2. Transfer the warm potatoes to a ricer or vegetable mill and pass into a medium bowl. Add the oil, vinegar, and Garlic Puree and stir until smooth. Season with salt and pepper. Transfer to a serving bowl. Drizzle with oil, garnish with chives, if desired, and serve.

NOTES Two small potatoes make more than you'd imagine of the pungent spread, enough for four people.

For an even fluffier result, dry out the boiled potatoes after Step 1: Bake them in a 375°F (190°C) toaster oven for about 5 minutes before continuing.

I've had excellent results cooking the potatoes, unpeeled and whole, in a microwave oven for 8 to 10 minutes instead of boiling them. Let the potatoes cool slightly, then halve them lengthwise, scoop the flesh into the ricer, and proceed with Step 2.

MAKE AHEAD The potato spread can be refrigerated for up to 5 days.

SERVE WITH As a side, skordalia is a classic with fried foods, especially Garlic-Cured Cod Fritters (page 70).

WINE Strong retsina from Attica or northern Greece.

Potato-Caper Spread

I am honored to be friends with Greek cooking expert Aglaia Kremezi. On one of her visits to Atlanta, she taught me how briny capers and a ton of fresh herbs transform the classic skordalia. • **MAKES ABOUT 2 CUPS (500 ML)**

1 medium (12-ounce/350 g) russet (baking) potato, peeled and sliced crosswise ¼ inch (6 mm) thick

½ cup (75 g) drained capers

¼ cup (60 ml) extra virgin olive oil, plus more for drizzling

2 tablespoons fresh lemon juice

2 scallions, thinly sliced

¼ cup (8 g) chopped parsley

1 tablespoon finely chopped fennel fronds (see Notes)

1 tablespoon finely chopped dill

Kosher salt and freshly ground white pepper

1. Cook the potato in a steamer until a paring knife slides in easily, about 10 minutes (see Notes). Transfer the warm potato to a ricer or vegetable mill and pass it into a medium bowl.

2. Thoroughly rinse the capers under warm water. Pat dry with paper towels. In a food processor, puree the capers with the oil until coarsely smooth. Add the caper puree, lemon juice, scallions, parsley, fennel, and dill to the potato and stir until smooth. Season with salt and pepper. Transfer to a serving bowl, drizzle with oil, and serve.

NOTES You can add extra dill instead of using fennel fronds.

For a lighter spread, dry out the steamed potato before ricing it: Bake in a 375°F (190°C) toaster oven for about 5 minutes, then continue.

Capers are plenty salty, so taste the spread before seasoning it in Step 2.

If the spread is too thick, loosen it with sparkling water a splash at a time.

MAKE AHEAD The spread can be refrigerated for up to 5 days.

WINE Light, fruity Savatiano from Attica.

THE CREAMY, DREAMY SPREADS OF GREECE

Spreads are a defining staple of Greek cuisine. Mostly vegetarian and light enough to start a meal, these velvety, room-temperature recipes provide a good flavor, temperature, and texture match for the meatier choices in a meze spread. Every Greek household has its card file of dips, and, additionally, every region offers local specialties.

Spreads also have applications beyond the small-plates category. For instance, they can become a fast dinner. Since they keep for days, they allow cooks to compose a meal in minutes along with pantry items like olives, yogurt, a selection of cheeses, and bread.

Plus, they can act as terrific accompaniments. I serve Cucumber Yogurt Spread (page 20) as a cooling sidekick to Grilled Lamb Chops with Greek Fries (pages 172–173). They can be the building blocks of more complex recipes, too. In Sautéed Scallops with Yellow Split Pea Puree (page 63), the puree creates a soft, lemony bed for seafood. And there are endless ways to deploy traditional spreads outside the Greek tradition, such as a topping for toast; a creamy base for sandwiches; a stuffing for peppers, tomatoes, or tubes of squid; and a garnish for grain bowls and salads. They may be Greek but these versatile spreads deserve a place in every cook's repertoire.

Coriander-Spiced Chickpea Spread

I've been to the island of Sifnos only once, but I knew before going that it's the land of dreamy beaches and chickpeas—chickpea soups, stews, purees. This hummus-type dip borrows from a revelatory revithosalata (chickpea spread) I sampled there.

• **MAKES ABOUT 2 CUPS (500 ML)**

⅔ cup (125 g) dried chickpeas, soaked overnight and drained

1 teaspoon coriander seeds

1 small bay leaf

1 small carrot, cut into 2-inch (5 cm) lengths

½ small onion

¼ cup (60 ml) fresh lemon juice

½ teaspoon Garlic Puree (page 219)

⅓ cup (100 ml) extra virgin olive oil

1¼ teaspoons ground coriander

Kosher salt

Pinch of cayenne pepper

Diced tomatoes, thinly sliced chives, and sliced olives, for garnish, optional

1. In a medium saucepan, cover the chickpeas with 2 inches (5 cm) of water and bring to a simmer. Tie the coriander seeds and bay leaf in a cheesecloth bundle. Add the bundle, carrot, and onion half to the chickpeas, cover partially, and cook over medium-low heat, skimming occasionally, until tender, 1½ to 2 hours. Remove the carrot, onion half, and bundle and discard. Drain the chickpeas, saving the cooking liquid for another use (see page 143).

2. While the chickpeas are still hot, puree them in a food processor with the lemon juice and Garlic Puree until very smooth, about 3 minutes. With the machine on, gradually drizzle in the oil and puree for 2 minutes. Add the ground coriander and puree for 30 seconds. Season with salt and cayenne. Transfer to a serving bowl, garnish with tomatoes, chives, and olives, if desired, and serve.

NOTES The dried chickpeas need to soak overnight before cooking, so plan accordingly.

The cooking time for the chickpeas depends on how dried out they are.

For extra smoothness, pass the mixture through a fine sieve after seasoning it in Step 2.

If the spread is too thick, loosen it with up to 1 tablespoon of sparkling water.

MAKE AHEAD The spread can be refrigerated for up to 5 days. Press a piece of plastic wrap directly on the surface of the spread to prevent it from drying out and forming a skin.

WINE High-quality retsina.

Yellow Split Pea Spread

I visit Greece every other year and never miss Santorini. Some of the best wines, capers, and the beloved yellow split peas called fava (not to be confused with fava beans) come from here. I'll never forget my first plate of fava Santorini: The peas were pureed with olive oil and lemon juice and amped up with cayenne. Serve this meze at room temperature, as they do in Santorini, or warm as in Crete—both versions with a flourish of capers. • **MAKES ABOUT 2 CUPS (500 ML)**

¾ cup (155 g) yellow split peas, picked over and rinsed

2½ cups (625 ml) water

½ small Vidalia (sweet) onion, thinly sliced

3 garlic cloves, crushed

Pinch of saffron threads

¼ cup (60 ml) plus 2 tablespoons extra virgin olive oil

⅓ cup (100 ml) fresh lemon juice

Kosher salt

¼ teaspoon cayenne pepper

Marinated red onions (page 56) and drained capers, for garnish

1. In a small saucepan, combine the split peas with the water and bring to a simmer, skimming occasionally. Add the onion, garlic, and saffron and cook over medium-low heat, stirring occasionally and scraping all the way down to the bottom of the pan to make sure the mixture doesn't stick, until the peas are very soft and the water is absorbed, about 1 hour (see Notes). If the peas absorb all the water before they're cooked, add a little more. If the peas are soft and water remains, drain them.

2. While the peas are still hot, scrape them into a food processor and puree until very smooth. Add the oil and lemon juice and puree. Season with salt and cayenne. Transfer to a serving bowl, garnish with onions and capers, and serve.

NOTES If the peas stick to the bottom, transfer them to another saucepan.
    When the peas are done, they fall apart.

MAKE AHEAD Yellow Split Pea Spread can be refrigerated for up to 4 days. Taste it and, if needed, season with more lemon juice before serving.

WINE White stone fruit–tinged Vidiano from Crete or aromatic Malagousia.

Red Caviar and Brioche Spread

Creamy, salty taramasalata is prepared with the red or white roe from cod, mullet, or carp. The red variety is easier to find than the white, which is usually dyed for export. Boiled peeled potato can also be used as the binder in this spread, but I prefer my mother Georgia's bread version. My tweak is to use soft, buttery brioche, which creates a rich, ultrasmooth texture. • **MAKES ABOUT 2 CUPS (500 ML)**

6 ounces (180 g) brioche, crust removed

About ¼ cup (60 ml) sparkling water

4 to 5 ounces (125 to 150 g) tarama roe (see Notes)

½ cup (125 ml) extra virgin olive oil, plus more for drizzling

⅔ cup (160 ml) fresh lemon juice

Kosher salt and freshly ground white pepper

Tear the bread into pieces. In a food processor, pulse the bread into fine crumbs. Add the sparkling water and puree until smooth. Add the roe, oil, and lemon juice and puree until the texture resembles stiffly whipped cream. If it's too thick, add more sparkling water 1 tablespoon at a time. Season with salt and pepper. Transfer to a serving bowl, drizzle with oil, and serve.

NOTES The flavors in taramasalata really come together overnight, so plan accordingly.

Tarama roe is available at Greek and Mediterranean markets and online. The flavor is more or less pronounced depending on the brand, so start with the smaller amount and, if needed, increase to taste.

Taste the mixture before adding salt; the tarama roe is already salty.

VARIATIONS

For a slightly different taste and texture, sub egg bread, sourdough, or raisin bread for the brioche.

This creamy, from-the-sea spread can also be transformed into fritters. Simply replace the cod and potato in Step 4 of Garlic-Cured Cod Fritters (page 70) with the tarama spread and proceed with the recipe to turn the mixture into a delectable fried hors d'oeuvre.

MAKE AHEAD This spread can be refrigerated for up to 3 days. Check the seasoning and add more lemon juice, salt, or pepper to taste. It thickens on standing, so you may need to blend in more sparkling water, too, a tablespoon at a time.

SERVE WITH I especially enjoy taramasalata in a meze spread alongside Stuffed Grape Leaves with Cumin Yogurt (pages 30–31) and any octopus recipe (pages 52–59).

WINE Tsipouro, bone-dry Assyrtiko from Santorini, or lemony retsina.

VEGETARIAN

Stuffed Grape Leaves with Cumin Yogurt

My grandmother Theone used to fill her dolmades with rice and dill or rice and ground lamb, and for years that's what I did—until my right-hand man, Eric Cutillo, rolled a version with bulgur. These next-level stuffed grape leaves contain tomato compote (for moistening the bulgur), mint and parsley (for a fresh herb punch), and golden raisins (for a sweet note). It's like tabbouleh in a vine leaf. Alongside, I serve warmly spicy lemon- and cumin-infused yogurt for dipping. • **MAKES ABOUT 30**

STUFFED GRAPE LEAVES

1 cup (175 g) medium bulgur

2 cups (500 ml) Tomato Compote (page 221)

¼ cup (45 g) golden raisins

¼ cup (8 g) finely chopped mint

¼ cup (8 g) finely chopped parsley

1 cup (250 ml) extra virgin olive oil

One 2-pound (1 kg) jar of pickled grape leaves, drained (see Notes)

1 cup (250 ml) water

¼ cup (60 ml) fresh lemon juice

Kosher salt and freshly ground white pepper

CUMIN YOGURT

1 cup (250 ml) Greek yogurt, preferably homemade (page 223)

¼ cup (60 ml) fresh lemon juice

1 tablespoon ground cumin

Kosher salt and freshly ground white pepper

Extra virgin olive oil and diced lemon segments, for garnish, optional

PHOTOGRAPH ON PRECEDING SPREAD

1. STUFFED GRAPE LEAVES In a medium bowl, mix the bulgur with the Tomato Compote, raisins, mint, parsley, and ¼ cup (60 ml) of the oil.

2. Rinse the grape leaves in a colander under cold water. Using scissors, cut off the stems, if necessary. Line a 9-by-13-inch (23-by-33 cm) baking pan with a thick layer of about 20 grape leaves rib side down. Reserve the same number of leaves for the top. Arrange the remaining leaves rib side up on a work surface with the stem end toward you. Dollop 1 rounded tablespoon of bulgur mixture in the center of each leaf. Fold the stem end over the bulgur, then fold in the sides of the leaves and roll into bundles about 2 by 1 inch (5 by 2.5 cm). Arrange the rolls snugly seam side down in 3 rows in the prepared pan. Spread the reserved leaves on top, rib side down.

3. Heat the oven to 300°F (150°C). In a small bowl, whisk the water with the lemon juice and remaining ¾ cup (185 ml) of oil, season with salt and pepper, and pour into the pan. Set another baking pan on top as a weight and cover with foil. Transfer to the oven and bake until a cake tester slides easily into a roll, 3 to 4 hours (see Notes). Let cool slightly, then remove the foil and top baking pan. Cover with plastic wrap and refrigerate overnight.

4. CUMIN YOGURT In a small bowl, whisk the yogurt with the lemon juice and cumin until smooth. Season with salt and pepper and refrigerate until ready to use. If desired, garnish the yogurt with oil and diced lemon. Serve the stuffed grape leaves cold or at room temperature with the yogurt.

NOTES The dolmades need to be refrigerated overnight before serving, so plan accordingly.

Some pickled grape leaves come with the large stems already removed, saving a step.

When I stuff the dolmades, I cover the work surface with enough plastic wrap so all the grape leaves can be laid out at once. This also makes for easy cleanup.

As you sort through grape leaves when rinsing them, save any torn leaves for lining the baking pan.

If the cooked grape leaves and dolmades are tender, they are done. If not, bake another 30 minutes. If the liquid evaporates before they are done, add 1 cup (250 ml) of water and continue cooking.

Although expert dolmades and pie maker Monfilio Vargas has been popping out hundreds of these a week for 15 years, I still enjoy making the imperfectly rolled versions at home with my daughter, Sophia.

MAKE AHEAD The stuffed grape leaves and Cumin Yogurt can be refrigerated separately for up to 3 days.

WINE Flowery, crisp Moschofilero from Mantinia or pleasantly aromatic Sauvignon Blanc from the mainland.

CLOCKWISE FROM TOP LEFT: Classic Greek Salad (page 49); Braised Giant White Beans with Tomato Sauce (page 34); Stuffed Grape Leaves with Cumin Yogurt (pages 30–31); Eggplant Stew with Onions and Tomato Sauce (pages 36–37); Zucchini and Feta Fritters (pages 44–45); Warm Potato-Tomato Salad (page 48); Lemony Quinoa Salad (page 35); Wild Mushrooms "à la Grecque" (pages 40–41)

Braised Giant White Beans with Tomato Sauce

After tasting creamy gigantes plaki on the island of Santorini, I wanted to re-create those saucy beans. Today, my customers would riot if I ever took them off the menu. I like to walk into the restaurant cooler and help myself to a bowl for lunch. Yes, they're good cold, right out of the fridge. • **4 SERVINGS**

¾ cup (125 g) dried gigante beans, soaked overnight and drained

7 black peppercorns

1 bay leaf

1 small carrot, cut into 2-inch (5 cm) lengths

1 leek, white and light green parts only, cut into 2-inch (5 cm) lengths

1 small onion, halved

Kosher salt and freshly ground white pepper

3 tablespoons canola oil

4 garlic cloves, thinly sliced

1 cup (250 ml) Greek Tomato Sauce (page 220)

1½ tablespoons extra virgin olive oil

Chopped herbs, such as dill or parsley, for garnish

1. In a medium saucepan, cover the beans with 2 inches (5 cm) of water and bring to a simmer. Tie the peppercorns and bay leaf in a cheesecloth bundle. Add the bundle, carrot, leek, and 1 onion half to the beans, cover partially, and cook over medium-low heat, skimming occasionally, until tender, 45 minutes to 1½ hours. Season the cooking liquid with salt and pepper as if it were soup and let the beans cool in the liquid. Remove the carrot, leek, onion, and bundle and discard. Drain the beans; save the cooking liquid for another use.

2. Thinly slice the remaining onion half. In the same pan, warm the canola oil. Add the sliced onion and cook over medium heat, stirring occasionally, until golden brown, 12 to 15 minutes. Add the garlic and cook, stirring, until fragrant, about 30 seconds. Stir in the tomato sauce and drained beans and simmer for 5 minutes. Remove the pan from the heat and stir in the olive oil. Season with salt and pepper. Transfer the beans to a serving bowl or bowls, garnish with herbs, and serve.

NOTES The miraculously creamy gigante beans are available at Greek and Mediterranean markets and kalustyans.com. Alternatively, look for giant white beans or coronas; ranchogordo.com is a good source.

If dinner is running late, try cooking the beans in a pressure cooker, which uses steam to cook foods faster; that means beans go from dry to velvety in about 30 minutes.

Don't throw out that bean cooking liquid! Use it like stock; it can be the broth in a wonderful soup.

MAKE AHEAD The cooked beans can be refrigerated in the cooking liquid for up to 5 days. The finished recipe can be refrigerated for up to 5 days, and it tastes even better over time as the flavors meld.

WINE Crisp, fruity Greek rosé or light red Agiorgitiko from Nemea.

Lemony Quinoa Salad

One of my mentors, chef Eric Ripert of Manhattan's Le Bernardin restaurant, turned me on to quinoa. I was captivated by the fluffy, versatile grain that comes in red, black, and white and can be eaten cold, warm, or hot. This room-temperature salad has a Greek accent; Andean quinoa gets the treatment typically reserved for traditional Mediterranean grains. It's steamed like a pilaf and then tossed with rich olive oil, a ton of lemon juice (plus tangy preserved lemon), and herbs from the garden. • **4 SERVINGS**

¼ cup (60 ml) extra virgin olive oil

2 shallots, finely chopped

¾ cup (130 g) white quinoa, rinsed

1¼ cups (300 ml) water

Kosher salt

2 tablespoons pine nuts

3 tablespoons fresh lemon juice

1 tablespoon minced preserved lemon rind

Freshly ground white pepper

2 scallions, white and light green parts only, thinly sliced, plus more for garnish

¼ cup (8 g) torn mixed herbs, such as parsley, mint, and basil, plus more for garnish

½ medium tomato, diced

1. In a medium saucepan, warm 1 tablespoon of the oil. Add half of the shallots and cook over medium heat, stirring occasionally, until softened but not browned, 2 to 3 minutes. Add the quinoa and cook, stirring occasionally, until toasted, about 2 minutes. Add the water and a pinch of salt and bring to a boil. Cover and simmer over low heat until the water is absorbed and the quinoa is tender, about 15 minutes. Spread the quinoa on a rimmed baking sheet and let cool to room temperature.

2. Meanwhile, in a small dry skillet, toast the pine nuts over medium-high heat, shaking the pan occasionally, until fragrant, about 4 minutes. Transfer to a plate and let cool.

3. In a medium bowl, mix the lemon juice with the preserved lemon and remaining shallots. Whisk in the remaining 3 tablespoons of oil. Season with salt and pepper. Add the quinoa, scallions, herbs, tomato, and toasted pine nuts and toss to coat. Transfer to a serving bowl or bowls, garnish with scallions and herbs, and serve.

VARIATIONS

To turn the salad into a vegetarian (and gluten-free) entrée, add crunchy shaved vegetables, such as radishes and carrots, and thinly sliced sugar snap peas plus crumbled feta or shaved kefalotiri cheese.

Try other toasted nuts, such as almonds or pistachios, or pumpkin seeds.

MAKE AHEAD The cooked quinoa can be refrigerated for up to 2 days. The salad can be refrigerated overnight—the flavors are even better—but add the tomatoes just before serving.

SERVE WITH This light and flavorful salad also works as a side with any grilled fish, poultry, or meat recipe that benefits from a lemony kick, such as Grilled Lamb Chops with Greek Fries (pages 172–173).

WINE Medium-bodied, aromatic Malagousia with hints of stone fruit and botanical notes.

Eggplant Stew with Onions and Tomato Sauce

Greek friend and restaurateur John Lefkaditis inspired this meze I call "eggplant candy" because the longer it stands, the sweeter it becomes and the softer the texture. At the end of service, my staff lines up with spoons to dig into the leftovers! I sauté eggplant slices and sweet onion separately until golden and melting, then layer them with homemade tomato sauce. Small enough to be a side and hearty enough for an entrée, this versatile stew can be served hot, warm, at room temperature, or reheated. It all works, thanks to the delectable sauce that brings it all together. • **4 SERVINGS**

½ cup (125 ml) canola oil

1½ pounds (750 g) small Japanese eggplants, sliced crosswise on the diagonal ¾ inch (2 cm) thick (see Notes)

Kosher salt and freshly ground white pepper

4 thyme sprigs

4 garlic cloves, crushed

1 medium Vidalia (sweet) onion, halved and thinly sliced

1 cup (250 ml) Greek Tomato Sauce (page 220)

Chopped parsley, for garnish, optional

1. Heat the oven to 300°F (150°C). Line a baking sheet with paper towels. In a large skillet, warm 3 tablespoons of the oil. Add half of the eggplant slices, season with salt and pepper, and cook over medium heat, turning occasionally, until browned and tender, 12 to 15 minutes. Add 2 thyme sprigs and 2 garlic cloves, toss with the eggplant to mix, and cook, stirring, for 30 seconds. Transfer the eggplant to the prepared baking sheet; discard the thyme and garlic. Repeat with 3 tablespoons of the oil and the remaining eggplant, thyme, and garlic.

2. In the same skillet, warm the remaining 2 tablespoons of oil. Add the onion, season with salt and pepper, and cook over medium heat, stirring occasionally, until lightly browned, 12 to 15 minutes. Remove the skillet from the heat.

3. In a medium baking pan, spread ¼ cup (60 ml) of the tomato sauce. Layer one-third of the onions, one-third of the eggplant, and ¼ cup (60 ml) of the tomato sauce on top and repeat two more times, finishing with the tomato sauce. Cover with a lid or foil and bake until very hot, about 20 minutes. Let stand for 5 minutes, then garnish with parsley, if desired, and serve hot, warm, or at room temperature.

NOTES Because the eggplants are thickly sliced, the insides turn soft and pillowy.

You can also split the same ingredients between two 4½-inch (10.5 cm) round shallow baking pans, which is what I do at the restaurant to make it feel like a meze. Whatever size you choose, if the cookware is also pretty, you can serve the stew directly from the pan.

VARIATIONS

It's worth multiplying the recipe just for the leftovers; they're very good in a folded omelet.

For a variation of Mini Moussaka (pages 98–99), use the Eggplant Stew instead of plain sautéed eggplant.

MAKE AHEAD The stew can be refrigerated for up to 3 days. The flavors meld to deliciousness over time.

WINE Crisp Xinomavro rosé from Amynteo, Limniona from Thessaly, or spicy red made from the rare black Kalavryta grape in Achaia.

Roasted Beet Salad with Manouri Cream and Buttered Walnuts

Many chefs make a beet-and-cheese salad. I never wanted to join the club until one of my cooks presented me with an overabundance of manouri cheese. I placed it in the blender, heated some cream, and pureed the two. The result was an amazingly rich mixture with the texture of thick Greek yogurt. The upshot: a salad like no other, with three temperatures and four textures, including butter-toasted walnuts. • **4 SERVINGS**

1½ pounds (750 g) mixed small beets, such as red, golden, and candy-striped, scrubbed

1 tablespoon unsalted butter

½ cup (50 g) shelled walnuts, coarsely chopped

Kosher salt and freshly ground white pepper

½ cup (60 g) crumbled manouri cheese (see page 163) or shredded fresh mozzarella cheese

2 tablespoons heavy cream

¼ cup (60 ml) extra virgin olive oil

2 tablespoons red wine vinegar

4 small scoops Beet Sorbet (page 217), optional

Edible flowers, for garnish, optional

1. Heat the oven to 350°F (175°C). Wrap the beets individually in foil, transfer to a baking sheet, and roast until a cake tester slides easily into the center of a beet, about 1 hour. Let cool slightly, then peel. Halve or quarter the beets, depending on size.

2. Meanwhile, in a small skillet, melt the butter. Add the walnuts and cook over medium heat, stirring often, until lightly browned, 4 to 5 minutes. Remove the skillet from the heat and season the nuts with salt and pepper.

3. In a small saucepan, melt the cheese in the cream over medium heat, stirring often, 2 to 3 minutes. Remove the pan from the heat and let cool slightly. Using an immersion blender, puree the mixture until smooth.

4. In a medium bowl, whisk the oil with the vinegar. Season with salt and pepper. Add the beets and toss to coat. Mound the beets in serving bowls. Scatter the walnuts on top and add 1 tablespoon of the warm manouri cream to each bowl, and serve, with a scoop of sorbet and a flower garnish, if desired.

MAKE AHEAD The roasted beets can be refrigerated in the vinaigrette for up to 5 days.

WINE Fruity, demi-sec Xinomavro from Macedonia or aromatic white Assyrtiko–Sauvignon Blanc blend from Drama.

Wild Mushrooms "à la Grecque"

À la grecque is the French culinary nod to the Greek style of cooking vegetables in olive oil and vinegar or lemon juice. In this recipe, I—a Greek chef—pay my respects to the French by sautéing mushrooms, then tossing them with oil and vinegar. But you can't lump all mushroom varieties together. Some are firm and require longer cooking, some taste best when caramelized, and others are delicate and need gentle heat, so I cook each kind separately. I like to use shiitake and oyster mushrooms as a base and then add a seasonal mushroom, such as chanterelle, morel, black trumpet, or white beech.

- **4 SERVINGS**

3 tablespoons canola oil

7 ounces (200 g) baby oyster mushrooms, sliced

Kosher salt and freshly ground white pepper

6 garlic cloves, crushed

6 small thyme sprigs

7 ounces (200 g) baby shiitake mushrooms, stems discarded, caps sliced

¼ cup (60 ml) dry white wine

10 ounces (300 g) chanterelle mushrooms, sliced

2 tablespoons finely diced carrot

2 tablespoons finely diced leek, white parts only

3 tablespoons finely diced shallot

2 tablespoons finely diced peeled, seeded tomato

2 tablespoons extra virgin olive oil

1 tablespoon Banyuls vinegar (see Notes) or sherry vinegar

Finely sliced chives, for garnish, optional

1. In a medium skillet, warm 1 tablespoon of the canola oil. Add the oyster mushrooms, season with salt and pepper, and cook over medium heat, undisturbed, until lightly browned on the bottom, about 3 minutes. Stir the mushrooms and cook, stirring often and reducing the heat as needed to avoid scorching, until lightly browned all over, about 5 minutes more. Add 2 garlic cloves and 2 thyme sprigs and cook, stirring, for 1 minute. Transfer to a medium bowl.

2. In the same skillet, warm 1 tablespoon of the canola oil. Add the shiitake and cook over medium heat, stirring occasionally, until softened but not browned, 2 to 3 minutes. Add 2 garlic cloves, 2 thyme sprigs, and 2 tablespoons of the wine. Season with salt and pepper and cook, stirring, until the skillet is dry, about 1 minute. Transfer to the bowl with the oyster mushrooms.

3. In the same skillet, warm the remaining 1 tablespoon of canola oil. Add the chanterelles and cook over medium heat, stirring occasionally, until softened but not browned, 2 to 3 minutes. Stir in the remaining 2 garlic cloves, 2 thyme sprigs, and 2 tablespoons of wine. Season with salt and pepper and cook, stirring, until the skillet is dry, about 1 minute. Transfer to the bowl with the other mushrooms and refrigerate until cool.

4. In a small saucepan of boiling water, cook the carrot for 1 minute. Add the leek and cook until both vegetables are crisp-tender, about 1 minute. Drain the vegetables in a fine sieve, rinse in cold water, and drain again.

5. Remove the garlic and thyme from the mushrooms and discard. Add the carrot, leek, shallot, tomato, olive oil, and vinegar to the mushrooms and toss to coat; taste for seasoning. Transfer to a platter or serving bowls, garnish with chives, if desired, and serve.

NOTES This recipe makes about 2 cups (250 g). It can easily be scaled up or down.

I clean mushrooms by rinsing them in cool water, then drying them in a salad spinner.

Banyuls vinegar is a rich, oak-aged vinegar from the south of France. It can be found at specialty food stores and chefshop.com.

MAKE AHEAD The recipe can be prepared through Step 4 and refrigerated for up to 3 days. The mushroom salad can be refrigerated for up to 4 hours.

SERVE WITH These mushrooms would be great as a meze alongside Stuffed Grape Leaves with Cumin Yogurt (pages 30–31).

WINE Pairing wine with the salad's vinegar is tricky; go with floral Moschofilero with firm acidity.

Shirred Eggs with Wild Mushrooms

In this spin on a popular Greek recipe for fried eggs with wild asparagus, I swap in mushrooms and shower them with shaved truffles. • **4 SERVINGS**

1 tablespoon plus 1 teaspoon extra virgin olive oil

4 large eggs

¼ cup (30 g) Wild Mushrooms "à la Grecque" (pages 40–41)

Kosher salt and freshly ground white pepper

White truffle oil, for drizzling, optional (see Notes)

Thinly sliced chives and fleur de sel, for garnish

¼ ounce (8 g) black truffle (see Notes)

Heat the broiler on high. Warm the olive oil in a heatproof baking pan. Crack the eggs into the pan and cook over medium-low heat until the whites are set, 1 to 2 minutes. Sprinkle the mushrooms around the yolks, transfer the pan to the broiler, and cook to the desired doneness, about 30 seconds for yolks that are slightly set but still soft. Remove the pan from the broiler and season the eggs with kosher salt and pepper. Drizzle with truffle oil, if desired, and garnish with chives and fleur de sel. Shave the truffle on top and serve.

NOTES While I import truffles from Greece—yes, there are Greek truffles—black truffles and white truffle oil from France and Italy are available at specialty food shops and dartagnan.com.

As an alternative to the black truffles and fleur de sel, black truffle sea salt is available at specialty food shops and tfsnyc.com.

Instead of 1 larger heatproof baking pan, you can use two 6-inch (15 cm) shirred-egg pans or heatproof baking pans.

VARIATION

In the spring, try replacing the mushrooms with fava beans or asparagus, especially the wild variety.

SERVE WITH As a meze meal, try these eggs alongside Classic Greek Salad (page 49) and Warm Potato-Tomato Salad (page 48), or serve as a first course before Grilled Beef Rib Eye with Parsley Sauce (page 171).

WINE Light red with earthy aromas, such as a Kotsifali-Mandilaria blend; Syrah from Crete; or Limnio from Halkidiki.

Zucchini and Feta Fritters

Since experiencing my thea Stella's kolokithokeftedes, I've been hooked on the deep-fried zucchini balls' crispy exteriors and melting centers. I updated my aunt's recipe with an extra-crunchy tempura coating borrowed from Napa Valley's French Laundry restaurant and a saffron yogurt dipping sauce of my own invention.

• **MAKES ABOUT 18 FRITTERS/4 SERVINGS**

SAFFRON YOGURT

2 tablespoons whole milk

12 saffron strands

½ cup (125 ml) Greek yogurt, preferably homemade (page 223)

1 teaspoon fresh lemon juice

Kosher salt and freshly ground white pepper

FRITTERS

1 medium (8-ounce/250 g) green zucchini

1 tablespoon canola oil, plus more for frying

1 small Vidalia (sweet) onion, grated

Kosher salt and freshly ground white pepper

1 teaspoon Garlic Puree (page 219)

1 cup (125 g) crumbled feta cheese (see page 163)

½ cup (15 g) mint, finely chopped

¼ cup (8 g) parsley, finely chopped

1 large egg, lightly beaten

½ cup (20 g) fresh brioche breadcrumbs (see Notes)

¾ cup (100 g) cake flour

2½ tablespoons (25 g) cornstarch

¾ teaspoon baking powder

¼ teaspoon baking soda

About ¾ cup (185 ml) sparkling water

1. SAFFRON YOGURT In a small microwave-safe bowl, combine the milk and saffron. Microwave on high for about 25 seconds, until simmering. Let steep until deep yellow, about 30 minutes (see Notes). Add the yogurt and lemon juice and whisk until smooth. Season with salt and pepper.

2. FRITTERS Halve the zucchini crosswise. Using a box grater, coarsely shred each half lengthwise, working around the seedy core to get 4 sides. Discard the core. In a large skillet, heat the 1 tablespoon of oil until shimmering. Add the onion, season with salt and pepper, and cook over medium-high heat, stirring occasionally, until softened, 3 to 5 minutes. Add the zucchini, season with salt and pepper, and cook, stirring occasionally, until cooked through and dry, about 5 minutes. Add the Garlic Puree and cook, stirring, until fragrant, about 30 seconds. Remove the skillet from the heat and let cool slightly. Using your hands and working in batches, squeeze the zucchini dry.

3. In a medium bowl, combine the zucchini with the cheese, mint, parsley, and half of the egg (discard the remainder). Mix in the breadcrumbs. Using your hands, form 1-tablespoon (20 g) balls; transfer them to a large plate as they're shaped.

4. In a medium saucepan, heat 1 inch (2.5 cm) of the oil to 350°F (175°C). Line a baking sheet with paper towels.

5. Meanwhile, in a medium bowl, whisk the flour with the cornstarch, baking powder, and baking soda. Whisk in enough of the sparkling water until the tempura batter is as fluid as heavy cream.

6. Working in batches, drop the balls into the batter. Using a slotted spoon, lift them out, letting the excess batter drip back into the bowl. Fry the balls, turning them occasionally, until golden brown, 2 to 3 minutes. Transfer them to the prepared baking sheet as they're cooked and season with salt. Serve the fritters hot with the Saffron Yogurt.

NOTES Egg bread, sourdough, or raisin bread can be substituted for the brioche.

To get the deepest yellow color on the Saffron Yogurt, let the milk-and-saffron mixture steep in the refrigerator overnight before mixing it with the yogurt.

If your yogurt is thinnish, reduce the amount of saffron milk to keep the texture thick.

Make sure to whisk the sparkling water into the batter just before using or it will lose airiness.

VARIATIONS
For a change, try these fritters using yellow summer squash, butternut squash, or eggplant.

As an alternative dipping sauce, serve the fritters with Cucumber Yogurt Spread (page 20) or Coriander Yogurt (page 104).

MAKE AHEAD The Saffron Yogurt can be refrigerated for up to 3 days. The dry ingredients for the batter can be whisked and stored for up to 1 week.

SERVE WITH For a meze meal, try the fritters with Grilled Eggplant Spread (page 22) and Roasted Beet Salad with Manouri Cream and Buttered Walnuts (page 38).

WINE Refreshing, crisp Assyrtiko or Robola from Cephalonia.

Watermelon and Feta Salad

I grew up on melon and cheese—a typical Greek morning meal and midday snack—so I did a double take when I saw watermelon-and-goat-cheese salads being assembled in the Michelin-three-star kitchen at Jean-Georges in New York City. In my own restaurant, I add a Southern boost—sweet Vidalia onion—plus a spoonful of watermelon sorbet, which creates a savory, fruity sauce as it melts into the olive oil. Even without the sorbet, the juicy mix of sweet, salty, oniony, and lactic tastes is fantastic.

• **4 SERVINGS**

One 1-pound (500 g) wedge of seedless watermelon, rind removed, flesh cut into ¾-inch (2 cm) cubes

One 8-ounce (250 g) chunk of feta cheese (see page 163), cut into ¾-inch (2 cm) cubes

¼ small Vidalia (sweet) onion, halved and thinly sliced

Kosher salt and freshly ground white pepper

Extra virgin olive oil, for drizzling

Watermelon Sorbet (page 217), optional (see Note)

Edible flowers and mixed micro herbs, for garnish

In serving bowls, mound alternating cubes of watermelon and cheese. Sprinkle with the onion, season with salt and pepper, and drizzle with oil. Top the salads with small scoops of sorbet, if desired, garnish with flowers and herbs, and serve.

NOTE I make my own watermelon sorbet, but if you want to pick it up ready-made at an ice cream parlor, I won't tell.

WINE Aromatic sparkling rosé from Amynteo or Zitsa.

Warm Potato-Tomato Salad

I had one of my all-time favorite potato recipes at Domaine Spiropoulos in Mantinia on Greece's southern Peloponnese peninsula. After a wine tasting, the meze spread featured sliced potatoes baked in tomato puree, then stirred until coarsely smooth with homemade tomato sauce, lemon juice, and olive oil. It's simple but crazy good.

• **4 SERVINGS**

1 tablespoon canola oil

3 shallots, finely chopped

2 pounds (1 kg) russet (baking) potatoes, peeled, halved or quartered lengthwise, depending on size, and sliced crosswise ¼ inch (6 mm) thick

2 cups (500 ml) fresh tomato puree (see Note)

8 saffron threads

1 tablespoon ground coriander

Kosher salt and freshly ground white pepper

½ cup (125 ml) Greek Tomato Sauce (page 220)

2 tablespoons fresh lemon juice

1 tablespoon extra virgin olive oil

1. Heat the oven to 350°F (175°C). In a large ovenproof skillet, warm the canola oil. Add the shallots and cook over medium heat, stirring occasionally, until softened, 2 to 3 minutes. Stir in the potatoes, tomato puree, saffron, and coriander and season with salt and pepper. Cover with a lid or foil, transfer to the oven, and bake, stirring once or twice, until the potatoes are very tender and have absorbed the puree, 45 minutes to 1 hour.

2. Remove the skillet from the oven and stir in the tomato sauce, lemon juice, and olive oil, breaking up the potatoes. Season with salt and pepper, transfer to a serving bowl or bowls, and serve warm or at room temperature.

NOTE To make fresh tomato puree, peel raw tomatoes (you can use a vegetable peeler), puree them in a food processor, and then pass them through a food mill. Or use a high-quality store-bought tomato puree.

VARIATION
You could definitely add chopped fresh herbs to the mix in Step 1—thyme, rosemary, basil, oregano—whatever's on hand.

MAKE AHEAD The recipe can be prepared through Step 1 and refrigerated overnight. Reheat the potatoes in a 300°F (150°C) oven before continuing.

WINE Citrusy Roditis from the Peloponnese, central Greece, or Macedonia. Or peachy, crisp Vidiano from Crete.

Classic Greek Salad

There should be a law: horiatiki salata = no lettuce. Really, it's the super-high-quality tomatoes, cucumbers, and incredible Greek extra virgin olive oil that make this recipe wonderfully flavorful. The tomatoes are so crucial that my chef-restaurateur father still inspects one case of them a week, even though I've had the same purveyor (Dan "the Tomato Man" Darrington) for 15 years. • **4 SERVINGS**

⅓ European cucumber, peeled, halved lengthwise, and sliced into ½-inch (1 cm) half-moons

1 small green bell pepper, halved and thinly sliced

½ small red onion, halved and thinly sliced (see Notes)

¼ cup (60 ml) extra virgin olive oil

1 teaspoon red wine vinegar, optional (see Notes)

½ teaspoon dried oregano, plus more for sprinkling

Kosher salt and freshly ground white pepper

2 ripe medium heirloom tomatoes (1 pound/500 g total), each cut into 8 wedges

4 cracked green olives

4 dry-cured black olives (see Notes)

4 Kalamata olives

One 4-ounce (125 g) chunk of feta cheese (see page 163), sliced ¼ inch (6 mm) thick and cut into triangles

1. In a large bowl, combine the cucumber, bell pepper, and onion. Add the oil, vinegar, if desired, and oregano, season with salt and pepper, and toss to coat.

2. Add the tomatoes to the bowl and toss gently to mix. Season with salt and pepper. Transfer the salad to a serving bowl or bowls. Decorate with the olives and feta, sprinkle with oregano, and serve.

NOTES A fresh red onion from the farmers' market is almost sweet. To tame the pungency of a raw storage onion, soak the slices in ice water for 10 minutes, then drain and pat dry.

If your tomatoes are really spectacular, omit the vinegar.

Dry-cured olives are the intensely flavored wrinkly ones. My favorite variety is the Throuba from Thassos, an island in the northern Aegean.

VARIATION
When I was growing up, my father prepared this recipe at home, sopping up the fantastic juices with bread to make "sloppy sandwiches."

MAKE AHEAD The salad can be prepared through Step 1 and left to marinate for 15 minutes. Proceed to Step 2 just before serving.

WINE Apple-tinged Debina from Epirus. Or crisp Roditis from Achaia or Amyndeon.

OCTOPUS

Pickled White Octopus in a Jar

It was my aunt Maria who taught me how to cook octopus with white wine and sweet onions. Naturally, being from Georgia, I'm proud of our sweet Vidalias, so I couldn't wait to get home and try it with the local alliums. This recipe is the simplest and most versatile of the three pickled octopuses. • **8 SERVINGS**

3 tablespoons white peppercorns

One 6- to 8-pound (2.75 to 3.75 kg) tenderized octopus (see page 57)

2 cups (500 ml) dry white wine

5 cups (1.25 L) aged white wine vinegar

12 large thyme sprigs

6 bay leaves

6 cups (1.5 L) water

1 cup (200 g) sugar

1 medium Vidalia (sweet) onion, cut into julienne strips

1 pound (500 g) red radishes, sliced ⅛ inch (3 mm) thick on a mandoline

8 ounces (250 g) white mushrooms, halved or quartered, depending on size

Extra virgin olive oil, for drizzling

1. Heat the oven to 325°F (165°C). In a small dry skillet, toast the peppercorns over medium heat, shaking the pan occasionally, until fragrant, 2 to 3 minutes. Transfer to a small bowl and let cool.

2. In a large enameled cast-iron casserole, arrange the octopus, stretching the tentacles away from the head. Add the wine, 1 cup (250 ml) of the vinegar, 1 tablespoon of the toasted peppercorns, 6 thyme sprigs, and 3 bay leaves. Cover the casserole, transfer to the oven, and cook the octopus until a cake tester slides easily into the thickest part of a tentacle, 45 minutes to 2 hours.

3. Remove the casserole from the oven. Transfer the octopus to a large baking pan and let cool. Slice off the head and discard. Cut off the tentacles, being careful not to cut into the beak. Trim the rubbery flaps on the tentacles and discard; leave the suckers intact. Arrange the tentacles in a 4-quart (4 L) jar. Discard the braising liquid.

4. Tie the remaining 6 thyme sprigs, 3 bay leaves, and 2 tablespoons of toasted peppercorns in a cheesecloth bundle.

5. In a large saucepan, bring the water, the remaining 4 cups (1 L) of vinegar, the sugar, and herb bundle to a boil, stirring to dissolve the sugar. Remove the pan from the heat and discard the herb bundle. Add the onion, radishes, and mushrooms and let cool. Ladle the vegetables and brine into the jar. Seal and refrigerate. Slice the tentacles ¼ inch (6 mm) thick and serve with the vegetables and a drizzle of brine and oil.

MAKE AHEAD The pickled octopus can be refrigerated for up to 3 months.

Pickled Red Octopus in a Jar

I learned this recipe from my aunts, watching them slow-cook the cephalopod in their kitchens in Greece, then cut off the tentacles and pickle them in red wine vinegar, which lends a pale pink color. The tangy tentacles and vegetables taste great straight from the jar, but they're also the start of something grander, like Grilled Octopus with Olives, Capers, and Marinated Red Onions (following spread). • **8 SERVINGS**

3 tablespoons black peppercorns

3 tablespoons coriander seeds

One 6- to 8-pound (2.75 to 3.75 kg) tenderized octopus (see page 57)

6 cups (1.5 L) red wine vinegar

12 large thyme sprigs

6 bay leaves

6 cups (1.5 L) water

1 cup (200 g) sugar

8 ounces (250 g) pearl onions, preferably red, peeled and quartered lengthwise

8 ounces (250 g) carrots, peeled and thinly sliced crosswise (see Note)

8 ounces (250 g) white mushrooms, halved or quartered, depending on size

Extra virgin olive oil, for drizzling

1. Heat the oven to 325°F (165°C). In a dry medium skillet, toast the peppercorns and coriander seeds over medium heat, shaking the pan occasionally, until fragrant, 2 to 3 minutes. Transfer the spices to a small bowl and let cool.

2. In a large enameled cast-iron casserole, arrange the octopus, stretching the tentacles away from the head. Add 2 cups (500 ml) of the vinegar, 2 tablespoons of the toasted spices, 6 thyme sprigs, and 3 bay leaves. Cover the casserole, transfer to the oven, and cook the octopus until a cake tester slides easily into the thickest part of a tentacle, 45 minutes to 2 hours.

3. Remove the casserole from the oven. Transfer the octopus to a large baking pan and let cool. Slice off the head and discard. Cut off the tentacles, being careful not to cut into the beak. Trim the rubbery flaps on the tentacles and discard; leave the suckers intact. Arrange the tentacles in a 4-quart (4 L) jar. Discard the braising liquid.

4. Tie the remaining 6 thyme sprigs, 3 bay leaves, and ¼ cup (25 g) of toasted spices in a cheesecloth bundle.

5. In a large saucepan, bring the water, the remaining 4 cups (1 L) of vinegar, the sugar, and herb bundle to a boil, stirring to dissolve the sugar. Remove the pan from the heat and discard the herb bundle. Add the pearl onions, carrots, and mushrooms and let cool. Ladle the vegetables and brine into the jar. Seal and refrigerate. Slice the tentacles ½ inch (1 cm) thick and serve with the pickled vegetables and a drizzle of brine and oil.

NOTE To make carrot flowers, use a channel knife to cut 5 parallel grooves the length of the carrots before slicing them crosswise. I like the Victorinox rosewood channeler available at qualityknives.co.uk.

MAKE AHEAD The pickled octopus can be refrigerated for up to 3 months.

Pickled Orange Octopus in a Jar

I'm mad for the vibrant flavors of oranges, cracked green olives, and fennel, so I tried using them as aromatics for pickled octopus. Braising with saffron adds to the sunny, copper-tinted hue I'm looking for and lends a subtle spice. After simmering and quick fermenting, the result is a super-clean taste. • **8 SERVINGS**

3 tablespoons white peppercorns

3 tablespoons coriander seeds

One 6- to 8-pound (2.75 to 3.75 kg) tenderized octopus (see page 57)

4 cups (1 L) fresh orange juice

5 cups (1.25 L) Champagne vinegar

12 large thyme sprigs

6 bay leaves

2 pinches of saffron threads

4 cups (1 L) water

1 cup (200 g) sugar

2 cups (350 g) cracked green olives

1 fennel bulb, cut into julienne strips

8 ounces (250 g) white mushrooms, halved or quartered, depending on size

Extra virgin olive oil, for drizzling

1. Heat the oven to 325°F (165°C). In a dry medium skillet, toast the peppercorns and coriander seeds over medium heat, shaking the pan occasionally, until fragrant, 2 to 3 minutes. Transfer the spices to a small bowl and let cool.

2. In a large enameled cast-iron casserole, arrange the octopus, stretching the tentacles away from the head. Add 2 cups (500 ml) of the orange juice, 1 cup (250 ml) of the vinegar, 2 tablespoons of the toasted spices, 6 thyme sprigs, 3 bay leaves, and the saffron. Cover the casserole, transfer to the oven, and cook the octopus until a cake tester slides easily into the thickest part of a tentacle, 45 minutes to 2 hours.

3. Remove the casserole from the oven. Transfer the octopus to a large baking pan and let cool. Slice off the head and discard. Cut off the tentacles, being careful not to cut into the beak. Trim the rubbery flaps on the tentacles and discard; leave the suckers intact. Arrange the tentacles in a 4-quart (4 L) jar. Discard the braising liquid.

4. Tie the remaining 6 thyme sprigs, 3 bay leaves, and ¼ cup (25 g) of toasted spices in a cheesecloth bundle.

5. In a large saucepan, bring the water, the remaining 4 cups (1 L) of vinegar, the sugar, and herb bundle to a boil, stirring to dissolve the sugar. Remove the pan from the heat and discard the herb bundle. Add the olives, fennel, and mushrooms and let cool. Ladle the olives, fennel, brine, and remaining 2 cups (500 ml) of orange juice into the jar. Seal and refrigerate. Slice the tentacles ¼ inch (6 mm) thick and serve with the olives, fennel, mushrooms, and a drizzle of brine and oil.

MAKE AHEAD The pickled octopus can be refrigerated for up to 3 months.

Grilled Octopus Salad with Orange, Almonds, and Arugula

Here, I've riffed on the recipe of my friend, Greek food luminary Susanna Hoffman. The char on the tentacles from the grill combined with the flavors of the brine are amazing. • **4 SERVINGS**

CITRUS VINAIGRETTE

¼ cup (60 ml) extra virgin olive oil

1 tablespoon Champagne vinegar

2 tablespoons fresh orange juice

1 tablespoon fresh lemon juice

½ tablespoon fresh lime juice

Kosher salt and freshly ground white pepper

OCTOPUS SALAD

¼ cup (20 g) sliced almonds (see Notes)

2 oranges

2 tentacles from Pickled Orange Octopus in a Jar (page 54)

Fine sea salt and freshly ground white pepper

3 ounces (90 g) baby arugula

1. CITRUS VINAIGRETTE In a blender, emulsify the oil with the vinegar and orange, lemon, and lime juices. Season with kosher salt and pepper.

2. OCTOPUS SALAD Heat the oven to 350°F (175°C). Spread the almonds on a small baking sheet and toast in the oven, stirring occasionally, until lightly browned, 8 to 10 minutes.

3. Using a small, sharp knife, cut the skin and all of the white pith off the oranges. Working over a plate, cut in between the membranes to release the segments.

4. Heat a grill or a grill pan. Grill the tentacles over high heat, turning and brushing them occasionally with some of the vinaigrette, until lightly charred all over, about 4 minutes. Transfer to a carving board and let rest for 30 seconds. Slice crosswise ¼ inch (6 mm) thick.

5. Arrange the orange segments in a circle on a platter or plates. Top with half of the tentacle slices, drizzle with 2 tablespoons of the vinaigrette, and sprinkle with 2 tablespoons of the almonds. Season with sea salt and pepper. In a medium bowl, combine the arugula with 2 tablespoons of the vinaigrette and toss to coat. Scatter the arugula on top, garnish with the remaining tentacle slices, and sprinkle with the remaining 2 tablespoons of almonds. Season with sea salt and pepper and serve. Pass the remaining vinaigrette separately.

NOTES The recipe for Citrus Vinaigrette makes about ½ cup (125 ml). It can easily be scaled up to have extra on hand.

If you can find them, try the delicate green almonds available from farmers in their too-brief spring and early-summer season. You must cut open the green fuzzy husk to get at the nut. It splits where it naturally forms two halves. Use them raw instead of toasting them.

MAKE AHEAD The vinaigrette can be refrigerated for up to 3 days. The toasted almonds can be stored in an airtight container at room temperature for a week.

WINE Dry, elegant, and fruity Greek rosé.

Grilled Octopus with Olives, Capers, and Marinated Red Onions

I'll never forget the recipe-testing day before my restaurant Kyma launched. Stratos Lambos, then my sous chef, now a Charlotte, North Carolina, restaurateur, nervously gave me my first bite of this meze. As soon as he saw me smile, he wrapped me in a hug and said, "Now we can open a Greek restaurant, my brother!" Accolades followed: "It's the reason why Atlantans eat octopus." This recipe, with just the right balance of salt, sugar, and tang, is my number 1 menu item. • **4 SERVINGS**

RED WINE VINAIGRETTE

½ cup (125 ml) canola oil

¼ cup (60 ml) extra virgin olive oil

¼ cup (60 ml) red wine vinegar

Kosher salt and freshly ground white pepper

OCTOPUS SALAD

1 medium red onion, halved and thinly sliced

Kosher salt and freshly ground white pepper

4 tentacles from Pickled Red Octopus in a Jar (page 53)

8 Kalamata olives

8 cracked green olives

Drained capers and chopped parsley, for garnish

1. RED WINE VINAIGRETTE In a blender, emulsify both oils with the vinegar. Season with salt and pepper. Scrape the vinaigrette into a 1-cup (250 ml) jar with a lid and seal. Shake well before using.

2. OCTOPUS SALAD In a medium bowl, combine the onion with ¾ cup (185 ml) of the vinaigrette. Let stand at room temperature for at least 1 hour and preferably 24 hours. Season with salt and pepper.

3. Heat a grill or a grill pan. Grill the tentacles over high heat, turning and brushing them occasionally with the remaining ¼ cup (60 ml) of vinaigrette, until lightly charred all over, about 4 minutes. Transfer to a carving board and let rest for 30 seconds. Slice crosswise ½ inch (1 cm) thick.

4. Spread half of the marinated onion on a platter or plates. Arrange the octopus, olives, and remaining onion on top. Drizzle the vinaigrette remaining from the onions over the octopus, garnish with capers and parsley, and serve.

NOTES The red onion needs to marinate for at least 1 hour, preferably 24 hours, so plan accordingly.

The recipe for Red Wine Vinaigrette makes about 1 cup (250 ml) and can easily be multiplied to have extra on hand.

MAKE AHEAD The vinaigrette can be refrigerated for up to 5 days. The marinated onions can be refrigerated in the vinaigrette for up to 2 days; they're best after 24 hours.

WINE Crisp Robola from Cephalonia or Roditis from the Peloponnese or northern Greece.

DO NOT FEAR THE OCTOPUS

When Kyma first opened, my servers tried different tactics to get timid patrons to sample the octopus. They insisted: "This octopus is very tender." They pleaded: "You're missing out on something special." They promised: "If you don't like it, we'll gladly replace it."

Now we sell octopus like crazy—at least 500 servings every week. Still, whenever I'm in the dining room, guests pull me aside with questions: Is octopus a kind of squid (calamari)? I'm allergic to shellfish. Can I eat it?

I tell them octopus and squid are both cephalopods meaning "feet around the head," so they're cousins. And, yes, they are both shellfish. If you are allergic to mollusks (a kind of shellfish), your doctor may advise you to stay clear of them.

I also tell patrons who want to cook octopus that they can't just throw it on the grill or it will be chewy. It must be braised first, which is easy and mostly hands-free. Once the octopus is tender, I suggest cutting off and pickling the tentacles.

Although not strictly necessary, preserving them in a savory liquid gives you options. You can make more than you need for a single recipe and save the rest in the marinade. Or you can serve the octopus pickled and grilled at the same meal. In any event, the mild-tasting sea creature benefits from absorbing extra flavor.

I offer three kinds of pickling liquid because each lends itself to different secondary preparations. My white pickle cleans up the octopus flavor, great for a salad or pasta. The robust red pickle is especially good for grilling. The orange pickle works well for both cold recipes and gentle grilling to keep the delicate flavors.

TIPS FOR COOKING WITH OCTOPUS

1. Look for octopus at well-stocked grocery stores and fish markets; you may need to pre-order it. Of course, it's also available online. My favorite species are the frozen octopuses from Spain, Morocco, and Portugal.

2. These recipes work for both small and large octopus, so if you can't find one that's 6 to 8 pounds (2.75 kg to 3.75 kg), buy enough smaller ones to make up this weight.

3. Thaw frozen octopus in the refrigerator, which can take up to a couple of days. You can run cold water over it in the sink to speed the process.

4. Size does not matter. A small octopus can take longer to get tender than a large one. Even octopuses of similar weight may require considerably different cooking times.

5. There are no hard and fast rules for timing: anywhere from 45 minutes to 2 hours. Be patient. Start checking for doneness at 45 minutes. When a cake tester slides easily into the thickest part of a tentacle, it's ready. You can also use a thin metal skewer; it just makes a larger hole.

6. You don't need to remove the lovely gelatinous skin or the suction cups. During grilling, the suckers get nicely charred, leaving the tentacles tender.

Braised Octopus with Pasta and Tomato Sauce

Combining the long-simmered flavors of braised octopus and oregano-scented tomato sauce with lashings of lemon juice, olive oil, and ouzo makes this pasta something special. I've refined my aunt Maria's makaronada, adding the pure white tentacles just before serving so they stand out against the dark red background. • **4 SERVINGS**

Kosher salt

¾ cup (100 g) ditalini pasta

2 tentacles from Pickled White Octopus in a Jar (page 52), sliced crosswise ½ inch (1 cm) thick

2 cups (500 ml) Greek Tomato Sauce (page 220)

2 rosemary sprigs

Freshly ground white pepper

Pinch of crushed red pepper

2 tablespoons fresh lemon juice

2 tablespoons ouzo

2 tablespoons extra virgin olive oil

Micro herbs, for garnish, optional

1. In a large saucepan of salted boiling water, cook the pasta until al dente. Drain in a colander.

2. In the same saucepan, combine the pasta with the octopus, Greek Tomato Sauce, and rosemary. Bring to a simmer and cook over medium heat to heat through, about 1 minute. Season with salt, white pepper, and crushed red pepper. Discard the rosemary. Spoon into a serving bowl or bowls and drizzle with the lemon juice, ouzo, and oil. Sprinkle with herbs, if desired, and serve.

VARIATIONS

This recipe is incredibly versatile: Grill the tentacles whole before slicing and adding them to the sauce. Or replace them, singly or in combination, with sliced squid, whole shrimp, and steamed mussels in the shell. And you can always add a crumbled-feta topping.

SERVE WITH I think lamb is the perfect entrée to follow. Try Grilled Lamb Chops with Greek Fries (pages 172–173), Braised Leg of Lamb with Sour Pasta Pearls (pages 175–176), or Braised Lamb and Roasted Tomatoes in Thieves' Purses (pages 180–181).

WINE Crisp, aromatic Agiorgitiko rosé from Nemea or citrusy Savatiano from Attica.

SEAFOOD

Tuna Tartare with Wild Mushrooms and Shredded Phyllo

In this multitiered appetizer, a sprightly mushroom salad underneath the tartare provides all the acidity the tuna needs without turning it gray. For crunch, it's topped with a kataifi (shredded phyllo) cracker. You break off a piece of the kataifi and use it to push the silky tuna and mushroom salad onto your fork. • **MAKES 2 TARTARES/4 SERVINGS**

1½ ounces (40 g) frozen shredded phyllo (kataifi), thawed (see Notes)

¼ cup (60 ml) clarified butter (see Step 3, page 199)

6 ounces (180 g) sushi-grade tuna fillet, cut into ¼-inch (6 mm) dice

2 teaspoons thinly sliced chives

1 teaspoon extra virgin olive oil, plus more for drizzling

Kosher salt and freshly ground white pepper

½ cup (60 g) Wild Mushrooms "à la Grecque" (pages 40–41)

Mushroom powder, for dusting, optional (see Notes)

1. Heat the oven to 325°F (165°C). Line a baking sheet with parchment paper and set a 3-inch (7.5 cm) ring mold on top (see Notes). In a small bowl, toss the phyllo with the clarified butter until coated. Pat half of the phyllo into the mold; remove the mold. Make a second disk with the remaining phyllo. Cover the disks with another sheet of parchment and set a second baking sheet on top. Bake until golden brown, about 25 minutes. Remove from the oven and let cool.

2. In a small bowl, toss the tuna with the chives and oil. Season with salt and pepper.

3. Set the same mold on a salad plate. Pat in half of the mushrooms, then half of the tuna and smooth the top; remove the mold. Repeat with the remaining mushrooms and tuna on a second plate. Top each with a phyllo disk and drizzle oil around the tartares. Dust the plates with mushroom powder, if desired, and serve.

NOTES Shredded phyllo (kataifi) is available at Greek and Mediterranean markets.

Mushroom powder is available at specialty food shops and online, but I make my own using dried black trumpet mushrooms. Pick through the dried mushrooms, discarding any leaves, twigs, or pebbles, then grind them to a fine powder.

Instead of a ring mold, feel free to use a tuna can with the bottom and top removed Or try a ramekin brushed with oil; you'll need to pat in the tuna first, then the mushrooms to get the order of the layers right, because you'll invert them onto a salad plate. Running a table knife around the inside edge of the ramekin helps the filling slide out nicely.

MAKE AHEAD The baked phyllo disks can be stored in an airtight container overnight.

WINE Sparkling Xinomavro rosé from Amynteo or dry, crisp Moschofilero from Mantinia.

Sautéed Scallops with Yellow Split Pea Puree

At a small Santorini restaurant overlooking the port, I settled in with a bowl of yellow split pea spread and a cold beer. Right in front of me, one of the cooks was grilling everything from oysters and scallops to octopus and giant squid. I ordered all of it. But it was the sweet scallops paired with the earthy, lemony split pea puree that stuck with me. • **4 SERVINGS**

¼ small red onion, cut into julienne strips

¼ cup (60 ml) Red Wine Vinaigrette (page 56)

Kosher salt and freshly ground white pepper

4 medium scallops, side muscle removed

1 tablespoon canola oil

1 cup (250 ml) Yellow Split Pea Spread (page 26)

Drained capers, micro arugula, and edible flowers for garnish, optional

1. In a small bowl, combine the red onion with the vinaigrette. Let stand for at least 1 hour and preferably 24 hours. Season with salt and pepper.

2. Pat the scallops dry using paper towels and season with salt and pepper. In a small skillet, heat the oil until shimmering. Add the scallops and cook over medium-high heat until they have released their moisture, about 20 seconds. Using a slotted spatula, lift the scallops, then return them to the skillet and cook until browned on the bottom, about 2 minutes. Turn them over and cook until a cake tester inserted into the thickest part of a scallop feels warm when touched to your lower lip, for medium-rare, about 2 minutes.

3. Spread the split peas on a platter or plates and garnish with capers, if desired. Drain the marinated onion, reserving the vinaigrette for another use, and scatter it on the split peas. Slice each scallop in half horizontally and shingle the slices on top of the peas, alternating the browned outside with the medium-rare center. Garnish with arugula and flowers, if desired, and serve.

NOTES The red onion needs to marinate for at least 1 hour, preferably 24 hours, so plan accordingly. Prepare the Yellow Split Pea Spread right after the onion in Step 1; the peas can cook while the onion is marinating.

To get a uniform crust on scallops, make sure to dry them well, season them, and then lift them up and replace them in the skillet after cooking them for 20 seconds.

VARIATIONS

You can grill the scallops or replace them with shrimp or grilled octopus.

SERVE WITH I like these scallops in a meze spread with Zucchini and Feta Fritters (pages 44–45) and Steamed Mussels with Feta Sauce (page 67).

WINE Apricot-scented Vidiano from Crete, minerally Savatiano from Attica, or fresh Assyrtiko from Santorini.

Oven-Roasted Oysters with Champagne Avgolemono

This update of the iconic Greek lemon emulsion avgolemono unites three of my favorite ingredients—Champagne, oysters, and caviar. • **4 SERVINGS**

2 cups (1 kg) rock salt

8 small cold-water oysters, such as Wellfleet or Kumamoto, shucked, on the half shell (see Notes)

1 large egg yolk

1 tablespoon Champagne or another sparkling white wine

1 tablespoon fresh lemon juice

Freshly ground white pepper

Extra virgin olive oil, for drizzling

2 teaspoons (12 g) osetra caviar or hackleback or paddlefish roe

1. Heat the oven to 350°F (175°C). Spread 1 cup (300 g) of the rock salt in a 9-by-11-inch (23- by-28 cm) shallow baking pan. Transfer the oyster meat and liquor to a small bowl. Scrub the oyster shells and nestle them into the salt. Transfer each oyster to a shell, reserving the liquor.

2. Strain the reserved liquor through a fine sieve into a small saucepan, leaving the grit behind. Add the egg yolk and cook over medium heat, whisking constantly and moving the pan on and off the heat, until the sauce thickens slightly, 1 to 2 minutes. Add the Champagne and lemon juice and season the sauce with pepper. Remove the pan from the heat.

3. Drizzle the oysters with oil and bake until they are warm to the touch, about 3 minutes. Spread the remaining 1 cup (300 g) of salt on a platter or plates. Nestle the oysters on the half shell into the salt. Using an immersion blender or a whisk, whip the sauce until frothy. Spoon some of the froth on each oyster and top with ¼ teaspoon of caviar. Serve immediately.

NOTES Whether you or your fishmonger shucks the oysters, make sure they do not lose a drop of their liquor in the process. If a fishmonger does the work, the oysters will be juicy by the time you get home. If opening your own, add the meat and liquor to a small bowl set in a medium bowl of half ice, half water; reserve the bottom shells. Let the oysters stand until they release all of their liquor, 20 to 30 minutes, before continuing. You should have about 3 tablespoons of oyster liquor; if you're short, add water.

MAKE AHEAD The shucked oysters can be refrigerated for up to 6 hours.

SERVE WITH For an all-seafood meze spread, serve these oysters alongside a dish of Calamari Pasta with Saffron Yogurt (page 75), Tuna Tartare with Wild Mushrooms and Shredded Phyllo (page 62), and Grilled Octopus with Olives, Capers, and Marinated Red Onions (pages 56–57).

WINE Minerally, crisp Assyrtiko from Santorini. Or sparkling white Debina from Epirus or sparkling Moschofilero from Mantinia.

Mussels Diane with Sour Pasta Pearls

I am honored to be friends with food and wine expert Diane Kochilas, who prepared this recipe for me when I visited her in Thessaloniki in northern Greece. What I love most about it is the way the flavors of the mussel broth (made by steaming the bivalves with white wine, garlic, and basil) are soaked up by the nicely tart trahana (sour pasta pearls). • **4 SERVINGS**

½ teaspoon Garlic Puree (page 219)

1 cup (250 ml) white wine

1¼ pounds (625 g) mussels, scrubbed and debearded

3 basil leaves

½ cup (60 g) sour trahana pasta (see Notes)

¼ cup (60 ml) Tomato Compote (page 221)

1 tablespoon fresh lemon juice

1 tablespoon ouzo

1 tablespoon chopped mint

2½ tablespoons extra virgin olive oil

Freshly ground white pepper

Thinly sliced chives, for garnish

Crumbled feta cheese (see page 163), optional, for garnish

1. In a large saucepan, cook the Garlic Puree over medium heat, stirring, until fragrant, about 30 seconds. Add the wine, mussels, and basil, cover, and cook over high heat, shaking the pan a few times, until the mussels open, 3 to 5 minutes. Remove the pan from the heat. Using a slotted spoon, transfer the mussels to a large bowl. Discard any that do not open.

2. Strain the cooking liquid through a fine sieve into a medium glass measuring cup, leaving the grit behind. You should have at least 1 cup (250 ml) of liquid; if not, add water. Rinse out the pan. Return the cooking

liquid to the pan and bring to a simmer. Add the pasta and cook over medium-low heat, whisking to break it up, until tender, about 10 minutes. If needed, add water a splash at a time and cook until the pasta is cooked and saucy. Add the Tomato Compote and cook, whisking occasionally, until heated through, 1 to 2 minutes. Remove the pan from the heat and whisk in the lemon juice, ouzo, mint, and 1 tablespoon of the oil. Transfer to a serving bowl or bowls, add the mussels, and drizzle with the remaining 1½ tablespoons of oil. Season with pepper. Garnish with chives and, if desired, cheese and serve.

NOTES Trahana, a Greek pasta made from bulgur wheat, has a pebbly appearance similar to couscous. There are two types, sweet and sour; the sour variety is mixed with goat's milk yogurt before it's dried, giving it a distinctive tangy flavor. Trahana is available at Greek and Middle Eastern markets and online. I like the Vlaha brand.

In a pinch, you could swap in couscous for the trahana, but you'd miss the intriguing element that really makes this recipe transcendent.

The pasta will continue to absorb liquid, so add more water to make it saucy if needed.

MAKE AHEAD The recipe can be prepared through Step 1 up to 2 hours ahead.

WINE Tsipouro.

Steamed Mussels with Feta Sauce

The common name for this classic meze is mussels Constantinople, one of the megahits on my menu. The steamed mussels are shucked and served in a creamy, ouzo-spiked sauce made from the intensely flavorful mussel cooking liquid. To keep things texturally interesting, I add feta cheese three times: first, completely melted into the sauce; next, stirred into the warm sauce once it comes off the heat to produce soft curds; then, crumbled fresh on top just before serving. • **4 SERVINGS**

2 thyme sprigs

2 dill sprigs

2 parsley sprigs, plus chopped parsley for garnish

1 bay leaf

1 tablespoon canola oil

2 shallots, finely chopped

2 garlic cloves, finely chopped

¼ teaspoon crushed red pepper

2 pounds (1 kg) small mussels, scrubbed and debearded

¼ cup (60 ml) dry white wine

½ cup (125 ml) heavy cream

¾ cup (90 g) crumbled feta cheese (see page 163)

½ cup (125 ml) Vidalia Onion Stew (page 159)

2 tablespoons ouzo

Freshly ground white pepper

Minced green bell pepper, for garnish

Extra virgin olive oil, for drizzling

Grilled sliced bread, for serving

1. Tie the herb sprigs and bay leaf in a bundle. In a large saucepan, warm the canola oil. Add the shallots, garlic, herb bundle, and crushed red pepper and cook over medium heat, stirring occasionally, until the vegetables soften, 2 to 3 minutes. Add the mussels and wine, cover, and cook over high heat, shaking the pan a few times, until the mussels open, 3 to 5 minutes. Remove the pan from the heat. Using a slotted spoon, transfer the mussels to a large bowl. Shuck the mussels and discard the shells and any unopened mussels.

2. Strain the cooking liquid through a fine sieve into a small glass measuring cup, leaving the grit and solids behind. Rinse out the pan and return the cooking liquid to the pan. Add the cream, bring to a simmer, and cook over medium-low heat until reduced by half, about 10 minutes. Add ½ cup (60 g) of the cheese and cook over medium heat, stirring often, until melted, 2 to 3 minutes.

3. Add the Vidalia Onion Stew, mussels, ouzo, and 2 tablespoons of the cheese to the pan. Season with white pepper. Transfer to a serving bowl or bowls. Garnish with minced bell pepper, chopped parsley, and the remaining 2 tablespoons of cheese. Drizzle with olive oil and serve with bread.

MAKE AHEAD The mussels can be prepared through Step 1 and refrigerated overnight. The sauce can be prepared through Step 2 and refrigerated overnight. Reheat gently before continuing to Step 3.

WINE Floral Moschofilero with firm acidity or herbaceous, lemon-tinged retsina.

CLOCKWISE FROM TOP LEFT: Mussels Diane with Sour Pasta Pearls (page 66); Steamed Mussels with Feta Sauce (page 67); Garlic-Cured Cod Fritters (pages 70–71); Sautéed Scallops with Yellow Split Pea Puree (page 63); Baked Pasta with Lobster and Cauliflower (page 72); Seafood and Tomato Stew (page 73); Tuna Meatballs with Chickpea Stew (pages 76–77)

Garlic-Cured Cod Fritters

Bakaliarokeftedes have a texture somewhere between crunchy and tender. While they're traditionally prepared with salt cod, they're as good—or even better—with freshly cured cod. My recipe is influenced by the Provençal brandade I cooked at Le Bernardin in New York City, with its shamelessly high ratio of cream to cod and mashed potato, but I replace the dairy with olive oil. My tip: Folding whipped egg white into the cod-potato mixture helps the fish balls hold their shape. • **4 SERVINGS**

3 tablespoons (45 g) Garlic Puree (page 219)

12 ounces (350 g) skinless cod fillet

Kosher salt

1 cup (250 ml) extra virgin olive oil

1 cup (250 ml) canola oil, plus more for frying

½ small onion, thinly sliced

1 large garlic clove, crushed

2 thyme sprigs

1 medium (12-ounce/350 g) russet (baking) potato, peeled and cut into equal chunks

1 large egg white

3 tablespoons thinly sliced chives

Freshly ground white pepper

Garlicky Potato Spread (page 23) and lemon wedges, for serving

1. On a large plate, rub the Garlic Puree all over the fish. On another large plate, spread a layer of salt ¼ inch (6 mm) thick. Set the fish on the salt and spread a layer of salt ¼ inch (6 mm) thick on top. Refrigerate for 1 hour. Rinse the cure off the fish and pat dry.

2. In a medium skillet, combine the olive oil with the 1 cup (250 ml) of canola oil, the onion, garlic, and thyme. Add the fish and bring to a simmer, then cover and cook over medium-low heat, turning the fish halfway through, until a cake tester inserted into the thickest part of the fish feels warm when touched to your lower lip, about 10 minutes. Remove the skillet from the heat and let the fish cool to room temperature in the cooking liquid.

3. Meanwhile, heat the toaster oven to 375°F (190°C). Line the toaster's baking sheet with foil. In a medium saucepan, cover the potato with 2 inches (5 cm) of cold water. Bring to a boil and cook until tender, about 15 minutes. Spread the potato on the prepared sheet and bake for 5 minutes to dry it out. Transfer the warm potato to a ricer or vegetable mill and pass it into a medium bowl.

4. In a small bowl, whip the egg white until stiff. Fold the egg white and chives into the potato mixture and season with pepper. Using a slotted spatula, transfer the cod to the potatoes, flake the fish, and fold it into the potatoes; discard the cooking liquid. Using your hands, form 2-tablespoon balls of the cod-potato mixture; transfer them to a plate as they're shaped.

5. In a large saucepan, heat 1 inch (2.5 cm) of canola oil to 350°F (175°C). Line a baking sheet with paper towels. Working in batches, fry the balls, turning them occasionally, until golden brown, 3 to 4 minutes. Using a slotted spoon, transfer them to the prepared baking sheet as they're cooked. Serve the fritters hot with Garlicky Potato Spread and lemon wedges.

VARIATIONS

After curing the cod in Step 1, I also like to cut the fish into perfect fingers, dip them in a tempura batter, and fry them until golden brown (see Zucchini and Feta Fritters, pages 44–45).

After the cod is cooked in Step 2, it's good enough to eat straight out of the skillet with a green salad.

MAKE AHEAD The cod can be prepared through Step 2 and refrigerated for up to 5 days. The fritters can be prepared through Step 4 and refrigerated overnight.

SERVE WITH Garlicky Potato Spread is the traditional accompaniment for cod fritters, but I also like to pass Spicy Red Pepper–Feta Spread (page 21) alongside.

WINE Zesty Assyrtiko with firm acidity or minerally Robola from Cephalonia.

Baked Pasta with Lobster and Cauliflower

Time-honored pastichio (baked pasta) is made with ground beef (or lamb), long maca-roni noodles, and béchamel (white sauce). To shake up routine, I created this all-white lobster pastichio with short ditalini pasta, tangy yogurt, and earthy cauliflower.

• **4 SERVINGS**

Kosher salt

¼ cup plus 2 tablespoons (50 g) ditalini pasta

1 cup (250 ml) water

1 tablespoon (15 g) unsalted butter

Freshly ground white pepper

¾ cup (75 g) finely chopped cauliflower florets

4 ounces (125 g) cooked lobster meat, sliced crosswise ¼ inch (6 mm) thick

¼ cup (60 ml) vegetable stock

¼ cup (60 ml) crème fraîche or sour cream

2 tablespoons Greek yogurt, preferably homemade (page 223)

1 tablespoon finely chopped shallot

¼ ounce (8 g) black truffle, finely diced, optional

1 cup (250 ml) Béchamel Sauce (page 222)

Freshly grated nutmeg, for sprinkling, optional

1. Heat the oven to 325°F (165°C). In a small saucepan of salted boiling water, cook the pasta until al dente; drain in a colander.

2. In the same saucepan, bring the water and butter to a simmer and season with salt and pepper. Add the cauliflower and cook until tender, about 5 minutes. Drain in the colander with the pasta.

3. In the same saucepan, combine the pasta and cauliflower with the lobster, 2 table-spoons of the stock, the crème fraîche, yogurt, shallot, and, if desired, truffle. Bring to a simmer over medium heat, stirring constantly. If needed, add more stock by the tablespoon to loosen the texture. Season with salt and pepper.

4. In each of two 4½-inch (10.5 cm) round shallow baking pans, spread half of the pasta mixture. Spread the Béchamel Sauce on top. Transfer to the oven and bake until bubbling, about 10 minutes. Heat the broiler and broil until golden brown, 2 to 3 minutes. If not using the truffle, sprinkle nutmeg on top. Let stand for 5 minutes before serving.

NOTE The same ingredients can also be baked in a single medium baking pan.

VARIATIONS
Instead of lobster, substitute braised meat. Or try another seafood and introduce a touch of lobster stock for flavor.

Swap root vegetables or summer squash for the cauliflower, depending on the season.

MAKE AHEAD The baked pasta can be prepared through Step 3 and refrigerated for up to 4 hours.

SERVE WITH I like this baked pasta alongside Roasted Beet Salad with Manouri Cream and Buttered Walnuts (page 38) and Yellow Split Pea Spread (page 26), or before Braised Whole Fish with Tomatoes, Garlic, and Onions (pages 119–120).

WINE Nykteri from Santorini or oak-aged Greek Chardonnay.

Seafood and Tomato Stew

Saganaki is the name for a two-handled baking pan and for the food that's served in it. There are many variations, including the dramatic flaming cheese saganaki and shrimp saganaki (shrimp baked with tomato and feta). My version, saganaki tou posidonia, calls for mixed seafood, which poaches simply in salted water, because all the other ingredients are super flavorful. • **4 SERVINGS**

4 cups (1 L) water

Kosher salt

4 jumbo shrimp, peeled and deveined

3½ ounces (110 g) skinless halibut fillet, cut into 1-inch (2.5 cm) pieces

2 ounces (60 g) calamari, cut into rings

2½ ounces (70 g) bay scallops, side muscle removed

½ cup (125 ml) Greek Tomato Sauce (page 220)

1 teaspoon fresh lemon juice

½ teaspoon ouzo

Extra virgin olive oil, for drizzling

Crumbled feta cheese (see page 163), micro herbs, and edible flowers, for garnish

1. Heat the oven to 325°F (165°C). In a medium saucepan, generously season the water with salt and heat to 140°F (60°C). Add the shrimp and cook for 30 seconds, adjusting the heat to maintain the temperature. Add the fish and calamari and cook for 30 seconds. Add the scallops and cook for 1 minute, for a total cooking time of 2 minutes. Drain the seafood. Cut the shrimp into 1½-inch (4 cm) pieces.

2. Spoon the Greek Tomato Sauce into a heat-proof platter or serving bowls and transfer to the oven until warmed through, about 3 minutes. Remove from the oven and drizzle with the lemon juice, ouzo, and oil. Garnish with cheese and arrange the seafood on top. Return to the oven until warmed through, about 3 minutes. Drizzle with oil, garnish with herbs and flowers, and serve.

NOTE It is important to maintain a temperature of 140°F (60°C) in Step 1, so adjust the heat accordingly.

VARIATIONS
Grouper or another thick whitefish fillet can be substituted for the halibut. Diced sea scallops can stand in for bay scallops when they're out of season. Clams, mussels, or lobster meat can be added or substituted for another ingredient in the stew. Or feature only one variety of seafood.

SERVE WITH I like eating saganaki tou posidonia with Zucchini and Feta Fritters (pages 44–45).

WINE Fresh Assyrtiko from Santorini, apple-tinged Debina, or citrusy Roditis from the mountains.

Calamari "Pasta" with Saffron Yogurt

Treating calamari like pasta is fun—and you don't have to make a dough. At first I cut the bodies into stubby squares to resemble hilopites (Greek egg pasta), but I prefer these thin, elegant strands. Once you cut the "pasta" (a chore, it's true), the rest is a breeze. The strands are sautéed, then tossed with the remaining ingredients as if making a salad. • **4 SERVINGS**

3 tablespoons extra virgin olive oil

1 garlic clove, crushed

1 small yellow squash, skin only, cut into thin julienne strips

1 small green zucchini, skin only, cut into thin julienne strips

Kosher salt and freshly ground white pepper

7 ounces (200 g) cleaned calamari tubes, 4 to 6 inches (10 to 15 cm) long, sliced lengthwise into strips ⅛ inch (3 mm) wide

½ teaspoon crushed red pepper

2 tablespoons (15 g) Kalamata olive julienne

2 tablespoons (20 g) finely diced peeled, seeded tomato

1 tablespoon (9 g) drained capers

2 teaspoons chopped parsley

2 teaspoons fresh lemon juice

2 tablespoons Saffron Yogurt (page 44)

Edible flowers, for garnish, optional

1. In a medium skillet, heat 1 tablespoon of the oil until shimmering. Add the garlic and 1 ounce (30 g) each of the yellow squash and zucchini julienne, season with salt and white pepper, and cook over medium-high heat, stirring often, until the squash and zucchini are softened but not browned, about 1 minute. Remove the skillet from the heat and discard the garlic. Using a slotted spoon, transfer the squash and zucchini to a plate. Wipe out the skillet.

2. In the same skillet, heat 1 tablespoon of the oil until it begins to smoke. Add the calamari, season with salt, white pepper, and crushed red pepper, and cook over medium-high heat, stirring, until just cooked, about 10 seconds. Remove the skillet from the heat and pour off any liquid. Add the squash and zucchini, olives, tomato, capers, parsley, lemon juice, and remaining 1 tablespoon of oil. Toss to mix and taste for seasoning.

3. Brush a serving bowl or bowls with the Saffron Yogurt. Mound the calamari mixture in the bowl, garnish with edible flowers, if desired, and serve.

NOTE Before sautéing the calamari, I pour 4 cups (1 L) of boiling water over it, refrigerate it until cool, and drain. This technique makes for a cleaner presentation.

SERVE WITH As part of a meze spread, serve this calamari alongside Grilled Eggplant Spread (page 22), Steamed Mussels with Feta Sauce (page 67), and Roasted Beet Salad with Manouri Cream and Buttered Walnuts (page 38). It's also nice as a first course before Braised Lamb and Roasted Tomatoes in Thieves' Purses (pages 180–181).

WINE Herbaceous, crisp Sauvignon Blanc from northern Greece or flowery Moschofilero from Mantinia.

Tuna Meatballs with Chickpea Stew

On one of my trips to Crete, I sampled veal meatballs served with a cozy chickpea and tomato stew. It brought to mind a similar recipe with tuna created by one of my best friends, chef Piero Premoli of Pricci, our Italian restaurant in Atlanta. When I got home, I met with Piero and came up with this piquant version. • **4 SERVINGS**

CHICKPEAS

½ cup (100 g) dried chickpeas, soaked overnight and drained

½ teaspoon coriander seeds

1 small bay leaf

1 small carrot, cut into 2-inch (5 cm) pieces

½ small onion

Kosher salt and freshly ground white pepper

¾ cup (185 ml) Greek Tomato Sauce (page 220)

2 teaspoons ground cumin

½ teaspoon Garlic Puree (page 219)

MEATBALLS

8 ounces (250 g) skinless tuna fillet

2 tablespoons Greek Tomato Sauce (page 220)

2 tablespoons heavy cream

½ ounce (15 g) focaccia or other plain bread without crust

2½ teaspoons pureed oil-packed Calabrian chiles (see Note)

1 clove of Garlic Confit (page 219)

1 teaspoon minced preserved lemon rind

1 teaspoon ground coriander

½ teaspoon chopped parsley

Canola oil, for frying

1 or 2 scoops Greek yogurt, preferably homemade (page 223)

Micro herbs, for garnish, optional

1. CHICKPEAS In a medium saucepan, cover the chickpeas with 2 inches (5 cm) of water and bring to a simmer. Tie the coriander seeds and bay leaf in a cheesecloth bundle. Add the bundle, carrot, and onion to the chickpeas, cover partially, and cook over medium-low heat, skimming occasionally, until tender, 1 to 1½ hours. Season the cooking liquid with salt and pepper as if it were soup and let the chickpeas cool in the liquid. Remove the carrot, onion, and bundle and discard. Drain the chickpeas, saving the cooking liquid for another use, and return to the pan. Just before serving, stir in the tomato sauce, cumin, and Garlic Puree and simmer for 5 minutes. Season with salt and pepper.

2. MEATBALLS Pass the tuna through the small plate of a grinder or coarsely chop it; keep cold. In a food processor, puree the tomato sauce with the cream, bread, Calabrian chiles, Garlic Confit, preserved lemon, coriander, and parsley until smooth. Add the tuna and pulse until smooth. Using your hands, form the tuna mixture into ½-tablespoon balls; transfer them to a plate as they're shaped.

3. Line a baking sheet with paper towels. In a medium skillet, heat ½ inch (1 cm) of oil to 350°F (175°C). Working in batches, fry the meatballs, turning them occasionally, until golden brown, 2 to 3 minutes. Using a slotted spoon, transfer them to the prepared baking sheet as they're cooked.

4. Spoon the chickpeas into a serving bowl or bowls. Arrange the meatballs on top in a circle and season with salt and pepper. Dollop the yogurt in the center, garnish with herbs, if desired, and serve.

NOTE Spicy Calabrian chiles come whole in jars. You'll need to drain a couple and puree them to a chunky paste. Or try 1 teaspoon of harissa, Sriracha, or chili-garlic paste instead.

MAKE AHEAD The cooked chickpeas can be refrigerated in the cooking liquid for up to 5 days.

WINE Medium-bodied, spicy red (Liatiko, Kotsifali-Mandilaria, or Kotsifali-Syrah) from Crete or Xinomavro from northern Greece.

PHYLLO PASTRIES

Spinach-and-Feta Phyllo Triangles

There isn't a single family gathering where my mother doesn't make at least one or two pie-crust versions of spanakopita, and they're always the first appetizers to go. In Greece, my thea Stella prepares a recipe using a rough puff pastry dough that she calls fila (with an "a"). I use store-bought no. 10 phyllo, a.k.a. country phyllo, and make two-bite triangles. • **MAKES 12 PASTRIES/4 SERVINGS**

1 tablespoon canola oil

4 ounces (125 g) spinach leaves, thick stems removed

Kosher salt and freshly ground white pepper

¾ cup (60 g) halved lengthwise and thinly sliced leeks, white and light green parts only

4 scallions, thinly sliced (½ cup)

1 tablespoon plus 1 teaspoon finely chopped dill

2 teaspoons finely chopped parsley

1 large egg, lightly beaten

¾ cup (90 g) crumbled feta cheese (see page 163)

2 frozen country-style (extra-thick) phyllo sheets (no. 10), thawed

¼ cup (60 ml) clarified butter (see Step 3, page 199)

1. Line a baking sheet with paper towels. In a large saucepan, warm 1 teaspoon of the oil. Add the spinach, season with salt and pepper, and cook over medium heat, stirring occasionally, until wilted, 3 to 5 minutes; transfer to the prepared baking sheet. Repeat with the leeks and scallions, cooking them each in 1 teaspoon of the oil.

2. Coarsely chop the spinach and squeeze dry in cheesecloth. In a medium bowl, mix the spinach with the leeks, scallions, herbs, and half of the egg. Stir in the cheese and season with salt and pepper. Transfer to the refrigerator and chill until firm, at least 1 hour.

3. Line a baking sheet with parchment paper. For each phyllo sheet, lay it on a work surface with a long side in front of you. Brush with clarified butter. Using a pizza cutter or a sharp knife, cut the phyllo crosswise into 6 equal strips. Mound 1½ tablespoons (25 g) of the spinach filling at the bottom of each phyllo strip. Fold the bottom left corner of a phyllo strip over the filling to meet the right edge of the dough, making a triangle. Fold up the triangle to meet the right edge of the dough. Continue folding over and up to the end (see Note). Transfer the triangle to the prepared baking sheet and brush all over with clarified butter. Repeat with the remaining spinach filling and phyllo strips. Transfer to the refrigerator and chill until the butter is firm, at least 30 minutes.

PRECEDING SPREAD, CLOCKWISE FROM CENTER: Spinach-and-Feta Phyllo Triangles (this spread); Cheese Phyllo Cigars (page 82); Cheese and Wild Mushroom Shredded-Phyllo Pies (page 83); Salmon-and-Leek Phyllo Spirals with Tarama Mousse (pages 86–87)

4. Heat the oven to 350°F (175°C). Brush a large skillet with clarified butter and warm over medium heat. Add the pastries in batches and cook, turning them every 20 to 30 seconds so they don't burn, until lightly browned, 3 to 4 minutes. Return the pastries to the baking sheet, spacing them well apart, and bake, turning them once, until a cake tester inserted in a pastry is warm when touched to your lower lip, about 10 minutes. Let cool slightly and serve.

NOTE If you know how to fold a paper football, use the same technique for shaping the phyllo triangles.

MAKE AHEAD The triangles can be prepared through Step 3 and refrigerated for up to 2 days.

WINE Crisp Moschofilero, Greek Sauvignon Blanc, or dry Malvasia from Crete.

SAVORY GREEK PIE, WHENEVER YOU WANT IT

I used to walk three or four miles home from elementary school with my brother, Niko, and our friends, but, if we were lucky, my grandmother's spinach pie would already be out of the oven and cooling on the counter. It takes a whole hour to cool a hot pie enough for a tender mouth—that's forever in kid time. So when I could smell the filling from the doorway, I'd drop my book bag and bolt to the kitchen, hoping like crazy that the afternoon treat was ready to eat.

Pites, Greek "pies," are something like a double-crusted fruit pie in that they're encased in dough. But they're eaten more like pizza or sandwiches. For the most part, pites are savory. I grew up with the spinach-and-cheese variety, but in Greece, my relatives serve innumerable fillings, such as meat, often lamb or pork; seafood; melted leeks; wild greens; and leftover combinations of all of the above. As for sweet versions, my aunt Elaine Tissura prepares a pumpkin-and-rice pite, and my pastry chef, Daniela Ascencio, has created a variation, Phyllo-Wrapped Banana with Flourless Chocolate Cake (pages 200–201).

Greek pies take many forms. They can be round (like apple pie), half-moon turnovers, spirals, or the hefty baking-pan slabs you see at diners. At Kyma, there's a lot of sharing, so we get into the little shapes, like two-bite triangles and "cigars."

And the pastry crust varies. My mother usually prepares a no-fuss pie dough. But my aunt Stella goes all out, stacking balls of dough and rolling them into a kind of puff pastry. The layers of flour and fat create a really flaky crust. Also, there's no shame in buying readymade sheets of phyllo dough—I use it at Kyma—as well as kataifi, shredded phyllo dough.

Being savory, pites are more a food staple than an occasional indulgence. They can be a prelude to a meal, a meal in itself, and a side dish, as well as iconic, crowd-pleasing party food. My kids wake up and have pie for breakfast or eat it for lunch at school. For big Easter dinners, my mother will crank out multiple "feeds ten"-size pies, at least two spinach and two cheese. And since it's wrapped in pastry, it's easily portable for a potluck or any kind of gathering. In Greece, if you're walking around hungry and there isn't any pie waiting for you at home, you can always pick up some at a bakeshop. You don't need an excuse to eat pie.

Cheese Phyllo Cigars

One of the first things I do when I arrive in Greece is hunt down freshly made tiropita, cheese-stuffed pastries. For Greeks, these creamy, crispy hand pies are soul food. They come in many shapes—triangles, half-moons, spirals, or, as here, cigars.

• **MAKES 8 PASTRIES/4 SERVINGS**

¾ cup (90 g) shredded graviera cheese (see page 163) or Swiss-type cheese

¼ cup plus 2 tablespoons (40 g) shredded kasseri cheese (see page 163) or provolone cheese

¼ cup plus 2 tablespoons (40 g) crumbled manouri cheese (see page 163) or shredded fresh mozzarella cheese

3 tablespoons mascarpone cheese or cream cheese

1 large egg, lightly beaten

⅛ teaspoon freshly ground white pepper

1 tablespoon thinly sliced chives

1 frozen country-style (extra-thick) phyllo sheet (no. 10), thawed

¼ cup (60 ml) clarified butter (see Step 3, page 199)

1. In a food processor, puree the four cheeses with half of the egg and the pepper until smooth. Scrape the mixture into a small bowl and fold in the chives. Transfer to the refrigerator and chill until firm, at least 1 hour.

2. Line a baking sheet with parchment paper. Lay the phyllo sheet on a work surface with a long side in front of you. Brush with clarified butter. Using a pizza cutter or a sharp knife, cut the phyllo in half lengthwise, then cut crosswise into 8 equal rectangles. Using your hands, shape 1½ tablespoons (30 g) of the cheese filling into a 3-inch (7.5 cm) tube and place it along the bottom of a rectangle, leaving a 1-inch (2.5 cm) border. Fold the phyllo

tightly over the filling and roll up to the end. Pinch the ends to seal. Transfer the cigar to the prepared baking sheet and brush all over with clarified butter. Repeat with the remaining cheese filling and phyllo rectangles. Transfer to the refrigerator and chill until the butter is firm, at least 30 minutes.

3. Heat the oven to 350°F (175°C). Brush a medium skillet with clarified butter and warm over medium heat. Add the pastries and cook, turning them every 20 to 30 seconds so they don't burn, until lightly browned, 3 to 4 minutes. Return the pastries to the baking sheet, spacing them well apart, and bake, turning them once, until a cake tester inserted in a pastry is warm when touched to your lower lip, about 10 minutes. Let cool slightly and serve.

NOTE If you're comfortable using a pastry bag, spoon the filling into a bag fitted with a ¼-inch (6 mm) tip (or a plastic bag with a bottom corner cut off to make a tip) and pipe 3-inch (7.5 cm) tubes along the bottom of each rectangle, leaving a 1-inch (2.5 cm) border.

MAKE AHEAD The cheese filling can be refrigerated for up to 5 days. The cigars can be prepared through Step 3 and refrigerated for up to 2 days.

SERVE WITH I like these cheese pastries with Classic Greek Salad (page 49).

WINE Crisp, citrus-scented Robola from Cephalonia or barrel-aged Malagousia.

Cheese and Wild Mushroom Shredded-Phyllo Pies

My Athens-based cousin Sofia Perpera introduced me to one of the best meals in the city, at Rena tis Ftelias. I'll never forget chef-owner Rena Togia's melted cheese under a thatch of shredded phyllo (kataifi). It's beautiful to look at and fun to share, so for my version—I add a layer of sautéed mushrooms in vinaigrette—each cheese pie makes enough to serve two. • **MAKES TWO 4½-INCH (10.5 CM) PASTRIES/4 SERVINGS**

3 ounces (90 g) frozen shredded phyllo (kataifi), thawed, cut into four 8-inch (20 cm) sections (see Notes)

10 ounces (300 g) kasseri cheese (see page 163) or provolone cheese, shredded

1 cup (125 g) Wild Mushrooms "à la Grecque" (pages 40–41)

¼ cup plus 2 tablespoons (100 ml) clarified butter (see Step 3, page 199)

2 tablespoons water

Truffle oil, for drizzling, optional (see Notes)

NOTES Shredded phyllo (kataifi) is available at Greek and Mediterranean markets.
Truffle oil is available at specialty food shops and dartagnan.com.

VARIATION
To make a cheese-only pie, omit the mushrooms and double the cheese.

MAKE AHEAD The assembled pies can be wrapped in plastic and refrigerated for up to 3 days before baking.

SERVE WITH I like this pie alongside Wilted Greens (page 114) and Eggplant Stew with Onions and Tomato Sauce (pages 36–37).

WINE Oak-aged Assyrtiko with pronounced acidity or Assyrtiko–Sauvignon Blanc or Assyrtiko-Sémillon blend.

1. For each pie, spread 1 section of the phyllo over a 4 ½-inch (10.5 cm) round shallow baking pan, leaving about 2 inches (5 cm) of overhang on both ends. Repeat with another section of the phyllo, making a cross.

2. For each pie, mound half of the cheese on the phyllo. Spread half of the mushrooms on top. One at a time, fold the phyllo sections over the mushrooms. Brush with the clarified butter. Transfer to the refrigerator and chill until the butter is firm, at least 30 minutes.

3. Heat the oven to 350°F (175°C). Add 1 tablespoon of water to each pie and bake until golden brown, about 30 minutes. Tilt the pies to drain off any oil. Drizzle with truffle oil, if desired, and serve.

Lamb Phyllo Spirals

This recipe pays homage to the Greek exohiko pie, described by my friend John Lefkathitikis as having a filling of leftover meats that have been crisped in oil and garnished with onions, garlic, thyme, and oregano. How much thyme and oregano? "Enough so it smells throughout the kitchen," he said. I serve this lamb version with tangy yogurt and a citrusy salad of arugula and olives. • **MAKES 2 PASTRIES/4 SERVINGS**

One 1¼-pound (625 g) lamb shank (see Note)

Kosher salt and freshly ground white pepper

3 tablespoons canola oil

1 small Vidalia (sweet) onion, thinly sliced

3 garlic cloves, thinly sliced

2 thyme sprigs, plus 1 tablespoon chopped thyme

2 cups (500 ml) chicken stock

1 tablespoon dried oregano

1 tablespoon all-purpose flour

2 tablespoons extra virgin olive oil

1½ ounces (50 g) graviera cheese (see page 163) or Swiss-type cheese, cut into ¼-inch (6 mm) dice

4 frozen phyllo sheets (no. 4), thawed

¼ cup plus 2 tablespoons (100 ml) clarified butter (see Step 3, page 199)

1 cup (30 g) baby arugula

2 scallions, thinly sliced

4 pitted Kalamata olives, quartered lengthwise

1½ teaspoons fresh lemon juice

3 tablespoons Greek yogurt, preferably homemade (page 223)

Dill sprigs and parsley sprigs, large stems removed, for garnish

1. Heat the oven to 325°F (165°C). Season the lamb with salt and pepper. In a small enameled cast-iron casserole, heat 1 tablespoon of the canola oil until shimmering. Add the lamb and cook over medium-high heat until browned on all sides, about 10 minutes. Transfer the lamb to a plate. In the same pot, heat 1 tablespoon of the canola oil until shimmering. Add the onion and garlic, season with salt and pepper, and cook over medium-high heat, stirring occasionally, until lightly browned, 5 to 8 minutes. Return the lamb to the pot along with the thyme sprigs and stock. Press a parchment paper lid on top, cover, and bring to a simmer. Transfer the pot to the oven and cook the lamb, turning it once, until a cake tester slides easily into the meat, 1½ to 3½ hours. Remove the pot from the oven and

let cool to room temperature. Transfer the lamb to a carving board. Strain the braising liquid through a fine sieve into a small bowl, and reserve the onion mixture.

2. In a medium bowl, remove the meat from the bone and discard the fat. Shred the meat and combine it with the oregano, chopped thyme, and flour. Season with salt and pepper. In a small skillet, heat the remaining 1 tablespoon of canola oil until shimmering. Add the lamb mixture and cook over medium-high heat, stirring and scraping up the browned bits stuck to the bottom, until crispy, about 4 minutes. Add ¼ cup (60 ml) of the braising liquid and cook, stirring and scraping up the browned bits, until the liquid evaporates, about 1 minute. Remove the skillet from the heat. Using a wooden spoon, beat in 1 tablespoon of the olive oil. Stir in the reserved onion mixture and let cool completely. In the same bowl, combine 2 cups (160 g) of the lamb mixture with the cheese; save any remaining meat for another use.

3. Line a baking sheet with parchment paper. For each spiral, lay 1 phyllo sheet on a work surface with a long side in front of you. Brush with clarified butter. Cover with a second phyllo sheet and brush with clarified butter. Spoon half of the filling along the bottom long side of the phyllo, leaving a 1-inch (2.5 cm) border.

4. Roll the phyllo over the filling and continue rolling to the end, brushing with clarified butter as you go. Starting with one end, curl the roll into a spiral. Transfer the spiral to the prepared baking sheet and brush all over with clarified butter. Transfer to the refrigerator and chill until the butter is firm, at least 30 minutes.

5. Heat the oven to 350°F (175°C). Brush a large skillet with clarified butter and warm over medium heat. Add the pastries and cook, turning them once and watching carefully so they don't burn, until lightly browned, 3 to 4 minutes. Return the pastries to the baking sheet, spacing them well apart, and bake, turning them once, until a cake tester inserted in a pastry is warm when touched to your lower lip, about 10 minutes.

6. In a medium bowl, combine the arugula with the scallions, olives, lemon juice, and remaining 1 tablespoon of olive oil and toss to coat. Season with salt and pepper. Spread half of the yogurt in the center of each plate and set the lamb pastries on top. Mound the salad on the pastries, garnish with dill and parsley, and serve.

NOTE Don't have lamb shanks for this recipe? Substitute 12 ounces (350 g) of shoulder lamb chops or 8 ounces (250 g) of boneless lamb shoulder.

MAKE AHEAD The lamb can be prepared through Step 1 and refrigerated in the braising liquid for up to 5 days. The assembled pastries can be refrigerated for up to 2 days before baking.

SERVE WITH I like this pastry alongside Lemony Quinoa Salad (page 35) and Wild Mushrooms "à la Grecque" (pages 40–41). It also makes an excellent first course before whole grilled fish (pages 110–111; 114–115).

WINE Earthy Xinomavro from northern Greece or spicy Syrah from Crete or the mainland.

Salmon-and-Leek Phyllo Spirals with Tarama Mousse

Salmon and leeks are one of my favorite ingredient combos, so when my aunt Stella taught me how to make leek pie, prasopita, I was excited to put a seafood spin on it. The pastry filled with gently cooked salmon and velvet-textured leeks, plus a touch of melty kasseri, reminds me of a seaside grilled cheese sandwich. This rich pastry needs a spicy green salad, so I top it with peppercress and whipped tarama mousse.

• MAKES 2 PASTRIES/4 SERVINGS

PHYLLO SPIRALS

2 teaspoons canola oil

½ cup (35 g) halved lengthwise and thinly sliced leeks, white and light green parts only

Kosher salt and freshly ground white pepper

2 scallions, thinly sliced

¼ cup (30 g) shredded kasseri cheese (see page 163) or provolone cheese

¼ cup (30 g) crumbled feta cheese (see page 163)

1 tablespoon thinly sliced chives

1 large egg, lightly beaten

8 ounces (250 g) skinless salmon fillet, cut into ¼-inch (6 mm) dice

4 frozen phyllo sheets (no. 4), thawed

¼ cup plus 2 tablespoons (100 ml) clarified butter (see Step 3, page 199)

TARAMA MOUSSE

¼ cup (60 ml) crème fraîche or ¼ cup (60 ml) heavy cream plus 1 tablespoon sour cream (see Notes)

1½ tablespoons tarama roe (see Notes)

1½ teaspoons fresh lemon juice

Freshly ground white pepper

Micro peppercress or watercress, for garnish

Kosher salt

Extra virgin olive oil, for drizzling

1. PHYLLO SPIRALS In a small skillet, warm 1 teaspoon of the canola oil. Add the leeks, season with salt and pepper, and cook over medium heat, stirring occasionally, until softened but not browned, about 5 minutes. Transfer the leeks to a paper towel–lined plate. In the same skillet, heat the remaining 1 teaspoon of canola oil. Add the scallions, season with salt and pepper, and cook over medium heat, stirring occasionally, until softened, about 5 minutes. Transfer to the plate with the leeks and let cool.

2. In a medium bowl, combine the leek mixture with both cheeses, the chives, and half of the egg. Fold in the salmon. Transfer to the refrigerator and chill until firm, at least 1 hour.

3. Line a baking sheet with parchment paper. For each spiral, lay 1 phyllo sheet on a work surface with a long side in front of you. Brush with clarified butter. Cover with a second phyllo sheet and brush with clarified butter. Spoon half of the filling along the bottom long side of the phyllo, leaving a 1-inch (2.5 cm) border.

4. Roll the phyllo over the filling and continue rolling to the end, brushing with clarified butter as you go. Starting with one end, curl the roll into a spiral. Transfer to the prepared baking sheet and brush all over with clarified butter. Transfer to the refrigerator and chill until the butter is firm, at least 30 minutes.

5. TARAMA MOUSSE Meanwhile, in a small bowl, combine the crème fraîche with the tarama roe, lemon juice, and a pinch of pepper. Whisk until it holds a soft peak. Transfer to the refrigerator and chill until firm, at least 30 minutes.

6. Heat the oven to 350°F (175°C). Brush a large skillet with clarified butter and warm over medium heat. Add the pastries and cook, turning them once and watching carefully so they don't burn, until lightly browned, 3 to 4 minutes. Return the pastries to the baking sheet, spacing them well apart, and bake, turning them once, until a cake tester inserted in a pastry is warm when touched to your lower lip, about 10 minutes.

7. In a medium bowl, season the peppercress with salt and pepper and drizzle with olive oil. Transfer the pastries to plates. Mound half of the peppercress on each and set a spoonful of tarama mousse on top. Serve warm.

NOTES This pastry can be made year-round, but it's especially good in the spring, when leeks are at their peak and spring onions can replace the scallions.

Sour cream can't replace the crème fraîche here, because it doesn't whip on its own.

Tarama roe is available at Greek and Mediterranean markets and online.

Don't cook the pastries past when the cake tester feels warm to your lower lip, or the salmon will be overcooked.

VARIATION
For a version of my thea Stella's leek-only pie, omit the salmon.

MAKE AHEAD The tarama mousse can be refrigerated overnight. The assembled pastries can be refrigerated overnight before baking.

SERVE WITH I like this pastry alongside Lemony Quinoa Salad (page 35) and Warm Potato-Tomato Salad (page 48). It also makes an excellent first course before Grilled Beef Rib Eye with Parsley Sauce (page 171).

WINE Fresh, aromatic Agiorgitiko from Nemea or crisp Assyrtiko from Santorini.

MEAT

Spiced Red Wine–Braised Rabbit

After a night's drinking and eating in Greece, one of my favorite things to do is cruise the early-morning food markets. I'm looking for one last meal before bed—stifado, a pungent stew that's marinated for more than 24 hours in wine, vinegar, and copious spices. On my hunt, I'm always amused to see a grandma with a squirming chicken or rabbit in tow for slaughtering at home. How crazy that would seem in North America.

• **4 SERVINGS**

½ cup (125 ml) canola oil

1 medium Vidalia (sweet) onion, thinly sliced

1 head of garlic, cloves thinly sliced

3 tablespoons tomato paste

2 cinnamon sticks

3 bay leaves

1 tablespoon black peppercorns

1 tablespoon allspice berries

1 teaspoon whole cloves

2 cups (500 ml) red wine vinegar

4 cups (1 L) dry red wine

2 whole rabbit legs (see Notes)

Kosher salt and freshly ground white pepper

12 cipollini onions (8 ounces/250 g total), peeled

6 cherry tomatoes, halved

5 thyme sprigs

2 rosemary sprigs, plus small sprigs for garnish

1. In a medium skillet, warm ¼ cup (60 ml) of the oil. Add the Vidalia onion and cook over medium heat, stirring occasionally, until lightly browned, 12 to 15 minutes. Add the garlic and cook, stirring, until fragrant, about 30 seconds. Add the tomato paste and cook, stirring, for 1 minute. Add the cinnamon, bay leaves, peppercorns, allspice, cloves, and vinegar and cook, scraping up the browned bits on the bottom, until reduced by half, about 5 minutes. Add the wine and bring to a simmer, then cook over low heat for 20 minutes. Remove the skillet from the heat and let the marinade cool.

2. Transfer the marinade to a medium bowl, add the rabbit, and turn to coat. Cover and refrigerate overnight.

3. Heat the oven to 325°F (165°C). Remove the rabbit from the marinade and scrape off the spices; reserve the marinade. Pat the rabbit dry with paper towels and season with salt and pepper. In a medium skillet, warm the remaining ¼ cup (60 ml) of oil. Add the rabbit and cook over medium heat, turning the legs every 20 to 30 seconds, until mahogany brown, about 5 minutes.

PHOTOGRAPH ON PRECEDING SPREAD

4. Transfer the rabbit to a small enameled cast-iron casserole. Add the marinade, cipollini onions, tomatoes, thyme, and rosemary. Cover and bring to a simmer, then transfer to the oven and braise until a cake tester slides easily into the meat, about 2 hours.

5. Transfer the rabbit to a medium saucepan. Strain the braising liquid through a medium sieve into the pan. Reserve 4 tomato halves and 4 cipollini onions and discard the remaining solids in the sieve. Let the rabbit cool completely (see Notes). Reheat the rabbit in the braising liquid. Transfer to a serving bowl or bowls, garnish with rosemary, and serve with the reserved tomatoes and onions.

NOTES The rabbit needs to marinate for at least 24 hours, so plan accordingly.

Rabbit is available at butcher shops, farmers' markets, and dartagnan.com.

While I serve this version of stifado as a meze, it can also be doubled to make a deeply flavored entrée.

Letting the rabbit cool in the braising liquid makes it extra juicy.

The meat should be falling-apart tender; if it starts to shred when you plate it, that's a good sign.

VARIATIONS

Instead of rabbit, try this rustic stew with chicken, venison, quail, pheasant, or even octopus.

Shallots can be swapped in for the cipollini onions.

MAKE AHEAD The marinade can be prepared through Step 1 and refrigerated for up to 3 days. The braised meat can be refrigerated for up to 5 days.

WINE Greek Merlot or Agiorgitiko, singly or blended with Cabernet Sauvignon or Syrah, from the Peloponnese.

Drunk Man's Stew

Bekri meze is marinated, braised, and finished with glugs of Metaxa, Greece's golden brandy. **4 SERVINGS**

8 ounces (250 g) boneless braising lamb, such as top round or shoulder, cut into 1-inch cubes

1¼ cups (300 ml) brandy, preferably Metaxa (see Note)

Kosher salt and freshly ground white pepper

2 tablespoons (16 g) all-purpose flour

3 tablespoons canola oil

1 small (3½-ounce/100 g) onion, grated

1 teaspoon Garlic Puree (page 219)

1 tablespoon tomato paste

2 cups (500 ml) chicken stock

1 thyme sprig

1 rosemary sprig

1 bay leaf

¼ cup (50 g) small-diced carrot

¼ cup (50 g) small-diced parsnip

¼ cup (50 g) small-diced celery root

2 tablespoons chopped mixed herbs, such as parsley and chives

Micro herbs, for garnish, optional

1. In a medium bowl, combine the lamb with 1 cup (250 ml) of the brandy and refrigerate overnight.

2. Strain the brandy into a small glass measuring cup and reserve. Return the lamb to the bowl and pat dry with paper towels. Season with salt and pepper, add the flour, and toss to coat.

3. In a medium saucepan, heat 2 tablespoons of the oil until shimmering. Working in two batches, cook the lamb over medium-high heat until browned on all sides, about 5 minutes per batch. Transfer the lamb to a plate. Add the remaining 1 tablespoon of oil and the onion and cook over medium heat, stirring occasionally, until softened, 2 to 3 minutes. Add the Garlic Puree and cook until fragrant, about 30 seconds. Add the tomato paste and cook, stirring, for 45 seconds. Return the lamb to the pan along with the reserved brandy, the stock, thyme, rosemary, and bay leaf. Bring to a simmer and cook over medium-low heat until the lamb is tender, 1 to 1½ hours. Discard the thyme, rosemary, and bay leaf.

4. Meanwhile, in a medium saucepan, cover the diced carrot, parsnip, and celery root with 2 inches (5 cm) of water and season with salt. Bring to a simmer and cook until tender, about 5 minutes; drain.

5. Add the diced vegetables to the lamb stew along with the chopped herbs and remaining ¼ cup (60 ml) of brandy. Spoon the stew into a serving bowl or bowls, garnish with micro herbs, if desired, and serve.

NOTES Metaxa is a spirit distilled from the wine of sun-dried grapes that's aged in barrels and then blended with Muscat wine, herbs, and spices.

MAKE AHEAD The stew can be prepared through Step 3 and refrigerated for up to 5 days. The cooked diced vegetables can be refrigerated overnight.

WINE Xinomavro from Naoussa or Amynteo, Xinomavro-Krassato-Stavroto blend from Rapsani, or Xinomavro-Negoska blend from Goumenissa.

Chicken with Yogurt Barley and English Peas

This recipe is inspired by a traditional Greek chicken that's smeared with tangy walnut-studded yogurt and then roasted. But coating the skin keeps it from getting crisp, so instead, I slow-simmer skin-on chicken thighs to get succulent meat, then broil them until golden. The braising liquid is saved to prepare a barley accompaniment, which gets enriched with yogurt. My version is especially popular in late winter, when it's garnished with the last fresh black truffles of the season and the first sweet peas. Once the peas are gone, I swap in navy beans, which echo the earthy flavor of the walnuts. • **4 SERVINGS**

CHICKEN

1 tablespoon canola oil

1 small Vidalia (sweet) onion, thinly sliced

2 garlic cloves, thinly sliced

2 cups (500 ml) dry white wine

1 teaspoon coriander seeds

1/2 teaspoon black peppercorns

2 skin-on, bone-in chicken thighs

2 cups (500 ml) chicken stock

2 bay leaves

2 oregano sprigs

BARLEY AND ASSEMBLY

1 tablespoon canola oil

1 teaspoon finely chopped shallot

1/4 cup (50 g) pearl barley

Kosher salt and freshly ground white pepper

1/4 cup (30 g) shelled walnuts

1/4 cup (60 g) shelled fresh peas or thawed frozen baby peas

1/2 cup (125 ml) Greek yogurt, preferably homemade (page 223)

2 tablespoons thinly sliced chives

1 tablespoon white truffle oil (see Notes) or walnut oil

Fleur de sel, for sprinkling

1/4 ounce (8 g) black truffle, diced, optional (see Notes)

1. CHICKEN Heat the oven to 325°F (165°C). In a small enameled cast-iron casserole, warm the canola oil. Add the onion and cook over medium heat, stirring occasionally, until softened, about 5 minutes. Add the garlic and cook, stirring occasionally, for 1 minute. Add the wine, coriander seeds, and peppercorns, bring to a boil, and cook over medium-high heat until reduced by half, about 5 minutes. Add the chicken thighs, stock, bay leaves, and oregano. Press a parchment paper lid on top, cover, and bring to a simmer. Transfer to the oven and braise until a cake tester slides easily into the meat, 1 1/2 to 2 hours.

2. Transfer the chicken thighs to a medium bowl and slide out the bones, keeping the thighs intact; discard the bones. Leave the oven on. Strain the braising liquid through a fine sieve over the chicken; discard the solids in the sieve. Let cool to room temperature.

3. BARLEY In a small saucepan, warm the canola oil. Add the shallot and cook over medium heat until softened but not browned, about 2 minutes. Add the barley and cook, stirring, for 30 seconds. Add ¾ cup (185 ml) of the braising liquid and season with kosher salt and pepper. Cover and bring to a simmer, then cook over low heat until the barley is tender, about 30 minutes.

4. Spread the walnuts in a pie plate and toast in the oven, stirring occasionally, until fragrant, 8 to 10 minutes. Coarsely chop the walnuts. In a small saucepan of boiling water, cook the peas until tender, 1 to 3 minutes. Drain the peas, rinse in cold water, and drain again. Stir the yogurt, walnuts, peas, chives, and truffle oil into the barley. Season with kosher salt and pepper. If needed, add more braising liquid a tablespoon at a time until the barley is saucy.

5. ASSEMBLY Heat the broiler. Transfer the chicken to a small shallow baking pan. Add ½ cup (125 ml) of the remaining braising liquid to the pan; save the remaining liquid for another use. Broil the chicken skin side up until golden brown, 3 to 5 minutes. Spoon the barley into a serving bowl or bowls and set the chicken on top. Sprinkle with fleur de sel and, if desired, the truffle and serve.

NOTES White truffle oil and black truffles are available at dartagnan.com.

As an alternative to the fresh black truffle and fleur de sel, black truffle sea salt is available at specialty food shops and tfsnyc.com.

The chicken should be falling-apart tender; if it starts to shred when you plate it, that's a good sign.

The barley will continue to absorb liquid, so add more of the braising liquid to loosen the texture if needed.

VARIATION

The same amount of cooked navy beans can be substituted for the peas.

MAKE AHEAD The chicken can be prepared through Step 2 and refrigerated for up to 5 days; reheat it in its braising liquid before broiling. The barley can be prepared through Step 3 and refrigerated for up to 3 days.

SERVE WITH To make a meze meal, pair the chicken with Roasted Beet Salad with Manouri Cream and Buttered Walnuts (page 38) and Wilted Greens (page 114).

WINE Oak-aged Greek Chardonnay or spicy rare red Mavro from Achaia in the Peloponnese.

CLOCKWISE FROM TOP LEFT: Spiced Red Wine–
Braised Rabbit (pages 90–91); Grilled Spiced Pork
Ribs with Coriander Yogurt (pages 104–105); Drunk
Man's Stew (page 92); Mini Moussaka (pages 98–99);
Braised Red Wine Meatballs with Tomato Compote
(page 103)

Mini Moussaka

Moussaka is a Sunday special at Kyma. I prepare it à la minute, sautéing the eggplant the moment the order comes in and layering it with homemade meat sauce and béchamel (white sauce). To achieve the lofty height of a normal, large pan of moussaka, I fold whipped egg whites into the béchamel. • **4 SERVINGS**

MEAT SAUCE

1 tablespoon (15 g) unsalted butter

1 tablespoon extra virgin olive oil

¾ small Vidalia (sweet) onion, thinly sliced

6 ounces (180 g) ground beef sirloin

1 cinnamon stick

Kosher salt and freshly ground white pepper

2 tablespoons plus 1 teaspoon (40 g) tomato paste

2 tablespoons brandy, preferably Metaxa (see page 90)

⅓ cup (100 ml) water

EGGPLANT AND ASSEMBLY

¼ cup (60 ml) canola oil

14 ounces (425 g) small Japanese eggplants, sliced crosswise ½ inch (1 cm) thick

Kosher salt and freshly ground white pepper

2 garlic cloves, crushed

2 thyme sprigs

¼ cup (30 g) shredded graviera cheese (see page 163), preferably aged, or mozzarella cheese

2 tablespoons chopped mint

1 cup (250 ml) Béchamel Sauce (page 222)

Freshly grated nutmeg, for sprinkling

1. MEAT SAUCE In a small saucepan, melt the butter in the olive oil. Add the onion and cook over medium heat, stirring occasionally, until lightly browned, 12 to 15 minutes. Add the meat and cinnamon, season with salt and pepper, and cook, breaking up the clumps, until browned, about 5 minutes. Add the tomato paste and cook, stirring, for 1 minute. Add the brandy and cook until evaporated, about 20 seconds. Add the water and cook over medium-low heat until the sauce is semi-dry, about 10 minutes. Discard the cinnamon stick.

2. EGGPLANT Line a baking sheet with paper towels. In a large skillet, warm 2 tablespoons of the canola oil. Add half of the eggplant slices, season with salt and pepper, and cook over medium heat, turning them once, until browned and tender, 12 to 15 minutes. Add 1 garlic clove and 1 thyme sprig and cook, stirring, for 30 seconds. Transfer the eggplant to the prepared baking sheet and discard the garlic and thyme. Repeat with the remaining 2 tablespoons of oil and eggplant, garlic, and thyme.

3. ASSEMBLY Heat the oven to 325°F (165°C). In each of two 4½-inch (10.5 cm) round shallow baking pans, arrange one-fourth of the eggplant slices in a layer. Layer one-fourth each of the meat sauce, cheese, and mint on top. Repeat the layering and spread with the Béchamel Sauce. Sprinkle the nutmeg on top and bake until bubbling, about 10 minutes. Heat the broiler and broil the moussaka until golden brown, 2 to 3 minutes. Let stand for 5 minutes before serving.

NOTES I use a potato masher to break up the clumps of ground beef when I'm making the meat sauce.

If all your moussaka components are hot, you can layer them and place the pans under the broiler immediately (without baking first).

VARIATIONS

My yia yia Theone didn't use béchamel; she baked her moussaka with just shredded cheese on top.

Instead of eggplant, try yellow squash and/or green zucchini.

The mixture can also be baked in a single medium-small shallow baking pan.

MAKE AHEAD The Meat Sauce and Béchamel can be refrigerated for up to 3 days; just make sure to fold the egg whites into the Béchamel right before assembling the moussaka. The cooked eggplant can be refrigerated for up to 4 hours.

SERVE WITH My ideal meze spread with Mini Moussaka: Classic Greek Salad (page 49), Cucumber Yogurt Spread (page 20), and Stuffed Grape Leaves with Cumin Yogurt (pages 30–31).

WINE Fruity Agiorgitiko from Nemea or Limniona from central Greece. Or dry Mavrodaphne or Avgoustiatis blend from the Peloponnese or Ionian Islands.

Lamb Meatballs with White Bean Stew and Preserved Lemon Yogurt

This recipe is a combination of homey lamb keftedes, meatballs that are pan-fried instead of braised, and fasolatha, white bean soup. Both can be prepared and served separately or, as here, together. My grandmother's version of fasolatha was brothier, while mine is more like a stew. • **4 SERVINGS**

BEAN STEW

¼ cup (50 g) dried navy beans, soaked overnight and drained

1 small bay leaf

Pinch of black peppercorns

1 small thyme sprig

Kosher salt and freshly ground white pepper

1 tablespoon canola oil

½ carrot, peeled and thinly sliced

½ small onion, thinly sliced

½ celery rib, thinly sliced

2 small plum tomatoes, peeled, seeded, and diced

1½ tablespoons extra virgin olive oil

PRESERVED LEMON YOGURT

3 tablespoons Greek yogurt, preferably homemade (page 223)

1 teaspoon fresh lemon juice

1 teaspoon minced preserved lemon rind

Kosher salt and freshly ground white pepper

MEATBALLS

1 teaspoon canola oil, plus more for frying

½ small Vidalia (sweet) onion, finely chopped

8 ounces (250 g) ground lamb

½ cup (20 g) fresh brioche breadcrumbs (see Notes, page 102)

1 tablespoon finely chopped parsley

1 tablespoon finely chopped mint

1 teaspoon dried oregano

1 teaspoon Garlic Puree (page 219)

½ teaspoon ground cumin

½ teaspoon kosher salt

½ teaspoon freshly ground white pepper

1 large egg, lightly beaten

Thinly sliced scallion and finely diced peeled, seeded tomato, for garnish

1. BEAN STEW In a medium saucepan, cover the beans with 2 inches (5 cm) of water and bring to a simmer. Tie the bay leaf, peppercorns, and thyme in a cheesecloth bundle. Add the bundle to the beans, cover partially, and cook over medium-low heat, skimming occasionally, until tender, about 1 hour. Season the cooking liquid with salt and pepper as if it were soup and let the beans cool in the liquid. Remove the bundle and discard.

2. Meanwhile, in a small saucepan, warm the canola oil. Add the carrot, onion, and celery, season with salt and pepper, and cook over medium heat, stirring occasionally, until softened, about 5 minutes. In a food processor, puree the softened vegetables with the tomatoes until smooth.

3. Drain the beans, reserving the broth, and return them to the pan. Stir in the vegetable puree and ¼ cup (60 ml) of the bean broth;

save the remaining broth for another use. Simmer the beans over low heat for 5 minutes. Remove the pan from the heat and stir in the olive oil. Season with salt and pepper.

4. PRESERVED LEMON YOGURT In a small bowl, whisk the yogurt with the lemon juice and preserved lemon until smooth. Season with salt and pepper.

5. MEATBALLS In a small skillet, warm the 1 teaspoon of canola oil. Add the onion and cook over medium heat, stirring occasionally, until softened, about 3 minutes.

6. In a medium bowl, combine the onion with the lamb, breadcrumbs, herbs, Garlic Puree, cumin, salt, pepper, and half of the egg. Using your hands, form the lamb mixture into 1½-tablespoon (30 g) balls; transfer them to a plate as they're shaped.

7. Line a baking sheet with paper towels. In a medium saucepan, heat ½ inch (1 cm) of canola oil to 350°F (175°C). Working in batches, fry the meatballs, turning them occasionally, until golden brown, about 3 minutes. Using a slotted spoon, transfer them to the prepared baking sheet as they're cooked.

8. Spoon the bean stew into a serving bowl or bowls. Garnish with scallion and tomato. Arrange the meatballs on top in a circle, dollop the yogurt in the center, and serve.

NOTES The beans need to soak overnight, so plan accordingly.

Let the beans cool in the cooking liquid. And don't throw it out! Use it like stock; it can be the broth in a wonderful soup.

Egg bread, sourdough, or raisin bread can be substituted for the brioche.

VARIATIONS

To make the bean stew into a soup, just add more broth.

My grandmother would load up a plate of these meatballs alongside Cucumber Yogurt Spread (page 20). Or, instead of the bean stew, serve Greek Fries (pages 172–173).

MAKE AHEAD The bean stew can be refrigerated for up to 3 days; save the broth for reheating.

SERVE WITH I like this meaty meze alongside Roasted Beet Salad with Manouri Cream and Buttered Walnuts (page 38) and before Roast Chicken with Warm Potato-Tomato Salad (pages 164–167).

WINE Spicy Kotsifali-Mandilaria blend from Crete, Greek Merlot or Limniona, or hearty, dry Greek rosé.

Braised Red Wine Meatballs with Tomato Compote

When I make these torpedo-shaped meatballs (soutzoukakia) and close my eyes, I'm back in my grandmother's kitchen. Of course, my yia yia was cooking for six or eight of us every day and prepared a double or triple batch of this recipe to feed everyone. But the wonderful aromas of cumin and garlic don't change, no matter how many people you're serving. • **4 SERVINGS**

8 ounces (250 g) ground beef

½ small Vidalia (sweet) onion, finely chopped

½ cup (20 g) fresh brioche breadcrumbs (see Notes)

2 tablespoons dry red wine

1 teaspoon Garlic Puree (page 219)

½ teaspoon kosher salt

½ teaspoon freshly ground white pepper

½ teaspoon ground cumin

I large egg, lightly beaten

1 tablespoon chopped parsley

1½ cups (375 ml) Tomato Compote (page 221)

2 teaspoons extra virgin olive oil

8 cloves of Garlic Confit (page 219)

1 tablespoon (10 g) green olive julienne

Long chives, for garnish, optional

1. Heat the oven to 350°F (175°C). In a medium bowl, combine the beef with the onion, breadcrumbs, wine, Garlic Puree, salt, pepper, cumin, half of the egg, and the parsley. Using your hands, form the beef mixture into 1½-tablespoon (30 g) ovals; transfer them to a medium baking pan as they're shaped. Transfer to the oven and bake until firm, about 15 minutes.

2. In a medium saucepan, combine the Tomato Compote and the meatballs and simmer over medium-low heat for 15 minutes; keep warm.

3. In a small skillet, heat the oil. Add the Garlic Confit and cook over medium heat until golden brown, 2 to 3 minutes.

4. Spoon the meatballs and compote into a serving bowl or bowls. Sprinkle with the olive julienne and the Garlic Confit and oil. Garnish with chives, if desired, and serve.

NOTE Egg bread, sourdough, or raisin bread can be substituted for the brioche.

My yia yia wasn't afraid of garlic. She would double the amount in this recipe, so go for the full effect if you dare!

MAKE AHEAD The meatballs can be refrigerated in the sauce for up to 4 days. Warm them gently before garnishing them with the Garlic Confit, olives, and chives.

SERVE WITH I like these meatballs alongside Lemony Quinoa Salad (page 35), Classic Greek Salad (page 49), and Spicy Red Pepper–Feta Spread (page 21).

WINE Velvety Agiorgitiko or spicy, dry Mavrodaphne from the Peloponnese or Cephalonia.

Grilled Spiced Pork Ribs with Coriander Yogurt

Can you make grilled ribs even better? Yes—if you braise them first until fork-tender. What I thought would be a fleeting summer special has been on the menu now for seven years; I run through 24 racks a week! So here you have them: crispy, succulent, and full of earthy pork flavor. • **4 SERVINGS**

3 tablespoons canola oil

Four 3-rib portions of St. Louis–style pork ribs or baby back pork ribs

Kosher salt and freshly ground white pepper

1 small Vidalia (sweet) onion, thinly sliced

6 garlic cloves, chopped

2 cups (500 ml) chicken stock

12 thyme sprigs

1 tablespoon coriander seeds

1½ tablespoons dried oregano

¼ cup (60 ml) Lemon Vinaigrette (recipe follows)

½ cup (125 ml) Greek yogurt, preferably homemade (page 223)

1 teaspoon fresh lemon juice

Extra virgin olive oil, for drizzling

Chopped parsley, for garnish

1. Heat the oven to 325°F (160°C). In a large enameled cast-iron casserole, heat 2 tablespoons of the canola oil until shimmering. Season the pork ribs with salt and pepper. Working in two batches, cook the ribs over medium-high heat until browned all over, about 5 minutes per batch; transfer to a plate. Discard the fat in the pot.

2. Add the onion, garlic, and remaining 1 tablespoon of canola oil to the pot and season with salt. Cook over medium heat, stirring occasionally, until the vegetables are lightly browned, about 5 minutes. Add the stock and bring to a simmer, scraping up the browned bits on the bottom of the pot. Return the ribs to the pot along with the thyme and bring to a simmer. Cover and cook over low heat until a cake tester slides easily into the meat, 1½ to 2½ hours. Remove the pot from the heat and let cool slightly. Transfer the ribs to a broiler pan. Save the braising liquid for another use.

3. Meanwhile, in a small dry skillet, toast the coriander seeds over medium heat, shaking the skillet occasionally, until fragrant, 2 to 3 minutes. Transfer to a spice mill or coffee grinder and let cool, then grind to a powder. In a small bowl, stir ½ tablespoon of the ground coriander with ½ tablespoon of the oregano.

4. In another small bowl, stir the Lemon Vinaigrette with the remaining 1 tablespoon of oregano.

5. In a small serving bowl, stir the yogurt with the lemon juice and remaining ½ tablespoon of ground coriander until smooth. Season with salt and pepper. Drizzle with olive oil.

6. Heat a grill or a grill pan. Grill the ribs over medium-high heat, turning them once and basting occasionally with some of the oregano-lemon vinaigrette, until charred, about 3 minutes. Return the ribs to the broiler pan meaty side up.

7. Heat the broiler to high. Sprinkle the ribs with the spice mix and drizzle with the remaining oregano-lemon vinaigrette. Broil until crispy, about 2 minutes. Transfer to a carving board and slice into individual ribs. Arrange on a platter and season with salt and pepper. Garnish with parsley, if desired, and serve. Pass the yogurt separately.

NOTE The leftover braising liquid can be used like a flavorful stock—for cooking pearl onions, carrots, and potatoes; and for deglazing the browned bits on the bottom of a pan to make a simple sauce.

MAKE AHEAD The pork ribs can be prepared through Step 2 and refrigerated in the braising liquid for up to 3 days. Warm through before continuing.

SERVE WITH The best thing to eat along-side these ribs is Cheese and Wild Mushroom Shredded-Phyllo Pies (page 83). That's a pretty hefty start to a meal, so to follow, I'm partial to the light and bright-tasting Grilled Shrimp with Cabbage Salad (page 143).

WINE Spicy Xinomavro from Naoussa or red blend from Crete.

Lemon Vinaigrette

Whizzing this Greek mother sauce (ladolemono) in the blender for a full two minutes keeps it from breaking.

MAKES ABOUT 1 CUP (250 ML)

¼ cup (60 ml) fresh lemon juice
Pinch of saffron threads
Pinch of dry mustard
⅔ cup (160 ml) canola oil
¼ cup (60 ml) extra virgin olive oil
Kosher salt and freshly ground white pepper

In a blender, emulsify the lemon juice with the saffron and dry mustard. Add both oils and blend at high speed for 2 minutes. Season with salt and pepper. Scrape the vinaigrette into a 1-cup (250 ml) jar with a lid and seal.

MAKE AHEAD The vinaigrette can be refrigerated for up to 3 days.

ENTRÉES

WHOLE FISH

Trout Stuffed with Spinach Pilaf | 110

Fish Baked in a Salt Crust | 113

Grilled Fish with Wilted Greens
and Lemon Potatoes | 114

Braised Whole Fish with Tomatoes,
Garlic, and Onions | 119

Steamed Fish in Grape Leaves | 123

SEAFOOD

Oil–Poached Cod with
Clams and Melted Leeks | 126

Arctic Char in Mushroom Broth | 129

Poached Halibut with Tomato Broth | 134

Red Snapper with Greek Tomato Sauce
and Vegetables | 136

Swordfish with Homemade Sausage
and Bell Pepper Stew | 138

Grouper with Braised Flageolets
and Haricots Verts | 140

Pan-Roasted Skate with Lentils | 145

Grilled Shrimp with Cabbage Salad | 147

AVGOLEMONO

Cabbage-Wrapped Salmon
with Cabbage Pilaf | 150

Braised Veal with Romaine Lettuce
and Dill | 152

Roasted Monkfish with Artichoke
and Fava Bean Stew | 155

Braised Pork with Celery | 157

MEAT

Layered Baked Pasta with Meat Sauce | 162

Roast Chicken with Warm
Potato-Tomato Salad | 164

Braised Rabbit with Tomato and Orzo | 169

Grilled Beef Rib Eye with
Parsley Sauce | 171

Grilled Lamb Chops with Greek Fries | 172

Braised Leg of Lamb with
Sour Pasta Pearls | 175

Cheese-Stuffed Rack of Lamb with
Eggplant Stew | 177

Braised Lamb and Roasted Tomatoes
in Thieves' Purses | 180

VEGETARIAN

Melted Leeks with Bell Pepper Stew | 184

Caramelized Fennel with
Sour Pasta Pearls | 186

Zucchini-and-Eggplant-
Stuffed Tomatoes | 189

Pan-Roasted Eggplant with
Bulgur and Tomato Compote | 191

Softly Scrambled Eggs with
Tomato and Feta | 193

WHOLE FISH

Trout Stuffed with Spinach Pilaf

Spinach rice (spanakorizo) is one of the most popular vegetable pilafs in Greece. And grilling trout head-on but with the bones removed is a favorite in the American South. So why not turn two old recipes into something new? Here, spanakorizo becomes a stuffing for grilled butterflied trout, and the combination just melts in your mouth.

• **4 SERVINGS**

¼ cup (60 ml) plus 2 tablespoons extra virgin olive oil, plus more for drizzling

½ small Vidalia (sweet) onion, finely chopped

½ cup (100 g) long-grain rice

1 bay leaf

1 cup (250 ml) water

1½ ounces (50 g) baby spinach, thinly sliced (1⅓ cups)

⅓ cup (10 g) chopped dill

3 tablespoons chopped parsley

1 tablespoon fresh lemon juice

Kosher salt and freshly ground white pepper

Four 10- to 12-ounce (300 to 350 g) whole trout, cleaned and butterflied, head on

Canola oil, for brushing

Lemon Vinaigrette (page 105), for basting

2 cups (500 ml) Greek Tomato Sauce (page 220)

2 scallions, thinly sliced (¼ cup)

¼ cup (35 g) drained capers

1 tablespoon minced preserved lemon rind

1 tablespoon finely chopped shallot

1. In a small saucepan, warm 2 tablespoons of the olive oil. Add the onion and cook over medium heat, stirring occasionally, until softened, about 5 minutes. Add the rice and cook, stirring, until translucent, about 1 minute. Add the bay leaf and water and bring to a boil. Cover and simmer over low heat until the rice is tender and the liquid is absorbed, about 20 minutes. Remove the pan from the heat. Using a rubber spatula, fold in the spinach, dill, and parsley. Add the lemon juice and remaining ¼ cup (60 ml) of olive oil and season with salt and pepper. Line a baking sheet with parchment paper. Spread the spinach rice on the prepared baking sheet and let cool completely. Discard the bay leaf.

2. On another baking sheet, open 1 fish like a book and season with salt and pepper. Spread ½ cup (110 g) of the spinach rice on the bottom fillet. Sandwich with the top fillet, pressing lightly, and close. Repeat with the remaining fish and spinach rice.

3. Heat a grill or a grill pan until hot. Brush the fish with canola oil and season with salt and pepper. Grill over medium-high heat, turning the fish once and basting often with Lemon Vinaigrette, until a cake tester inserted into the thickest part of a bottom fillet feels hot when touched to your lower lip, about 7 minutes per side. Return the fish to the baking sheet.

(CONTINUED)

4. In a small saucepan, warm the Greek Tomato Sauce until heated through. Spoon the sauce into a serving bowl. Sprinkle with the scallions, capers, preserved lemon, and shallot. Transfer the fish to a platter or plates and drizzle with olive oil. Serve with the sauce.

VARIATIONS

Try a different leafy green (Swiss chard!) in lieu of the spinach, or sub in chickpeas or chickpeas and shelled chopped shrimp. Another grain, such as quinoa, barley, farro, or brown rice, can also be used; you'll need to adjust the amount of water and cooking time.

MAKE AHEAD The spinach pilaf can stand, covered, at room temperature for 30 minutes. Or it can be refrigerated overnight; let it come to room temperature before continuing.

SERVE WITH For starters, I like Braised Giant White Beans with Tomato Sauce (page 34), Sautéed Scallops with Yellow Split Pea Puree (page 63), and/or Classic Greek Salad (page 49).

WINE Fruity and crisp Greek Sauvignon Blanc or citrusy Roditis with good acidity from mountainous Achaia.

WHOLE FISH AT KYMA

As you walk through Kyma's front door, your eyes are drawn to the white marble walkway and, at the end of it, a glistening display of whole fish from around the world. It's easy to be seduced by the array and quality of the seafood imported from Greece (dorade, St. Pierre, sea bass, and red porgy, to name a few) as well as from Iceland (arctic char) and Holland (Dover sole), plus, of course, local varieties. It's all fresh—18 to 36 hours out of the water—and, yes, wild caught.

Guests pick a fish and a preparation. The most popular cooking style is grilled whole fish, which arrives at the table filleted, needing nothing more than a spoonful of latholemono (lemon vinaigrette). But some diners prefer whole fish baked in a salt mixture that hardens in the oven, producing incomparably tender and moist flesh. Others love their fish wrapped in pickled grape leaves and steamed; braised in wine and topped with layers of sweet onions and tomatoes; or stuffed with tangy spinach pilaf.

Fish Baked in a Salt Crust

Cooking whole fish in a salt crust, a common technique in Greece, sounds advanced but really is straightforward: You combine salt with egg whites and spread half of the mixture on a parchment-lined baking sheet, then lay the fish on top and cover with the remaining mixture. The only trick is to let the fish rest before cracking open the crust and digging in. The result is one of the juiciest fish preparations you'll ever eat.

• **4 SERVINGS**

One 2-pound (1 kg) whole fish, such as branzino, black bass, or red snapper, cleaned

½ lemon, thinly sliced

6 thyme sprigs

2 bay leaves

1 large rosemary sprig

4 large egg whites

2 pounds (1 kg) kosher salt

Lemon Vinaigrette (page 105), for serving

Freshly ground white pepper

1. Heat the oven to 350°F (175°C). Stuff the fish cavity with the lemon slices, thyme, bay leaves, and rosemary.

2. In a large bowl, lightly whisk the egg whites. Add the salt and stir until the mixture resembles wet sand. Line a rimmed baking sheet with parchment paper or foil. Using half of the salt mixture, spread a fish-shaped layer on the baking sheet. Set the fish on top and cover with the remaining salt mixture, pressing to adhere.

3. Transfer the fish to the oven and bake until a cake tester inserted into the thickest part of the top fillet feels hot when touched to your lower lip, 20 to 25 minutes. Remove the baking sheet from the oven and let the fish rest for 5 minutes. Using a knife and fork, break the top crust into pieces and remove.

4. Using kitchen scissors, cut off the head and tail. Remove the backbone. Slide a large chef's knife horizontally into the back of the fish and open it like a book. Using tweezers, pull out the large belly bones and small pin bones. Arrange the fillets on a platter or plates. Drizzle some of the Lemon Vinaigrette over the fillets, season with pepper, and serve. Pass the remaining vinaigrette separately.

NOTE For a larger fish, reduce the oven temperature so the salt crust doesn't brown.

VARIATIONS

If you want to add chopped fresh herbs to the salt crust recipe, my faves are parsley and oregano.

Meats can also be roasted in a salt crust. Stirring Garlic Puree (page 219) into the crust mixture adds incredible flavor.

SERVE WITH A plate of horta, Wilted Greens (page 114), usually comes alongside. Lemon Potatoes (page 114) would also be nice with the fish.

WINE Crisp and minerally Assyrtiko from Santorini.

Grilled Fish with Wilted Greens and Lemon Potatoes

I can't tell you how many times I've gone to psarotavernes (fish tavernas) in Greece and devoured impeccably grilled whole fish with nothing but olive oil and lemon juice. Each restaurant has its own fishing boat and a display case that shows off the morning's catch, and patrons inspect and select their own fish. The chosen specimen goes into the kitchen, where it's cleaned and grilled, then returned whole or opened like a book with the bones removed. There's no improving on perfection. • **4 SERVINGS**

WILTED GREENS

3 tablespoons extra virgin olive oil

1 pound (500 g) cooking greens, such as kale, dandelions, beet greens, or Swiss chard, thick stems removed, leaves coarsely chopped

1 tablespoon fresh lemon juice

Kosher salt and freshly ground white pepper

LEMON POTATOES

12 small fingerling potatoes (12 ounces/350 g)

2 garlic cloves, crushed

2 thyme sprigs

1 bay leaf

¼ cup (60 ml) Lemon Vinaigrette

Fleur de sel and chopped parsley, for garnish

FISH AND ASSEMBLY

One 2-pound (1 kg) whole fish, such as black bass, striped bass, or red snapper, cleaned

Kosher salt and freshly ground white pepper

½ cup (125 ml) Lemon Vinaigrette (page 105)

Chopped parsley, drained capers, and lemon wedges, for garnish

1. WILTED GREENS In a medium, deep skillet, heat 1 tablespoon of the oil until shimmering. Add the greens a handful at a time and cook over medium-high heat, stirring, until tender, about 5 minutes. Pour off any liquid. Season with the lemon juice, kosher salt, pepper, and the remaining 2 tablespoons of oil.

2. LEMON POTATOES In a medium saucepan, cover the potatoes, garlic, thyme, and bay leaf with water and bring to a boil. Cook over medium-high heat until tender, 15 to 20 minutes. Drain and let cool slightly; discard the aromatics. Halve the potatoes lengthwise. In a small bowl, combine the warm potatoes with the ¼ cup (60 ml) of Lemon Vinaigrette and toss to coat. Just before serving, garnish with fleur de sel and parsley.

3. FISH AND ASSEMBLY Heat a grill or a grill pan. On a platter, season the fish inside and out with kosher salt and pepper and brush with some of the Lemon Vinaigrette. Grill over medium-high heat, turning the fish once, until a cake tester inserted into the thickest part of the bottom fillet feels hot when touched to your lower lip, 8 to 10 minutes per side. Return the fish to the platter and let rest for 5 minutes.

4. Using kitchen scissors, cut off the head and tail. Remove the backbone. Slide a large chef's knife horizontally into the back of the fish and open it like a book. Using tweezers, pull out the large belly bones and small pin bones. Arrange the fillets on a platter or plates. Season with kosher salt and pepper and drizzle with Lemon Vinaigrette. Garnish with parsley and capers and serve. Pass the Lemon Potatoes, greens, lemon wedges, and remaining vinaigrette separately.

VARIATION

For extra richness, sauté the boiled potatoes in olive oil until lightly browned before tossing them with the Lemon Vinaigrette.

MAKE AHEAD The greens can be prepared through Step 1 and refrigerated overnight. Serve warm or at room temperature.

WINE Minerally Savatiano from Attica, citrusy Roditis from the Peloponnese, crisp Assyrtiko from Santorini, or fresh Robola from Cephalonia.

Braised Whole Fish with Tomatoes, Garlic, and Onions

My yia yia Athanasia's baked fish layered with vegetables appeared in regular rotation at the dinner table. In my version, I slice the vegetables and arrange them directly on a whole fish to make "scales" and braise it in the oven, creating a natural broth that's the foundation of an intensely flavored sauce. The head, tail, and bones are removed, then the parts are reassembled to appear intact. • **4 SERVINGS**

½ **carrot, peeled and thinly sliced (see Note, page 120)**

Kosher salt

One 2-pound (750 g to 1 kg) whole fish, such as red snapper or black bass, cleaned, fins removed

Freshly ground white pepper

2 cups (500 ml) dry white wine

2 garlic cloves, crushed

2 bay leaves

2 thyme sprigs, plus chopped leaves for sprinkling

2 teaspoons extra virgin olive oil, plus more for drizzling

¼ **cup (60 ml) Vidalia Onion Stew (page 159)**

6 cloves of Garlic Confit (page 219), thinly sliced

2 plum tomatoes, thinly sliced

1 cup (250 ml) Greek Tomato Sauce (page 220)

¼ **cup (60 ml) fresh lemon juice**

1½ **tablespoons chopped dill**

Fleur de sel, for sprinkling

1. Heat the oven to 400°F (200°C). In a small saucepan, cover the carrot with 1 inch (2.5 cm) of water, season with kosher salt, and bring to a simmer. Cook over medium-high heat until tender, 3 to 5 minutes; drain and rinse in cold water.

2. Season the fish inside and out with kosher salt and pepper. Make 1 shallow horizontal cut along each side of the backbone. In a large ovenproof skillet, combine the fish, wine, crushed garlic, bay leaves, and thyme sprigs. Drizzle the fish with 1 teaspoon of the oil. Bring to a simmer over high heat, transfer to the oven, and braise the fish, basting twice, until a cake tester inserted into the thickest part of the bottom fillet feels warm when touched to your lower lip, 12 to 15 minutes.

3. Remove the skillet from the oven. Carefully turn the fish over. Spoon the Vidalia Onion Stew on the body below the head, pressing to adhere. Arrange the Garlic Confit in a layer on top, then the carrot slices. Cover with overlapping tomato slices to mimic fish scales. Drizzle the fish with the remaining 1 teaspoon of oil and season with kosher salt and pepper. Return to the oven and braise, basting once or twice, until a cake tester inserted into the thickest part of the bottom fillet feels hot when touched to your lower lip, 12 to 15 minutes.

(CONTINUED)

4. Spread a large sheet of plastic wrap on a work surface. Using a wide spatula, carefully transfer the fish to the plastic wrap. Strain the pan juices into a small saucepan. Add the tomato sauce, bring to a simmer over medium-high heat, and cook until reduced by half, 10 to 15 minutes. Remove the pan from the heat and add the lemon juice and dill. Season with kosher salt and pepper and keep warm.

5. Cover the top of the fish with the plastic wrap. With one hand on top of the fish and using the spatula as a guide, carefully turn the fish tomato side down. Using kitchen scissors, cut off the head and tail; reserve. Remove the backbone. Insert a large chef's knife horizontally into the back of the fish and turn the top fillet over. Using tweezers, pull out the large belly bones and small pin bones. Turn the top fillet over to re-form the fish, then carefully turn the whole fish over tomato side up. Rearrange any toppings that have shifted.

6. Spoon some of the sauce into a deep serving platter. Transfer the fish to the platter and return the head and tail to the body. Drizzle with oil and sprinkle with fleur de sel and chopped thyme. Serve, passing the remaining sauce separately.

NOTE I sometimes carve the carrot into flowers: Using a channel knife, cut 5 parallel grooves the length of the carrot before slicing it. I like the Victorinox rosewood channeler available at qualityknives.co.uk.

VARIATION
For a change, I alternate the tomato slices with rows of thinly sliced yellow squash and green zucchini.

SERVE WITH Pair with Lemon Potatoes (page 114), steamed fingerling potatoes, rice pilaf, bulgur, or quinoa to soak up the lemony sauce. As a first course, try Classic Greek Salad (page 49) and/or Braised Giant White Beans with Tomato Sauce (page 34).

WINE Roditis from the mountains with melon and citrus aromas or crisp rosé from Nemea, Amynteo, Crete, or Thessaly.

WHOLE FISH PEP TALK: YOU CAN DO IT!

Here are my whole-fish how-tos on everything from buying to butchering.

BUYING

• Look for blood-red gills and clear eyes. The flesh should spring back when you touch it.

• The fish should have a clean ocean smell.

• Per person, you need 12 ounces (350 g) to 1 pound (500 g) of fish on the bone. That's three pounds (1.5 kg) of fish for four entree servings, either one 3-pounder (1.5 kg) or two 1½-pound (750 g) fish. If you're serving two or three meze first, you can get away with ½ pound (250 g) per person.

• Ask your fishmonger to clean the fish. That means taking out the gills and belly and scraping off the scales.

STORING

• You should buy fish to use as soon as possible.

• Refrigerate the fish in the swimming position. You want to avoid laying it fillet-side down, because the pressure makes it deteriorate faster.

PREPARING

• Handle the fish like a baby. Gently hold it in the swimming position with one hand under the belly and the other by the head or tail.

• Carefully wash the fish in cold water to remove any blood. Place it gently on the work surface and pat it dry with paper towels.

• Before cooking, I make a ¼-inch (6 mm) incision along both sides of the dorsal spine from head to tail, which makes it easy to remove for serving.

TESTING FOR DONENESS

• I judge when a fish is cooked properly by inserting a cake tester into the flesh right near the spine and touching it to my bottom lip. It will feel warm when the fish is cooked properly.

• If you're cooking fish in a salt crust, push the cake tester through the crust to where you imagine the spine to be and test there.

• Instead of a cake tester, you can use a thin metal skewer.

FILLETING FOR SERVING

• If you are right-handed, position the fish with the head toward you and the dorsal spine to the right. Using a spoon and a fork, remove the dorsal spine. If you've cut along both sides of the spine before cooking, it will come out easily.

• Using heavy-duty kitchen shears or a chef's knife, cut the head off the fish where it meets the fillet. Do the same at the tail end. Reserve both head and tail for presentation or for guests who wish to pick out the flesh.

• To cut the fillets away from the central bone, slide the knife into the middle of the fish where you just removed the dorsal spine and under the skeleton moving toward the middle of the fish and as close as you can to the skeleton so you don't cut into the flesh. You will be able to open the fish like a book, resting the top fillet to the left. Remove the skeleton, from the left fillet by simply peeling it away from the flesh. Remove any bones or unwanted skin from the fillets. Transfer the fillets to a plate or platter.

Steamed Fish in Grape Leaves

Cooking fish wrapped in grape leaves is known as klimatofila. I prepare many variations on this technique—grilling whole mackerel, baking sardines in a slow oven—but this one is the simplest, because all it requires is lining a steamer basket with the leaves and rock salt to get truly moist flesh. • **4 SERVINGS**

Two pounds (1 kg) jarred pickled grape leaves, drained

4 cups (2 kg) rock salt

Two 1-pound (500 g) whole fish, such as dorade, porgy, or branzino, cleaned

Freshly ground white pepper

1 lemon, thinly sliced

6 thyme sprigs

6 oregano sprigs

4 bay leaves

Lemon Vinaigrette (page 105), for serving

1. In a large deep skillet or a wok, bring 3 inches (7.5 cm) of water to a boil over high heat. Using scissors, cut off the stems of the grape leaves, if necessary. For each fish, line a large bamboo steamer basket with overlapping grape leaves rib side up, leaving a ½-inch (1 cm) overhang. Spread 2 cups (1 kg) of the salt on the leaves to cover the bottom completely. Season the fish inside and out with pepper. Lay the fish on the salt and stuff each of the cavities with 1 lemon slice, 1 thyme sprig, and 1 oregano sprig. Lay 2 lemon slices, 2 thyme sprigs, and 2 oregano sprigs on each fish. Place 1 bay leaf on each side of the fish. Cover the fish with more grape leaves, rib side down. Fold the bottom leaves over the top, completely covering the fish. Use extra grape leaves, if needed.

2. Stack the steamer baskets over the boiling water, cover, and cook the fish over medium heat until a cake tester inserted into the thickest part of the top fillet feels hot when touched to your lower lip, 20 to 25 minutes.

3. Remove the baskets from the heat and unwrap the top leaves. Brush off the rock salt and carefully transfer the fish, clean side down, to a work surface. Brush off the remaining salt. Using kitchen scissors, cut off the head and tail. Remove the backbone. Slide a large chef's knife horizontally into the back of the fish and open it like a book. Using tweezers, pull out the large belly bones and small pin bones. Arrange the fillets on a platter or plates. Drizzle some of the Lemon Vinaigrette over the fillets. Serve, passing the remaining vinaigrette separately.

NOTES A 1-pound (500 g) dorade is perfect for one person, but if you're also serving an appetizer, sides, and dessert, this size easily feeds two.

You'll need two 12- to 14-inch (30 to 35 cm) bamboo steamer baskets with lids. I like the Helen Chen brand. Soak the steamer baskets in water for a few hours before using so they don't burn.

SERVE WITH To start, try Classic Greek Salad (page 49) and Braised Giant White Beans with Tomato Sauce (page 34). Pass Wilted Greens (page 114) and Lemon Potatoes (page 114) alongside the fish.

WINE Aromatic, herb-tinged Malagousia from northern Greece.

SEAFOOD

Oil-Poached Cod with Clams and Melted Leeks

I draw inspiration from Greek cuisine, but I also apply my own culinary experience. For instance, this elegant recipe is based on a rustic appetizer that's well known on Lefkada, an island in the Ionian Sea. I turned the original combination of steamed clams, wine, garlic, and leeks into a sauce for poached cod fillets; sometimes I add earthy snails to the plate. • **4 SERVINGS**

CLAMS AND LEEKS

2 tablespoons canola oil

2 shallots, thinly sliced, plus 1 tablespoon finely diced shallot

2 tablespoons chopped parsley stems

½ teaspoon black peppercorns

1 bay leaf

1 cup (250 ml) dry white wine

1 cup (250 ml) bottled clam juice

24 littleneck clams, scrubbed

3 thyme sprigs

3 tablespoons plus 1 teaspoon extra virgin olive oil

4 large garlic cloves, sliced

2 tablespoons fresh lemon juice

Freshly ground white pepper

2 cups (140 g) halved lengthwise and thinly sliced leek, white and light green parts only, plus 2 tablespoons finely diced dark green part

2 tablespoons finely diced carrot

¼ teaspoon ground cardamom

¼ teaspoon ground coriander

1 tablespoon finely diced peeled, seeded tomato

Thinly sliced chives, for garnish

COD

3 cups (750 ml) canola oil

1 cup (250 ml) extra virgin olive oil

2 garlic cloves, halved

4 thyme sprigs

1 large rosemary sprig

Kosher salt

Four 6-ounce (180 g) skinless cod fillets

Freshly ground white pepper

1. CLAMS In a large pot, warm the canola oil. Add half of the sliced shallots, the parsley, peppercorns, and bay leaf and cook over medium heat, stirring occasionally, until the shallots soften, 2 to 3 minutes. Add the wine and clam juice, bring to a simmer, and cook over medium heat until reduced to 1 cup (250 ml), 5 to 7 minutes. Add the clams, cover, and cook over medium-high heat, shaking the pot a few times, until they open, 5 to 10 minutes. Using a slotted spoon, transfer the clams to a large bowl as they're done (see Note, page 128); remove the clam meat and discard the shells and any unopened clams. Strain the clam broth through a fine sieve into a small saucepan, leaving the grit behind; discard the solids in the sieve.

(CONTINUED)

2. In a medium glass measuring cup, combine the thyme and remaining sliced shallots. Bring the clam broth to a boil, skimming off the foam. Pour the broth into the cup; wipe out the small saucepan. Cover the broth with plastic wrap and let stand to infuse, about 20 minutes. Strain through a fine sieve into a medium saucepan; discard the solids in the sieve. In the small saucepan, warm 1 teaspoon of the olive oil. Add the garlic, cover, and cook over low heat, stirring occasionally, until soft, about 10 minutes. Scrape into the broth. Bring to a simmer over medium heat, then remove the pan from the heat. Using an immersion blender, puree until very smooth. Add the lemon juice and remaining 3 tablespoons of olive oil to the sauce and season with pepper. Pour ¼ cup (60 ml) of the sauce into a small glass measuring cup and reserve.

3. LEEKS In a medium saucepan of salted boiling water, cook the sliced leeks until tender, about 3 minutes. Drain, rinse in cold water, and pat dry. Add the sliced leeks to the sauce in the pan along with the carrot, diced leek, diced shallot, cardamom, and coriander and keep warm. Just before serving, stir in the clams and tomato.

4. COD In a medium, deep skillet, heat the canola oil with the olive oil, garlic, thyme, rosemary, and 1½ teaspoons of salt to 145°F (65°C), stirring to dissolve the salt. Season the fish with salt and pepper, add to the skillet, and poach, turning halfway through, until an instant-read thermometer inserted in the center of a fillet registers 120°F (50°C), about 10 minutes. Using a slotted spatula, transfer the fish to a paper towel–lined plate to drain. Transfer to a carving board and cut each piece of fish crosswise into thirds.

5. Spoon the clam and leek sauce into wide serving bowls, garnish with chives, and set the fish on top. Using an immersion blender or a whisk, whip the reserved sauce until frothy. Spoon the froth around the bowls and serve.

NOTE Lift the lid on the clams occasionally and remove each littleneck as soon as it pops open to avoid tough, overcooked meat. To make them extra tidy, after steaming, pull off the thin mantle that surrounds each clam.

VARIATIONS
In the sauce, I like to serve half clams, half fresh petits escargots. I sauté the snails in olive oil with shallots and garlic, then deglaze the pan with a little ouzo.

To make a clam appetizer, steam the clams until they open and make the sauce. Reheat the clams in the sauce, garnish with thinly sliced scallions, and serve with toasted baguette slices cut on the diagonal.

MAKE AHEAD The recipe can be prepared through Step 3 and refrigerated overnight.

SERVE WITH As a first course, try a meze spread of Stuffed Grape Leaves with Cumin Yogurt (pages 30–31), Spinach-and-Feta Phyllo Triangles (pages 80–81), and Lamb Phyllo Spirals (pages 84–85). With the fish, have Lemon Potatoes (page 114), steamed fingerling potatoes, rice pilaf, bulgur, or quinoa to soak up the delicious sauce.

WINE Assyrtiko from the mainland or refreshing Debina from Epirus.

Arctic Char in Mushroom Broth

Cooking à l'unilatérale is the French technique of cooking meat or seafood on one side only and leaving the top slightly raw, like an egg sunny-side up. It's perfect for any fish you cook medium-rare. I love the melting texture of the char against the woodsy mushrooms, which grow wild in northern Greece. • **4 SERVINGS**

SHERRY MUSHROOM BROTH

2 tablespoons canola oil

14 ounces (400 g) portobello mushrooms, sliced

1 small Vidalia (sweet) onion, thinly sliced

1 carrot, thinly sliced

20 garlic cloves, thinly sliced

3 thyme sprigs

8 cups (2 L) water

2 tablespoons sherry vinegar

Kosher salt and freshly ground white pepper

PEARL ONIONS, FISH, AND ASSEMBLY

6 pearl onions, preferably red

1 tablespoon extra virgin olive oil, plus more for drizzling

About 1 cup (250 ml) dry white wine

1 medium shallot, finely chopped

Four 6-ounce (180 g) skinless arctic char fillets, halved crosswise

Kosher salt and freshly ground white pepper

Wild Mushrooms "à la Grecque" (pages 40–41), made with sherry vinegar

12 cloves of Garlic Confit (page 219)

Thinly sliced chives and fleur de sel, for garnish

1. SHERRY MUSHROOM BROTH In a medium skillet, heat the canola oil until shimmering. Add the sliced mushrooms and cook over medium-high heat, stirring occasionally, until golden brown, about 10 minutes. Add the sliced onion, carrot, and garlic and cook over medium heat, stirring, for 2 minutes. Scrape the vegetables into a large saucepan; wipe out the skillet. Add the thyme and water to the saucepan and bring to a simmer. Cook over medium-low heat for 45 minutes, then strain through a fine sieve into a small saucepan; discard the solids in the sieve. Simmer the broth over medium-high heat until reduced to 2 cups (500 ml), 5 to 7 minutes. Add the vinegar and season with kosher salt and pepper.

2. PEARL ONIONS In a small skillet, combine the pearl onions with the olive oil and just enough water to coat the bottom of the pan. Cover, bring to a simmer, and cook over medium heat until the onions are tender, 5 to 7 minutes. Let cool and halve lengthwise.

3. FISH In a large skillet, combine the wine and shallot. Season the fish with kosher salt and pepper and add skinned side down to the skillet; the wine should come halfway up the side of the fish. Bring to a simmer and cook over medium-low heat until the fish is still slightly raw on top, 5 to 7 minutes (see Note).

(CONTINUED)

Remove the skillet from the heat. Using a slotted spatula, transfer the fish to a paper towel–lined plate to drain.

4. ASSEMBLY In the medium skillet, combine the mushroom salad with the Garlic Confit and pearl onions and warm over medium heat. Spoon the mushroom mixture into shallow serving bowls, pour in the broth, and garnish with chives. Set the fish on top and drizzle with olive oil. Sprinkle the fish with fleur de sel and serve.

NOTE Gently cook the fish in the wine so it doesn't boil, or you'll lose the rare effect. If the wine evaporates before the fish is done, add more.

VARIATION

Try trout, branzino, or salmon fillets using the same technique.

MAKE AHEAD The Sherry Mushroom Broth can be refrigerated for up to 3 days.

SERVE WITH For starters, try Lamb Phyllo Spirals (pages 84–85), Grilled Eggplant Spread (page 22), and/or Zucchini and Feta Fritters (pages 44–45). With the fish, have rice pilaf, bulgur, or quinoa to soak up the broth.

WINE Fresh, aromatic Agiorgitiko from Nemea.

Poached Halibut with Tomato Broth

Like Braised Whole Fish with Tomatoes, Garlic, and Onions (page 119), this recipe owes a debt to my grandmother Athanasia's baked fish plaki. But this rendition uses firm fish fillets poached in herb-infused olive oil, and the tomato broth—surprisingly—has roots in the classic Greek salad. Inspired by the deeply flavored juices that collect in the salad bowl from tossing batch after batch of tomatoes with onions and herbs during service, I employ a similar technique to make tomato broth. • **4 SERVINGS**

¼ cup (60 ml) verjus (see Notes)

1½ teaspoons tomato paste

1½ pounds (750 g) beefsteak tomatoes, coarsely chopped

1 small Vidalia (sweet) onion, sliced

¾ cup (20 g) packed mint leaves, chopped

1½ cups (375 ml) extra virgin olive oil

¼ cup (60 ml) plus 2 tablespoons fresh lemon juice

Kosher salt and freshly ground white pepper

24 small cherry tomatoes, half red, half yellow, each scored with a small X in the stem end (see Notes)

12 small green seedless grapes, each scored with a small X in the stem end (see Notes)

3 cups (750 ml) canola oil

2 garlic cloves, halved

4 thyme sprigs

1 large rosemary sprig

Four 6-ounce (180 g) skinless halibut fillets

1 cup (250 ml) Vidalia Onion Stew (page 159)

Micro celery leaves or tender inner celery leaves, for garnish

1. In a large bowl, whisk the verjus with the tomato paste. Add the chopped tomatoes, onion, mint, and ½ cup (125 ml) of the olive oil and toss to coat. Cover and refrigerate for at least 6 hours and up to 24 hours. Pass through a food mill into a medium saucepan (see Notes). Just before serving, warm the tomato broth over medium-low heat. Stir in the lemon juice and season with salt and pepper.

2. In a medium saucepan of boiling water, blanch the cherry tomatoes and grapes until the skin begins to peel, about 10 seconds; drain. Rinse in cold water and peel.

3. In a large deep skillet, heat the canola oil with the remaining 1 cup (250 ml) of olive oil, 1½ teaspoons of salt, the garlic, thyme, and rosemary to 145°F (65°C). Season the fish with salt and pepper, add to the skillet, and poach, turning halfway through, until an instant-read thermometer inserted in the center of a fillet registers 120°F (50°C), about 10 minutes. Using a slotted spatula, transfer the fish to a paper towel–lined plate to drain.

4. In a small saucepan, warm the Vidalia Onion Stew over medium-low heat. Mound the stew into the center of wide serving bowls. Alternate the red cherry tomatoes, yellow cherry tomatoes, and grapes around the stew and garnish with celery leaves. Pour some of the tomato broth around the bowls, set the fish on top, and serve. Pass the remaining tomato broth separately.

NOTES Peeling the cherry tomatoes and grapes is optional.

The tomato broth needs at least 6 hours to steep and tastes better the next day, so plan accordingly.

Verjus is the pressed juice of unripe grapes. Its mild acidity heightens the flavor of marinades, dressings, and sauces. You can substitute ½ cup (125 ml) of white wine that's been simmered for 2 minutes and cooled.

Instead of using a food mill in Step 1, you can puree the tomato mixture in a food processor until smooth, then strain it through a medium sieve into the pan.

At the restaurant, I'm particular about peeling the grapes and tomatoes, but it's not absolutely necessary.

SERVE WITH As a first course, have Lemony Quinoa Salad (page 35). With the fish, a plate of horta, Wilted Greens (page 114), or Spinach Pilaf (Step 1, page 110) would be nice.

WINE Medium-bodied, fruity Malagousia with stone-fruit aromas or citrusy Vidiano from Crete.

Red Snapper with Greek Tomato Sauce and Vegetables

To make the vegetables (briam) for a version of this recipe, my aunt Stella simply tosses them with olive oil, salt, and pepper, then roasts them for hours until completely collapsed. Here, I reduce the cooking time and fat to keep the tastes fresh. • **4 SERVINGS**

1 cup (250 ml) plus 2½ tablespoons canola oil

2 garlic cloves

2 thyme sprigs

1 small (8-ounce/250 g) russet (baking) potato

½ small Japanese eggplant, sliced crosswise ¼ inch (6 mm) thick

½ small green zucchini, sliced crosswise ¼ inch (6 mm) thick

½ small yellow squash, sliced crosswise ¼ inch (6 mm) thick

6 mixed cherry tomatoes, halved

Kosher salt and freshly ground white pepper

Four 6-ounce (180 g) skin-on snapper fillets, halved crosswise

2 cups (500 ml) Greek Tomato Sauce (page 220)

12 cloves of Garlic Confit (page 219)

1. Line a baking sheet with paper towels. In a small saucepan, combine 1 cup (250 ml) of the oil with 1 garlic clove and 1 thyme sprig and heat to 140°F (60°C). Peel the potato and slice it crosswise ¼ inch (6 mm) thick. Using a 1½-inch (3.5 cm) round cookie cutter, stamp out a smaller round from each slice; save the trimmings in a container of water for another use. Add the potato rounds to the pan and cook until a cake tester slides in easily, 10 to 15 minutes. Transfer the potato to the prepared baking sheet.

2. Line another baking sheet with paper towels. In a large skillet, heat 2 tablespoons of the oil until shimmering. Add the eggplant, zucchini, squash, and tomatoes in a single layer, season with salt and pepper, and cook over medium heat, turning once, until golden brown, about 10 minutes. Add the remaining 1 garlic clove and 1 thyme sprig, toss, then remove the skillet from the heat. Transfer the vegetables to the prepared baking sheet.

3. Season the fish flesh with salt and pepper and season the skin with salt only. In a large skillet, heat the remaining ½ tablespoon of oil until shimmering. Add the fish skin side down and press with a spatula to flatten. Cook over medium heat, turning once, until lightly browned and a cake tester inserted into the thickest part of a fillet feels warm when touched to your lower lip, about 5 minutes. Transfer to a paper towel–lined plate to drain.

4. In a small saucepan, warm the Greek Tomato Sauce over medium heat. Spread some of the sauce on plates and top with the fish skin side up, vegetables, and Garlic Confit. Garnish with thyme and flowers, if desired, and serve. Pass the sauce separately.

WINE Crisp, aromatic Sauvignon Blanc from northern Greece or the Peloponnese, or dry, fruity Xinomavro rosé.

Swordfish with Homemade Sausage and Bell Pepper Stew

Like Italians, Greeks make a sausage-and-pepper appetizer, loukaniko spetzofai. Here, I've paired it with meaty swordfish to make an unconventional entrée. The sausage is a blend of ground pork and spices, predominantly cumin and orange. Typically, the mixture is stuffed into casings, but it's just as tasty in this no-fuss version, baked in a pan. • **4 SERVINGS**

SAUSAGE

1 teaspoon canola oil

¼ cup (25 g) halved lengthwise and thinly sliced leek, white and light green parts only

4 ounces (125 g) ground pork

2 teaspoons cold water

¾ teaspoon kosher salt

½ teaspoon ground cumin

¼ teaspoon fennel seeds

¼ teaspoon finely grated orange zest

⅛ teaspoon freshly ground white pepper

FISH AND ASSEMBLY

1½ tablespoons canola oil

Four 6-ounce (180 g) skinless, boneless swordfish steaks

1 teaspoon ground coriander

Kosher salt and freshly ground white pepper

Bell Pepper Stew (page 184)

Mixed bell pepper julienne, for garnish

1 tablespoon thinly sliced chives

1 teaspoon extra virgin olive oil

Finely grated zest of 1 orange, dried overnight on a plate, optional

1. SAUSAGE Heat the oven to 375°F (190°C). In a small skillet, warm the canola oil. Add the leek and cook over medium heat, stirring occasionally, until softened, about 5 minutes. Transfer to a paper towel–lined plate to drain.

2. In a small bowl, combine the pork and leek with the water, salt, cumin, fennel, orange zest, and pepper. Spread the mixture in a small shallow baking pan and smooth the top to make a layer about 1 inch (2.5 cm) thick. Transfer to the oven and bake until cooked through, about 30 minutes. Remove from the oven and let cool slightly. Cut the sausage into 1-inch (2.5 cm) cubes.

3. FISH In a large nonstick skillet, warm the canola oil. Season the fish with the coriander, salt, and pepper, add to the skillet, and cook over medium heat until browned on the bottom, about 5 minutes. Turn the fish over and cook until a cake tester inserted into the thickest part of a steak feels hot when touched to your lower lip, 3 to 4 minutes. Transfer the fish to a paper towel–lined plate to drain.

4. Meanwhile, in a small saucepan, warm the Bell Pepper Stew with the sausage cubes over medium heat. In a small bowl, toss the pepper julienne with the chives and olive oil.

5. ASSEMBLY Spread the Bell Pepper Stew on plates. Set the fish on top. Sprinkle with the dried orange zest, if desired, garnish with the pepper julienne, and serve.

VARIATIONS

Try this recipe using another fish, like cod, halibut, or salmon.

The Bell Pepper Stew is great with pork, lamb, or chicken, too. It can also be served on its own as a meze with the sausage.

MAKE AHEAD The sausage can be prepared through Step 2 and refrigerated for up to 4 days.

SERVE WITH Spinach Pilaf (Step 1, page 110), Lemon Potatoes (page 114), or Greek Fries (pages 172–173) would be nice alongside. I like to start the meal with Cucumber Yogurt Spread (page 20), Warm Potato-Tomato Salad (page 48), and/or Zucchini and Feta Fritters (pages 44–45).

WINE Fruity, oak-aged Agiorgitiko from Nemea or spicy Limniona from Thessaly.

Grouper with Braised Flageolets and Haricots Verts

This plate comes topped with chef-y foam, but I drew inspiration from my grandmother Athanasia, who loved mixing filet beans with shelling beans, especially small, pale green flageolets. When we went shopping, we didn't just grab a fistful of the filet beans and move on—we had to inspect every one. At home, we'd pinch off the ends and pull the strings down the sides. • **4 SERVINGS**

FLAGEOLETS

½ cup (100 g) dried flageolet beans, soaked overnight and drained (see Notes, page 142)

1 thyme sprig

½ teaspoon black peppercorns

1 bay leaf

Kosher salt and freshly ground white pepper

4 ounces (125 g) haricots verts, thinly sliced on the diagonal

4 ounces (125 g) boiling potatoes, preferably purple-fleshed, peeled and cut into thick julienne strips

2 tablespoons fresh lemon juice

¼ cup (60 ml) extra virgin olive oil

1½ ounces (50 g) black truffle, cut into thick julienne strips, plus 8 black truffle slices, for garnish, optional

FISH AND ASSEMBLY

Four 6-ounce (180 g) skinless grouper fillets, halved crosswise

Kosher salt and freshly ground white pepper

Wondra (quick-mixing) flour, for dusting

¼ cup (60 ml) canola oil

1. FLAGEOLETS In a medium saucepan, cover the flageolets with 2 inches (5 cm) of water and bring to a simmer. Tie the thyme, peppercorns, and bay leaf in a cheesecloth bundle. Add the bundle to the flageolets, cover partially, and cook over medium-low heat, skimming occasionally, until tender, about 1 hour. Season the cooking liquid with salt and pepper as if it were soup and let the beans cool in the liquid. Remove the bundle and discard.

2. Drain the flageolets, reserving the broth. In a blender, combine 1 cup (180 g) of the flageolets with 1½ cups (375 ml) of the reserved broth and puree until smooth. Season with salt and pepper. Reserve the remaining whole flageolets; save the remaining broth for another use.

3. In a medium saucepan of salted boiling water, cook the haricots verts until crisp-tender, about 3 minutes. Using a slotted spoon, transfer the haricots verts to a colander and rinse under cold running water. Drain and pat dry. In the same saucepan, cook the potatoes until tender, about 10 minutes; drain.

4. FISH Season the fish with salt and pepper and dust with flour, patting off the excess. In a large skillet, heat the canola oil until

shimmering. Add the fish skinned side down and press with a spatula to flatten. Cook over medium-high heat, turning once, until golden brown and a cake tester inserted into the thickest part of a fillet feels warm when touched to your lower lip, about 5 minutes. Transfer the fish to a paper towel–lined plate to drain.

5. In a small saucepan, combine the remaining whole flageolets with 1½ cups (375 ml) of the pureed flageolets. Add the haricots verts and potatoes to the pan and warm over medium heat, stirring constantly. Remove from the heat and whisk in the lemon juice and olive oil. Season the flageolet stew with salt and pepper.

6. ASSEMBLY Spoon the flageolet stew into serving bowls and add the truffle julienne, if desired. Stand 2 fillet halves cut side up in the center of each bowl. In a small saucepan, bring the reserved pureed flageolets to a simmer; using an immersion blender or a whisk, whip until frothy. Spoon the froth around the fish, garnish with the truffle slices, if desired, and serve.

NOTES The flageolet beans need to soak overnight, so plan accordingly.

Flageolet beans are available at specialty food shops and ranchogordo.com. Other, more common small dried beans, such as navy beans, can be substituted.

Pick out and discard any floating rehydrated beans before cooking them. Avoid boiling the rehydrated beans violently, because they'll fall apart.

The cooking time for the beans depends on how dried out they are.

VARIATION

Replace the haricots verts with other filet beans, such as yellow, wax, or romano beans. When fresh cranberry beans are in season, they can replace the flageolets; they don't need soaking and take only 20 minutes to cook.

MAKE AHEAD The cooked flageolets can be refrigerated in the broth for up to 4 days. The stew can be refrigerated for up to 3 days. Wake it up with a squeeze of lemon juice before serving.

SERVE WITH As first courses, I like Potato-Caper Spread (page 24) and Seafood and Tomato Stew (page 73).

WINE Hearty, oak-aged Greek Chardonnay or Viognier.

HOW TO COOK WITH DRIED BEANS

For deeply flavored, creamy beans, braising your own is the way to go. You're unlikely to get that incomparable mix of shapely beans and pillowy perfection from a can. Pulses—the term includes dried beans, peas, and lentils—can go right from the bag into the saucepan, but I always soak them first in water overnight. The extra step does require some advance planning, but it reduces the cooking time, and I find the beans cook more evenly and without cracking and peeling. You'll also need to factor in an hour or two of simmering. But when it's convenient, you can make a ton, because beans keep for up to five days in the refrigerator and freeze very well, so you'll have plenty leftover for quick meals later on.

Read on for more pointers on making beautifully cooked beans covered in their delicious pot liquor.

- Dried chickpeas, split peas, and navy beans are available at most supermarkets. But for the finest beans, commonplace as well as heirloom varieties like gigandes, beluga lentils, and flageolets, buy them at specialty food shops, Greek and Mediterranean markets, or ranchogordo.com. You want a source with good turnover so the supply is fresh, ideally less than a year old; older beans take longer to cook, and some get crumbly instead of creamy. That explains the wide range of cooking times you see.

- Put your dried beans in a roomy bowl and cover with 2 inches (5 cm) of water. (Split peas and lentils don't require soaking.) Let them stand overnight on the counter. They'll swell to twice their original size.

- Pick out and discard any floating beans or skins, because they won't soften at the same time as the rest. Drain the beans and transfer them to a saucepan large enough so they can expand even more. Add fresh water to cover by 2 inches (5 cm) and bring to a simmer over high heat. Avoid a hard boil to keep the beans from falling apart.

- Add your aromatics, like onion, carrot, garlic, and herbs, which infuse the beans with lots of flavor. Wrapping the aromatics first in a cheesecloth bundle makes it easy to fish them out later. Adjust the heat to keep the liquid at a gentle boil and simmer the beans until tender, which varies from 45 minutes to a couple of hours, depending on the size and age of the beans.

- I salt my beans in their cooking liquid when they are fully soft but still hot. Actually, I salt the cooking liquid, since it takes about half an hour for the flavor of the broth to make its way into the beans. How do I know when they're adequately seasoned? My rule is to season the broth as if it were soup.

- If you're flavoring the beans with wine, lemon juice, or tomatoes, stir them in only when the beans are completely tender. Adding acidic ingredients too early makes the beans take much longer to cook.

- Unless, you plan on using the warm beans immediately, let them cool completely in their cooking liquid. That way they'll be seasoned on the inside, plump, and very moist, with the skins intact. Store the beans in their broth in the refrigerator. Or divide the beans and broth into portions, transfer to sturdy resealable bags, and freeze; then defrost what you want as you need it.

- Don't throw out the bean cooking liquid! It's full of flavor and body. In Grouper with Braised Flageolets and Haricots Verts (page 140), I save some of the liquid to make a bean puree and whip the rest with a little of the bean puree to make a frothy sauce. It also serves as a broth for reheating whole beans. Any extra will stand in nicely for stock in another recipe: it can be the vegetarian broth in a wonderful soup, stew, or braise. Or add a ladleful to cooked pasta to make it saucy.

Pan-Roasted Skate with Lentils

Traditional lentil soup, fakes, is enjoyed yearlong but especially during Lent. In thinking about how to update it to accompany fish, I remembered a technique from Le Bernardin restaurant in New York, where we pureed lentils with heavy cream. My recipe borrows from both experiences: I swap in almond milk for the cream and replace the textbook-Greek red wine vinegar and extra virgin olive oil with sherry vinegar and foie gras. • **4 SERVINGS**

LENTILS

½ cup (100 g) beluga lentils or green lentils, rinsed and picked over (see Notes)

One 2-inch (5 cm) piece of leek, white and light green parts only

¼ small onion

1 small garlic clove

1 bay leaf

Kosher salt and freshly ground white pepper

1½ cups (375 ml) almond milk

1 ounce (30 g) foie gras or chicken liver terrine, diced, optional (see Notes)

3 tablespoons sherry vinegar

¼ cup (50 g) small-diced peeled carrot, plus thinly sliced carrot for garnish

¼ cup (50 g) small-diced peeled parsnip, plus thinly sliced parsnip for garnish

¼ cup (50 g) small-diced peeled celery root

1 tablespoon finely chopped shallot

½ medium tomato, peeled, seeded, and cut into ¼-inch (6 mm) dice

2 tablespoons chopped parsley

2 tablespoons thinly sliced chives

FISH

Four 10-ounce (300 g) bone-in skinless skate wings (see Notes)

Kosher salt and freshly ground white pepper

Wondra (quick-mixing) flour, for dusting

¼ cup (60 ml) canola oil

1. LENTILS In a small saucepan, cover the lentils with 2 inches (5 cm) of water and bring to a simmer. Tie the leek, onion, garlic, and bay leaf in a cheesecloth bundle. Add the bundle to the lentils, cover partially, and cook over medium-low heat, skimming occasionally, until tender, about 25 minutes. Season the cooking liquid with salt and pepper as if it were soup and let the lentils cool in the liquid. Remove the bundle and discard.

2. Drain the lentils in a sieve, saving the cooking liquid for another use, and wash them under cold running water until the water is clear. In a small saucepan, combine 1 cup (180 g) of the lentils with the almond milk and, if desired, foie gras and bring to a simmer. Transfer to a blender with the sherry vinegar and puree until smooth. Season with salt and pepper.

(CONTINUED)

3. In a medium saucepan, cover the diced carrot, parsnip, and celery root with 2 inches (5 cm) of water and season with salt. Bring to a simmer and cook until tender, about 3 minutes. Using a slotted spoon, transfer the vegetables to a small bowl. Add the sliced carrot and parsnip to the pan and cook until tender, about 3 minutes; drain.

4. FISH Heat the oven to 450°F (230°C). Season the fish with salt and pepper and dust with flour, patting off the excess. In a large ovenproof skillet, heat the oil until shimmering. Add the fish thicker side down and cook over medium-high heat until lightly browned on the bottom, 3 to 4 minutes. Transfer the skillet to the oven and roast the fish until a cake tester inserted into a bottom fillet feels warm when touched to your lower lip, 4 to 5 minutes. Remove from the oven and turn the fish over. Cook over medium-high heat until lightly browned on the bottom, 3 to 4 minutes. Return the fish to the oven and roast until a cake tester inserted into a bottom fillet feels hot when touched to your lower lip, 4 to 5 minutes. Transfer the fish to a rack or a paper towel–lined baking sheet.

5. In a small saucepan, combine the remaining whole lentils with 1½ cups (375 ml) of the pureed lentils; reserve the remaining pureed lentils. Add the diced root vegetables to the pan and warm over medium heat, stirring constantly. Remove from the heat and season the lentil stew with salt and pepper.

6. Remove the fillets from the bones. Spoon the lentil stew onto plates and sprinkle with the shallot, tomato, parsley, and chives. Garnish with the carrot and parsnip slices and set the fish on top. In a small saucepan, bring the reserved pureed lentils to a simmer; using an immersion blender or a whisk, whip until frothy. Spoon the froth around the fish and serve.

NOTES Unlike common brown lentils, tiny black belugas and green lentils keep their shape when cooked. They're available at specialty food shops and online.

If you want to omit the foie gras, substitute ¼ cup (60 ml) extra virgin olive oil.

If you can't find bone-in skinless skate, use four 6-ounce (180 g) skinless, boneless skate, salmon, grouper, cod, or halibut fillets and reduce the cooking time.

MAKE AHEAD The lentils can be prepared through Step 2 and refrigerated for up to 3 days. The diced and sliced vegetables can be prepared through Step 3 and refrigerated overnight.

SERVE WITH For an appetizer, I like Classic Greek Salad (page 49) or Lemony Quinoa Salad (page 35).

WINE Barrel-aged Assyrtiko from Santorini.

Grilled Shrimp with Cabbage Salad

Colossal shrimp are incredibly satisfying to eat because they're so huge and muscular. In this twist, their smoky, salty, lemon-basted goodness drips into and mixes with a slawlike salad (lahanosalata)—it's dressed with a bright lemon vinaigrette, not mayo, and tossed with Kalamata olives, herbs, and scallions for extra flavor. • **4 SERVINGS**

½ small green cabbage, core and thick ribs removed, leaves thinly sliced (see Notes)

8 pitted Kalamata olives, cut into julienne strips

2 scallions, thinly sliced

2 teaspoons chopped parsley

1 tablespoon chopped dill

¾ cup (185 ml) Lemon Vinaigrette (page 105)

Kosher salt and freshly ground white pepper

12 colossal shrimp, heads and tails intact, shelled (see Notes)

¼ teaspoon cayenne pepper

1. In a large bowl, toss the cabbage with the olives, scallions, parsley, 2 teaspoons of the dill, and ¼ cup (60 ml) of the Lemon Vinaigrette. Season with salt and white pepper.

2. Heat a grill or a grill pan. Season the shrimp with salt, white pepper, and cayenne and grill over medium heat, basting them with ¼ cup (60 ml) of the vinaigrette, until opaque, about 2 minutes per side. Transfer the shrimp to a plate. Mound the salad on plates and arrange the shrimp on top. Sprinkle with the remaining ¼ cup (60 ml) of vinaigrette and 1 teaspoon of dill and serve.

NOTES Here's my method for slicing the cabbage: Slice the root end and pull off the outer leaves until you reach the core. Stack 2 or 3 leaves at a time on a carving board, lining up the ribs; cut out the ribs, dividing the cabbage leaves in half. Stack the halved cabbage leaves and slice them crosswise into ⅛-inch (3 mm) julienne strips.

Shrimp are frequently sold without heads, so don't stress if you can't find them head-on.

VARIATION

If you omit the olives and replace the cabbage with romaine lettuce, you've got another popular Greek salad called maroulosalata.

MAKE AHEAD The cabbage salad can be refrigerated for up to 4 hours.

WINE Crisp, floral Moschofilero from the Peloponnese.

AVGOLEMONO

Cabbage-Wrapped Salmon with Cabbage Pilaf

Dolmades are typically cabbage or grape leaves wrapped around rice. These salmon rolls deliver a similar idea, with a twist that's uniquely my own: The fish is tucked into cabbage leaves while the rice is served separately. • **4 SERVINGS**

CABBAGE STOCK

½ tablespoon coriander seeds

½ tablespoon black peppercorns

1 pound (500 g) Savoy cabbage, thinly sliced (see Note)

1 medium Vidalia (sweet) onion, halved and sliced

8 garlic cloves, halved

3 thyme sprigs

3 dill sprigs

2 bay leaves

2 quarts (2 L) water

CABBAGE PILAF

1 tablespoon canola oil

½ cup (100 g) shredded Savoy cabbage

¼ medium Vidalia (sweet) onion, finely chopped

2 dill sprigs, plus chopped dill for garnish

1 bay leaf

½ cup (100 g) short-grain rice

Kosher salt and freshly ground white pepper

1 cup (250 ml) Cabbage Stock or other vegetable stock, plus more for moistening

2 tablespoons crème fraîche or sour cream

2 tablespoons Greek yogurt, preferably homemade (page 223)

2 tablespoons extra virgin olive oil

1 tablespoon fresh lemon juice

SALMON ROLLS, SAUCE, AND ASSEMBLY

Kosher salt

8 large Savoy cabbage leaves

Freshly ground white pepper

1¼ pounds (625 g) skinless center-cut salmon fillet, halved lengthwise

1 cup (250 ml) dry white wine

2 tablespoons finely chopped shallot

1½ cups (375 ml) Cabbage Stock or other vegetable stock

3 large egg yolks

3 tablespoons fresh lemon juice

Osetra caviar, for garnish, optional

1. CABBAGE STOCK In a small dry skillet, toast the coriander seeds and peppercorns over medium heat, shaking the pan occasionally, until fragrant, 2 to 3 minutes. Remove from the heat and let cool slightly. In a large saucepan, combine the toasted spices with the cabbage, onion, garlic, thyme, dill, bay leaves, and water. Bring to a simmer and cook over medium heat until well flavored, about 40 minutes. Strain through a colander into a medium saucepan, pressing on the solids; discard the solids. You should have about 4 cups (1 L) of stock.

2. CABBAGE PILAF In a medium saucepan, warm the canola oil. Add the cabbage, onion, dill sprigs, and bay leaf, then cover and cook over low heat, stirring occasionally, until the vegetables are softened but not browned, 5 to 10 minutes. Add the rice, season with salt and pepper, and cook, stirring, until translucent, about 1 minute. Add 1 cup (250 ml) of the stock and bring to a simmer, then reduce the heat to low, cover, and cook until the rice is tender and the liquid is absorbed, 16 to 18 minutes. Remove the pan from the heat, fluff the rice with a fork, and discard the herbs; cover. Just before serving, stir in the crème fraîche, yogurt, and, if needed to loosen the texture, more stock 1 tablespoon at a time. Stir in the olive oil, lemon juice, and chopped dill. Season with salt and pepper.

3. SALMON ROLLS In a large saucepan of salted boiling water, cook the cabbage leaves until tender, about 4 minutes. Drain the cabbage in a colander and rinse in cold water. Drain again and pat dry. Trim the thick center rib of each leaf so it's flat, keeping the leaf whole, and lightly pound the rib with the heel of a large knife handle to soften. Moisten a work surface with water and line with plastic wrap. Arrange the cabbage leaves rib side up on the plastic in 2 rows of 4 leaves, slightly overlapping them. Season with salt and pepper. Line up the salmon fillets end to end on the long side nearest you, leaving a 3-inch (7.5 cm) border. Season with salt and pepper. Fold the cabbage border over the salmon and tightly roll up; wrap in the plastic. Tightly wrap the salmon roll in 2 more layers of plastic. Using a sharp knife, cut the roll crosswise into twelve 1½-inch (4 cm) sections.

4. In a medium, deep skillet, combine the wine and shallot and bring to a simmer. Season the salmon roll ends with salt and pepper, stand them in the skillet, and cook over medium-low heat until medium-rare on top, about 12 minutes. Transfer to a carving board. Unwrap before serving.

5. SAUCE Meanwhile, in a medium saucepan, bring 1½ cups (375 ml) of the stock to a simmer. In a medium glass measuring cup, whisk the egg yolks. Gradually pour 1 cup (250 ml) of the stock into the egg yolks, whisking constantly, then whisk this mixture back into the remaining stock. Cook the sauce over medium heat, whisking constantly, until slightly thickened, 2 to 3 minutes. Remove the pan from the heat, add the lemon juice, and season with salt and pepper. Using an immersion blender or a whisk, whip the sauce until frothy.

6. ASSEMBLY Mound ¼ cup (60 ml) of the Cabbage Pilaf in the center of each plate. Place 3 salmon rolls on top. Spoon some of the sauce around each plate. Top with a spoonful of caviar, if desired, and serve. Pass the remaining pilaf and sauce separately.

NOTE You'll need 1 Savoy cabbage of about 1½ pounds (750 g) to make both the Cabbage Stock and cabbage rolls. Discard the 4 darkest outer leaves.

WINE Assyrtiko–Sauvignon Blanc blend from Drama or crisp rosé from Amynteo.

Braised Veal with Romaine Lettuce and Dill

Braising meats or seafood with romaine lettuce and dill and enriching the broth with an avgolemono is a traditional Greek method called fricassee. • **4 SERVINGS**

Two 2-pound (1 kg) veal shanks (see Notes)

Kosher salt and freshly ground white pepper

3 tablespoons canola oil

1 large Vidalia (sweet) onion, halved and sliced

1 large head of garlic, cloves peeled and sliced

2 heads of romaine lettuce (about 10 ounces/300 g total), sliced (9 cups)

2 large bunches of dill (8 ounces/250 g total), plus chopped dill for garnish

6 cups (1.5 L) chicken stock

1 large boiling potato, peeled and diced

4 to 6 large egg yolks (see Notes)

4 scallions, thinly sliced

1½ tablespoons chopped parsley

⅓ cup (100 ml) fresh lemon juice

1. Heat the oven to 325°F (165°C). Season the veal with salt and pepper. In a large skillet, heat the oil until shimmering. Add the veal, in batches if necessary, and cook over medium-high heat until browned on all sides, about 15 minutes. Transfer the veal to a large enameled cast-iron casserole. Add the onion and garlic to the skillet and cook over medium heat, stirring occasionally, until softened, about 5 minutes.

2. Add the onion mixture to the veal along with 6 cups (200 g) of the lettuce, the bunches of dill, and the stock. Press a parchment paper lid on top, cover, and bring to a simmer. Transfer the pot to the oven and cook the veal, turning it once, until a cake tester slides easily into the meat, about 2½ hours. Remove the pot from the oven and let cool slightly. Reduce the oven temperature to 275°F (135°C).

3. Transfer the veal to a carving board and slice the meat off the bones; discard the bones. Arrange the meat on a heatproof platter, cover with foil, and keep warm in the oven. Strain the braising liquid through a fine sieve into a medium bowl, pressing on the solids, and skim off the fat; discard the solids in the sieve.

4. In a small saucepan, cover the potato with 2 inches (5 cm) of cold water. Bring to a boil and cook until tender, about 7 minutes. Drain and rinse in cold running water. Transfer to a plate and pat dry with paper towels.

5. In a medium saucepan, bring 2 cups (500 ml) of the braising liquid to a simmer. In a medium glass measuring cup, whisk the egg yolks. Gradually pour 1 cup (250 ml) of the braising liquid into the egg yolks, whisking constantly, then whisk this mixture back into the remaining braising liquid. Cook the sauce over medium heat, whisking constantly, until slightly thickened, 2 to 3 minutes. Pour ½ cup (125 ml) of the sauce back into the measuring cup and reserve.

6. Add the potato, scallions, parsley, lemon juice, and remaining 3 cups (100 g) of lettuce to the pan, season with salt and pepper, and warm over medium heat. Spoon into shallow serving bowls. Using an immersion blender or a whisk, whip the reserved sauce until frothy.

Add the veal to the bowls and top with the froth. Garnish with chopped dill and serve.

NOTES Don't have veal shanks for the recipe? Substitute 4 pounds (2 kg) bone-in veal shoulder roast (or 2 pounds/1 kg boneless shoulder roast) and slice before serving.

At the restaurant, I use the larger proportion of egg yolks to make a richer sauce—3 large egg yolks per 1 cup (250 ml) of broth.

MAKE AHEAD The veal can be prepared through Step 2 and refrigerated in the braising liquid for up to 5 days.

WINE Crisp, fruity Xinomavro rosé from Amynteo or barrel-aged Assyrtiko from Santorini.

EGG AND LEMON ALCHEMY

Which came first, the chicken or the avgolemono? Sure, chickens arrived before the Greeks created avgolemono, the category of sauces and soups thickened with eggs and flavored with lemon juice. But to truly understand avgolemono, you have to grasp the wonderful Greek ethos of sustainability.

Food is precious. Water is precious. Sometimes, the scraps that most people consider trash can be the highlight of a wonderful meal. That's where avgolemono comes in. It's traditionally prepared with leftover stocks, braising liquids, or even the boiling water used to cook vegetables. So at Easter, while the men are spit-roasting whole lambs, the women are simmering the animals' spleens, hearts, and sweetbreads to make magiritsa, the traditional Greek Easter avgolemono soup served with rice. At one unforgettable taverna meal, the chef had boiled whole zucchini in water until the broth tasted like essence of the vegetable. The broth was strained and then I was served the whole soft vegetable with zuccchini-broth avgolemono sauce.

Here's how avgolemono is done: You "temper" eggs with some of the hot broth, whisking it in a thin, steady stream so it doesn't curdle the eggs. Then you gradually pour the tempered-egg mixture into the remaining barely simmering broth, whisking constantly, and cook until the sauce is silky and has some body. Finally, you brighten the sauce with an electric jolt of lemon juice and season it with salt and white pepper (to avoid black specks). The result is a fluffy mixture containing millions of bubbles—possibly the first foam sauce!

Be assured, there's little chance of ending up with scrambled eggs. If the egg starts to coagulate, just remove the pan from the heat and rapidly mix the sauce with an immersion blender to emulsify it again.

Now, about the eggs. Some cooks use the whole egg to make avgolemono; that's thrifty and you don't have any whites collecting in your freezer. A variation separates the yolks and whites, using the yolks to make the avgolemono and whisking in the whipped whites when you pour the tempered mixture into the remaining hot broth.

I make mine with egg yolks only. I save the whites mainly for omelets but also to whip when I want to lighten Béchamel Sauce (page 222). They can also go to make meringues. Freeze leftover whites in ice cube trays, one to a cup. That way you know how many whites you have without having to measure them. And you can defrost only as many as you need.

I use three large egg yolks per 1 cup (250 ml) of broth. They are why my sauces are so rich and delicious. But you can take that number down to two and you'll still get a creamy sauce.

I adopted the Greek no-waste philosophy at Kyma. When I prepare Mussels Diane with Sour Pasta Pearls (page 66) or Roasted Monkfish with Artichokes and Fava Bean Stew (page 154), for example, I purposely save the cooking liquid to make avgolemono sauce. Similarly, to prepare Oven-Roasted Oysters with Champagne Avgolemono (page 64), I reserve the oyster liquor to make the tangy sauce. I'm always thinking about how to get to the plated recipe, wasting as little as possible.

Roasted Monkfish with Artichoke and Fava Bean Stew

Firm white monkfish has a texture that reminds me of meat tenderloin, so I butcher it like a saddle of lamb and roast it on the bone. Filleting this large-format fish just before serving produces the best flavor and succulence and also makes an entrée to share. Alongside, I serve artichoke bottoms braised in enough liquid to create a luscious egg-lemon sauce (avgolemono). The addition of fava beans makes it a fine spring or summer recipe. • **4 SERVINGS**

ARTICHOKE STEW

½ lemon, plus 2 tablespoons fresh lemon juice

¼ cup (60 ml) plus 1 tablespoon extra virgin olive oil

4 large artichokes

1 small Vidalia (sweet) onion, halved and thinly sliced

1 medium carrot, sliced, plus 2 tablespoons finely diced carrot

½ cup (35 g) halved lengthwise and thinly sliced leeks, white and light green parts only, plus 2 tablespoons finely diced dark green part

2 large garlic cloves, crushed

½ cup (125 ml) dry white wine

¼ cup (60 ml) chicken stock

Kosher salt and freshly ground white pepper

2 or 3 large egg yolks (see Notes, page 156)

¼ cup (60 ml) Vidalia Onion Stew (page 159)

8 ounces (250 g) fava beans in the pod, shelled, peeled, and cut crosswise ⅛ inch (3 mm) thick (½ cup/125 g) (see Notes, page 156)

2 tablespoons finely diced shallot

½ medium tomato, peeled, seeded, and cut into ¼-inch (6 mm) dice

FISH

Two 1-pound (500 g) bone-in monkfish saddles, trimmed of outer membranes (see Notes, page 156)

Kosher salt and freshly ground white pepper

Wondra (quick-mixing) flour, for dusting

¼ cup (60 ml) canola oil

4 tablespoons (60 g) unsalted butter

4 garlic cloves, crushed

4 thyme sprigs

1. ARTICHOKE STEW Fill a bowl with water. Squeeze the juice from the lemon half into the water and add the lemon half and 2 tablespoons of the olive oil. Working with one artichoke at a time, peel off all of the dark green outer leaves. Using a large, sharp knife, cut off the leaves just above the bottom, then scoop out the choke. Trim and peel the base and stem and add the artichoke bottom to the water. Drain before using.

2. In a large saucepan, warm 1 tablespoon of the olive oil. Add the onion, sliced carrot, sliced leeks, and garlic and cook over medium heat, stirring occasionally, until softened, about 5 minutes. Add the drained artichokes and cook for 2 minutes. Add the wine and cook for 2 minutes. Add the stock and bring to a simmer. Season with salt and pepper as if it were soup. Press a parchment paper lid on top, cover, and braise the artichokes over medium-low heat until tender, 20 to 30 minutes. Remove the pan from the heat.

3. Meanwhile, in a small saucepan of salted boiling water, blanch the diced carrot for 1 minute. Add the diced leek and cook for 1 minute. Drain and rinse in cold water.

4. Using a slotted spoon, transfer the artichokes to a carving board and cut each into 8 wedges. Strain the artichoke braising liquid through a fine sieve into a medium saucepan, pressing on the vegetables; discard the vegetables in the sieve. Bring the braising liquid to a simmer. In a medium glass measuring cup, whisk the egg yolks. Gradually pour 1/2 cup (125 ml) of the braising liquid into the egg yolks, whisking constantly, then whisk this mixture back into the remaining braising liquid. Cook the sauce over medium heat, whisking constantly, until slightly thickened, 2 to 3 minutes. Pour 1/4 cup (60 ml) of the sauce back into the measuring cup and reserve.

5. Add the artichokes, Vidalia Onion Stew, favas, and diced carrot, leek, shallot, and tomato to the pan and warm over medium heat. Stir in the lemon juice and remaining 2 tablespoons of olive oil. Season the stew with salt and pepper and keep warm.

6. FISH Heat the oven to 400°F (200°C). Season the fish with salt and pepper and dust with flour, patting off the excess. In a large ovenproof skillet, heat the canola oil until shimmering. Add the fish and cook over medium-high heat until lightly browned on 3 sides, about 6 minutes total. Turn the fish fourth side down, transfer the skillet to the oven, and roast the fish until a cake tester inserted into the thickest part of a fillet feels

warm when touched to your lower lip, about 5 minutes.

7. Spoon off any fat in the skillet and set it over medium heat. Add the butter, garlic, and thyme and cook until the butter is foamy. Carefully tip the skillet and, using a large spoon, baste the fish for 45 seconds. Remove the skillet from the heat.

8. Using an immersion blender or a whisk, whip the reserved sauce until frothy. Transfer the Artichoke Stew to a serving bowl, top with the froth, and serve with the fish.

NOTES At the restaurant, I use the larger proportion of egg yolks to make a richer sauce—3 large egg yolks per 1 cup (250 ml) of broth.

No fava beans? Try shelled fresh peas or thawed frozen baby peas.

If you can't get monkfish saddles (monkfish on the bone), substitute four 6-ounce (180 g) monkfish loins.

VARIATIONS

Try subbing in salmon, halibut, or grouper fillets for the monkfish.

The Artichoke Stew is also very good served with roast chicken, pork chops, or—a luxe treat—veal tenderloin. Or try the stew as a meze alongside Sautéed Scallops with Yellow Split Pea Puree (page 63).

MAKE AHEAD The artichokes can be prepared through Step 2 and refrigerated in the cooking liquid for up to 5 days.

SERVE WITH Pair with Lemon Potatoes (page 114), steamed fingerling potatoes, rice pilaf, bulgur, or quinoa to soak up the lemony sauce. As an appetizer, I like Spicy Red Pepper–Feta Spread (page 21).

WINE Crisp, fruity Debina from Epirus or citrusy, minerally Robola from Cephalonia.

Braised Pork with Celery

My yia yia Theone often prepared braised pork with an abundance of celery, then used the heady cooking liquid to make a rich egg-lemon sauce (avgolemono). My tweak is to add fresh, blanched celery (and celery-like fennel) just before serving to brighten the flavors. • **4 SERVINGS**

Four 1¼-pound (625 g) whole pork shanks
  (see Notes, page 159)

Kosher salt and freshly ground white pepper

3 tablespoons canola oil

1½ pounds (750 g) celery ribs, thinly sliced
  (7½ cups)

2 cups (200 g) halved lengthwise and
  thinly sliced leeks, white and light
  green parts only

4 squeezed lemon halves (see Notes, page
  159), plus ⅓ cup (100 ml) fresh lemon
  juice

4 large garlic cloves, crushed

9 dill sprigs plus 1 tablespoon chopped dill

3 thyme sprigs

3 bay leaves

2 tablespoons coriander seeds

1 tablespoon black peppercorns

6 cups (1.5 L) chicken stock

1 small (8-ounce/250 g) fennel bulb,
  cut into ½-inch (1 cm) wedges

4 to 6 large egg yolks (see Notes, page 159)

½ cup (125 ml) Vidalia Onion Stew
  (page 159)

1. Heat the oven to 325°F (165°C). Season the pork with salt and pepper. In a large skillet, heat the oil until shimmering. Add the pork, in batches if needed, and cook over medium-high heat until browned on all sides, about 15 minutes. Transfer the pork to a large enameled cast-iron casserole.

2. Add 5 cups (500 g) of the celery, the leek, lemon halves, garlic, 6 of the dill sprigs, the thyme, bay leaves, coriander seeds, peppercorns, and stock to the pork. Press a parchment paper lid on top, cover, and bring to a simmer. Transfer the pot to the oven and cook the pork, turning it once, until a cake tester slides easily into the meat, 1½ to 3½ hours. Remove the pot from the oven and let cool slightly. Reduce the oven temperature to 275°F (135°C).

3. Transfer the pork to a large ovenproof platter and trim off the fat. Cover with foil and keep warm in the oven. Strain the braising liquid through a fine sieve into a medium bowl, pressing on the solids, and skim off the fat; discard the solids in the sieve.

4. Prepare a medium bowl of half ice, half water. In a medium saucepan of boiling water fitted with a colander, cook the remaining 2½ cups (250 g) of celery until tender, about 5 minutes. Using the colander, transfer the celery to the ice water. Repeat with the fennel. Drain the celery and fennel and dry with paper towels.

5. In a medium saucepan, bring 2 cups (500 ml) of the braising liquid to a simmer. In a medium glass measuring cup, whisk the egg yolks. Gradually pour 1 cup (250 ml) of the braising liquid into the egg yolks, whisking constantly, then whisk this mixture back into the remaining braising liquid. Cook the

sauce over medium heat, whisking constantly, until slightly thickened, 2 to 3 minutes. Pour ½ cup (125 ml) of the sauce back into the measuring cup and reserve.

6. Add the blanched celery and fennel, the Vidalia Onion Stew, chopped dill, and lemon juice to the pan, season with salt and pepper, and warm over medium heat. Spoon into shallow serving bowls. Using an immersion blender or a whisk, whip the reserved sauce until frothy. Set a pork shank in each bowl and top with the froth. Garnish with the remaining dill and serve.

NOTES Don't have pork shanks for this recipe? Substitute 2 pounds (1 kg) of boneless pork butt.

After juicing lemons, save the lemon halves and add to stews; they add enormous citrus flavor.

At the restaurant, I use the larger proportion of eggs yolks to make a richer sauce—3 large egg yolks per 1 cup (250 ml) of broth.

VARIATIONS
The pork shanks can be replaced with lamb shanks, boneless lamb shoulder, or a boneless braising cut of beef, such as chuck or short ribs. Or try a whole chicken, but reduce the cooking time to about 1 hour.

MAKE AHEAD The pork can be prepared through Step 2 and refrigerated in the braising liquid for up to 5 days. The celery and fennel can be blanched and refrigerated overnight.

SERVE WITH Pair with Lemon Potatoes (page 114), steamed fingerling potatoes, rice pilaf, bulgur, or quinoa to soak up the lemony sauce. Before the pork, I like Stuffed Grape Leaves with Cumin Yogurt (pages 30–31) and/or Roasted Beet Salad with Manouri Cream and Buttered Walnuts (page 38).

WINE Full-bodied, barrel-aged Assyrtiko from Santorini with crisp acidity or Greek Sauvignon Blanc from northern Greece, Crete, or the Peloponnese.

Vidalia Onion Stew

The trick to these sweet, melting onions is fully cooking them with salt and pepper in extra virgin olive oil, then whipping in fresh oil and lemon juice. • **MAKES ABOUT 2 CUPS (500 ML)**

1 cup (250 ml) extra virgin olive oil
2 medium Vidalia (sweet) onions, sliced ⅛ inch (3 mm) thick
1 teaspoon kosher salt
½ teaspoon freshly ground white pepper
¼ cup fresh lemon juice

In a small saucepan, warm ½ cup (125 ml) of the oil. Add the onions, salt, and pepper, cover, and cook over low heat, stirring every 5 minutes, until very tender, about 45 minutes. Remove the pan from the heat and, using a wooden spoon, beat in the remaining ½ cup (125 ml) of oil, then the lemon juice.

MAKE AHEAD The onions can be refrigerated for up to 2 weeks.

SERVE WITH I like to spoon the onions straight from the refrigerator on toast and garnish it with capers, dill, and pickled white anchovies. You can also pair the onions with any seafood or vegetable.

MEAT

Layered Baked Pasta with Meat Sauce

Nothing warms the Greek soul like a pan of fresh-baked pastichio. My right-hand man, Eric Cutillo, makes a terrific version for staff meal. It incorporates a brandy-spiked meat sauce I learned from my aunt Rena and is capped with a fluffy layer of next-wave béchamel sauce (lightened with whipped egg whites). • **15 TO 20 SERVINGS**

MEAT SAUCE

4 tablespoons (60 g) unsalted butter

2 tablespoons extra virgin olive oil

2 medium Vidalia (sweet) onions, grated

2 pounds (1 kg) ground beef sirloin

4 small cinnamon sticks

Kosher salt and freshly ground white pepper

1 cup (200 g) tomato paste

1 cup (250 ml) brandy, preferably Metaxa (see page 90)

2 cups (500 ml) water

PASTA AND ASSEMBLY

Kosher salt

1¼ pounds (600 g) 10-inch (25 cm) macaroni noodles (see Notes)

¼ cup (60 ml) extra virgin olive oil

10 cups (2.5 L) Béchamel Sauce (page 222)

3½ ounces (100 g) graviera cheese (see page 163), preferably aged, or Pecorino Romano cheese, shredded

1. MEAT SAUCE In a large saucepan, melt the butter in the oil. Add the onions and cook over medium-high heat, stirring occasionally, until lightly browned, 5 to 8 minutes. Add the meat and cinnamon sticks, season with salt and pepper, and cook, breaking up the clumps with a potato masher, until browned, about 5 minutes. Add the tomato paste and cook, stirring, for 3 minutes. Add the brandy and cook until evaporated, about 2 minutes. Add the water and cook over medium-low heat, scraping up the browned bits stuck to the bottom, until the sauce is semi-dry, about 20 minutes. Discard the cinnamon sticks.

2. PASTA In a large pot of salted boiling water, cook the pasta until al dente. Drain and transfer to a very large bowl with the oil and toss to coat.

3. ASSEMBLY Heat the oven to 350°F (175°C). Using your hands, mix 3 cups (750 ml) of the Béchamel Sauce into the pasta along with the cheese; it will clump. In an 11-by-14-inch (28-by-35.5 cm) shallow baking pan, line up half of the pasta in tight lengthwise rows. Add the meat sauce and spread in a layer. Line up the remaining pasta in rows on top. Add the remaining 7 cups (1.75 L) of Béchamel Sauce and spread in a layer. Bake until the filling bubbles, about 45 minutes. Let the pastichio cool slightly, cut into squares, and serve.

NOTES For the noodles, I like Misko brand pastitsio pasta no 2. In a pinch, you could use perciatelli or bucatini.

Like most baked pastas, this one is easier to cut if left to set for 10 minutes or so before serving.

VARIATIONS

You can replace the ground beef with another ground meat, such as lamb, pork, veal, rabbit, or turkey, or a mix.

This easy meat sauce is great with just about any pasta, not only in pastichio.

MAKE AHEAD The Meat Sauce can be refrigerated for up to 3 days. The pastichio can be assembled and refrigerated for 4 hours before topping with the béchamel and baking. The baked pasta can be refrigerated overnight and reheated in a 325°F (165°C) oven.

SERVE WITH I like a vegetable with the baked pasta, like Wilted Greens (page 114) or Classic Greek Salad (page 49).

WINE Fruity Agiorgitiko from Nemea or fresh Limniona from Thessaly.

GREEK CHEESE PRIMER

Nearly all Greek cheeses are fabricated from sheep's milk (mainly), goat's milk, or a combination, though a few are made from cow's milk. They're available at Greek and Mediterranean markets as well as the best cheese shops. Here are the types you'll find in these pages.

FETA: Outside of Greece, feta is often crafted from cow's milk. But Greek feta is produced only from sheep's or goat's milk. For the creamiest, tangiest examples, look for blocks in brine, not the pre-crumbled or vacuum-sealed varieties. I'm partial to the soft, moist, and slightly briny Dodoni brand from the region of Epirus in northwestern Greece.

GRAVIERA: Semihard, supple, mild, and yellow, usually made from cow's milk. Similar to Gruyère.

KASSERI: Firm, kneaded (like mozzarella), and yellow, with a mild flavor. Similar to provolone.

KEFALOTIRI: Hard, salty, pale yellow grating cheese. Similar to Pecorino Romano.

MANOURI: Dense, soft, stark-white cheese made from the whey that's drained during the production of feta or graviera. Similar to fresh ricotta salata.

MIZITHRA: Hard, nutty, salty whey cheese that's often grated. Similar to aged (dry) ricotta salata.

Roast Chicken with Warm Potato-Tomato Salad

At a winery in the Peloponnese, I enjoyed a simple lunch of roast chicken with an amazing recipe of potatoes cooked in tomato sauce and finished with olive oil and lemon. But magic happened when I reshaped it in my own kitchen. Instead of roasting a bird whole, I confit the legs with spices and herbs and, separately, roast the breast. The original also included roasted cherry tomatoes; here, I tart up the flavors on the plate with pickled tomatoes from my garden. • **4 SERVINGS**

PICKLED TOMATOES

1 cup (250 ml) water

⅓ cup (100 ml) white balsamic vinegar

2 tablespoons sugar

2 cups (300 g) grape tomatoes (see Note, page 167)

Thinly peeled zest of 1 large lemon

5 thyme sprigs

1 teaspoon canola oil

CONFIT CHICKEN LEGS

2 tablespoons coriander seeds

2 tablespoons black peppercorns

½ cup (80 g) kosher salt

5 thyme sprigs

2 whole chicken legs

Thinly peeled zest of 1 lemon

1 bay leaf

½ tablespoon canola oil, plus more for braising

CHICKEN JUS

1¾ pounds (800 g) chicken wings, split

1 small Vidalia (sweet) onion, sliced

1 carrot, sliced

1 small head of garlic, cloves peeled and sliced

6 parsley sprigs

3 thyme sprigs

5 cups (1.25 L) chicken stock

Kosher salt and freshly ground white pepper

PEARL ONIONS, ROASTED CHICKEN BREASTS, AND ASSEMBLY

4 white pearl onions

1 tablespoon (15 g) unsalted butter

Kosher salt

½ tablespoon canola oil

Two 8-ounce (250 g) skin-on boneless chicken breast halves

Warm Potato-Tomato Salad (page 48), warmed

Extra virgin olive oil, for drizzling

1. PICKLED TOMATOES In a small saucepan, combine the water with the vinegar and sugar and bring to a simmer over medium heat, stirring to dissolve the sugar. Remove the pan from the heat and let cool. Using a toothpick, pierce the bottom of each grape tomato. In a 2-cup (500 ml) container, combine the tomatoes with the pickling liquid, lemon zest, and thyme. Cover and refrigerate for at least 8 hours or overnight; drain.

2. CONFIT CHICKEN LEGS In a small dry skillet, toast the coriander seeds and peppercorns over medium heat, shaking the pan

occasionally, until fragrant, 2 to 3 minutes. Transfer the spices to a small bowl and let cool. Tie 2 tablespoons of the toasted spices in a cheesecloth bundle. Reserve the remaining spices.

3. In a medium baking pan, spread the ½ cup (80 g) of salt. Sprinkle with the reserved spices and 3 of the thyme sprigs. Arrange the chicken legs skin side up on top. Cover with a second medium baking pan to press the chicken into the salt and refrigerate for 4 hours. Rinse the salt off the chicken and pat dry with paper towels.

4. In a medium enameled cast-iron casserole, combine the cured chicken legs with the spice bundle, lemon zest, bay leaf, remaining 2 thyme sprigs, and canola oil to just cover the chicken. Bring to a simmer and cook over medium-low heat, turning the chicken halfway through, until a cake tester slides easily into a leg, about 1 hour. Remove from the heat and let cool completely. Using a slotted spoon, transfer the confit legs to a carving board and slide out the bones, keeping the meat intact. Discard the oil.

5. CHICKEN JUS Place a medium roasting pan in the oven and heat to 450°F (230°C). Add the chicken wings to the pan and roast, stirring two or three times, until the wings are deeply browned, about 45 minutes. Stir in the sliced onion, carrot, and garlic and roast for 5 minutes. Add the parsley, thyme, and stock and bake until the stock simmers, about 15 minutes. Reduce the oven temperature to 350°F (175°C) and bake for 30 minutes. Remove the pan from the oven and let cool slightly. Strain the stock through a fine sieve

into a medium bowl, pressing on the solids, and skim off the fat; discard the solids in the sieve. In a medium saucepan, simmer the stock over medium heat, skimming often, until syrupy and reduced to ¼ cup (60 ml), about 30 minutes. Season with salt and pepper. Reheat the jus before serving.

6. PEARL ONIONS In a small saucepan, combine the pearl onions with the butter, a pinch of salt, and just enough water to barely coat the bottom of the pan. Cover, bring to a simmer, and cook over medium heat until the onions are tender and glazed, 4 to 6 minutes. Transfer the onions to a paper towel–lined plate to drain. Halve them lengthwise, then separate into petals.

7. In a small skillet, heat the 1 teaspoon of canola oil until shimmering. Add 8 of the Pickled Tomatoes and cook over medium-high heat, shaking occasionally, until golden brown, 2 to 3 minutes; save the remaining Pickled Tomatoes for another use. Drain on a paper towel–lined plate.

8. ROASTED CHICKEN BREASTS Position racks in the upper and lower thirds of the oven and heat to 350°F (175°C). In a medium ovenproof skillet, heat the ½ tablespoon of canola oil until shimmering. Season the chicken breasts with salt. Add skin side down to the skillet and cook over medium-high heat, pressing with a spatula, until golden brown on the bottom, 3 to 5 minutes. Turn the chicken over, transfer to the upper rack in the oven, and roast until an instant-read thermometer inserted in the center of a breast registers 160°F (70°C), 10 to 15 minutes.

9. Meanwhile, in another medium ovenproof skillet, heat the remaining ½ tablespoon of canola oil until shimmering. Add the confit chicken legs skin side down and cook over medium-high heat, pressing with a spatula, until golden brown on the bottom, 3 to 5 minutes. Turn the chicken over, transfer to the lower rack in the oven, and roast until heated through, about 10 minutes. Remove both skillets from the oven and transfer the breasts and legs to a carving board.

10. ASSEMBLY Cut each leg crosswise into 4 pieces. Cut each breast crosswise in half. Mound some of the Warm Potato-Tomato Salad on each plate and nestle a breast half skin side up on top. Stand 2 pieces of confit leg alongside. Garnish with Pickled Tomatoes and pearl onion petals and drizzle with olive oil. Brush the plates with Chicken Jus. Serve, passing more Warm Potato-Tomato Salad and Chicken Jus separately.

NOTES The grape tomatoes pickle for at least 8 hours and the chicken legs cure for 4 hours, so plan accordingly.

Instead of buying chicken legs and breasts separately, you can buy one 3 ½- to 4-pound (1.75 kg) whole chicken and cut off the legs and breasts yourself. For the Chicken Jus, save the wings and carcass as a supplement to the additional chicken wings; you want a total of 1¾ pounds (800 g).

The Pickled Tomatoes make more than you need for this recipe but can be refrigerated for up to 1 week.

If you have time, make the Chicken Jus a day ahead and refrigerate it, so the fat can be easily removed.

VARIATION

Oven-roasted plum tomatoes (see Braised Lamb and Roasted Tomatoes in Thieves' Purses, Step 4, page 180) can replace the Pickled Tomatoes.

MAKE AHEAD The recipe can be prepared through Step 5 and refrigerated overnight.

SERVE WITH Round out the meal with Classic Greek Salad (page 49).

WINE Oak-aged Xinomavro from Naoussa or full-bodied Goumenissa.

Braised Rabbit with Tomato and Orzo

In traditional youvetsi, lamb slow-cooks in cinnamon-scented red wine (then the rice-shaped pasta accompaniment simmers in the braising liquid, absorbing all the sweet spice). But I love the same tastes with rabbit. Another thing I like about this rich version is the freshness added by stirring in homemade tomato compote, instead of the usual canned tomato paste, once the meat is tender. • **4 SERVINGS**

4 whole rabbit legs (see Note, page 170)

Kosher salt and freshly ground white pepper

¼ cup (60 ml) canola oil

2 yellow onions, sliced

6 garlic cloves, smashed

2 cups (500 ml) red wine

6 cups (1.5 L) chicken stock

2 cinnamon sticks

6 thyme sprigs

3 bay leaves

3 cherry tomatoes, preferably heirloom, quartered lengthwise

2 tablespoons extra virgin olive oil

4 white pearl onions

1 cup (140 g) orzo pasta

1 cup (250 ml) Tomato Compote (page 221)

Thinly sliced chives and mint sprigs, for garnish

1. Heat the oven to 325°F (165°C). Season the rabbit with salt and pepper. In a large enameled cast-iron casserole, warm 2 tablespoons of the canola oil. Add the rabbit, in batches if needed, and cook over medium heat, turning once, until lightly browned, 5 to 8 minutes. Transfer the rabbit to a plate. Add the sliced onions and remaining 2 tablespoons of canola oil to the casserole and cook, stirring occasionally, until slightly softened, about 2 minutes. Add the garlic and cook, stirring occasionally, until softened, about 2 minutes.

2. Add the wine to the pot and cook until evaporated, 15 to 20 minutes. Return the rabbit to the pot and add the stock, cinnamon sticks, thyme, and bay leaves. Press a parchment paper lid on top, cover, and bring to a simmer. Transfer the pot to the oven and cook the rabbit, turning it once, until a cake tester slides easily into the meat, about 2 hours. Remove the pot from the oven and let cool.

3. While the rabbit is braising, in a pie plate, season the cherry tomatoes with salt and pepper and drizzle with 1 tablespoon of the olive oil. Transfer to the oven and roast until lightly browned and wilted, about 20 minutes.

4. Transfer the rabbit to a large shallow baking pan. Strain the braising liquid through a fine sieve into a medium bowl, pressing on the solids, and skim off the fat; discard the solids in the sieve. In a medium saucepan, bring 2 cups (500 ml) of the braising liquid to a simmer. Add the pearl onions and cook until tender, about 5 minutes. Using a slotted spoon, transfer the onions to a carving board. Halve them lengthwise, then separate into petals.

5. Add enough of the remaining braising liquid to the saucepan to make 4 cups (1 L) and bring to a simmer. Add the pasta and cook until al dente. Strain through a fine sieve and add the pasta to the baking pan with the rabbit. Wipe out the saucepan. Transfer the rabbit to the oven and bake, basting every 2 minutes with the braising liquid, until glazed, about 10 minutes.

6. In the same saucepan, combine the pasta with the Tomato Compote and ½ cup (125 ml) of the braising liquid and bring to a simmer. Add the remaining 1 tablespoon of olive oil and season with salt and pepper. Spoon the pasta into shallow serving bowls. Garnish with chives and top with a rabbit leg. Alternate tomato quarters and onion petals around the rabbit, garnish with mint, and serve.

NOTE Rabbit is available at butcher shops, farmers' markets, and dartagnan.com.

VARIATIONS

The rabbit can be replaced with lamb shank, pork shank, or bone-in chicken thighs.

Showering the plates with grated cheese, such as mizithra (see page 163), kefalogtiri (see page 163), or Parmesan, is a nice touch.

MAKE AHEAD The recipe can be prepared through Step 3 and refrigerated for up to 5 days.

SERVE WITH To begin the meal, I like Cheese Phyllo Cigars (page 82) and Grilled Eggplant Spread (page 22).

WINE Oak-aged Assyrtiko from Santorini or northern Greece or fruity Agiorgitiko from Nemea.

Grilled Beef Rib Eye with Parsley Sauce

Serving Flintstone-size steaks is not very Greek, but basting them with oregano-lemon vinaigrette as they grill definitely is. I like the juicy meat with tangy parsley sauce, a bright green puree of herbs, anchovies, capers, and olive oil—another purely Greek note. • **4 SERVINGS**

1¼ cups (40 g) packed parsley leaves, plus chopped parsley for sprinkling

½ cup (125 ml) extra virgin olive oil

2 oil-packed anchovy fillets

2 teaspoons (10 g) drained capers

Kosher salt and freshly ground black pepper

Two 1¼- to 1½-pound (625 to 750 g) bone-in rib eye steaks (see Notes)

1 tablespoon dried oregano

¼ cup (60 ml) Lemon Vinaigrette (page 105)

Fleur de sel, for sprinkling

Lemon Potatoes (page 114), for serving

1. Set a small stainless steel bowl in a medium bowl of half ice, half water. In a blender, puree ¾ cup (25 g) of the parsley leaves with the oil, anchovies, capers, and a pinch each of kosher salt and pepper until very smooth, about 3 minutes. Add the remaining ½ cup (15 g) of parsley leaves and puree until smooth. Scrape into the prepared bowl and stir until cool.

2. Remove the steaks from the refrigerator and let stand at room temperature for 15 minutes. Heat a grill or a grill pan. In a small bowl, stir the oregano into the Lemon Vinaigrette. Season the steaks with kosher salt and pepper and grill over medium-high heat, turning them 90 degrees and brushing them with 2 tablespoons of the oregano-lemon vinaigrette halfway through, until charred on the bottom, about 8 minutes. Turn the steaks over and repeat with the remaining 2 tablespoons of oregano-lemon vinaigrette, grilling until a cake tester inserted in the center of a steak is lukewarm when touched to your lower lip, about 8 minutes for medium-rare (see Notes). Transfer the steaks to a carving board and let rest for 10 minutes.

3. Slice the steaks off the bone, then cut crosswise into slices. Transfer to a platter or plates, sprinkle with fleur de sel, and spoon some of the parsley sauce on top. Sprinkle the Lemon Potatoes with chopped parsley. Serve the steak with the Lemon Potatoes, passing the remaining parsley sauce separately.

NOTES Grade prime, dry-aged cowboy steak is best.

Those with hearty appetites will require an entire steak; for most others, half of one of these giant cuts is probably plenty.

For medium meat, the cake tester will be a true warm, warm/hot for medium-well, and hot for well done.

SERVE WITH I like to serve Wilted Greens (page 114) alongside. As a first course, try Braised Giant White Beans with Tomato Sauce (page 34) or Roasted Beet Salad with Manouri Cream and Buttered Walnuts (page 38).

WINE Full-bodied Cabernet Sauvignon blends with Agiorgitiko, Merlot, or Limnio from the Peloponnese or northern or central Greece.

Grilled Lamb Chops with Greek Fries

These lemony, fire-licked chops are a standout in my family's recipe box. They're simple to prepare: Marinate the lamb in vinaigrette seasoned with fresh herbs and dried oregano for three days, then grill. The crispy, twice-cooked fried potatoes, however, do require some work but are definitely worth it. Thick, cooling cucumber yogurt finishes the plate. • **4 SERVINGS**

2 cups (500 ml) fresh lemon juice

3 tablespoons (12 g) rosemary leaves

3 tablespoons (12 g) thyme leaves

5 tablespoons (10 g) dried oregano

2 cups (500 ml) extra virgin olive oil

4 cups (1 L) canola oil, plus more for deep-frying

12 lamb loin chops (about 2¼ pounds/1 kg total)

2 large (1-pound/500 g) russet (baking) potatoes

Kosher salt and freshly ground white pepper

¼ teaspoon crushed red pepper

Finely grated graviera cheese (see page 163) or Pecorino Romano cheese, for sprinkling

¾ cup (185 ml) Cucumber Yogurt Spread (page 20), for serving

Lemon wedges, for serving

1. In a blender, working in two batches, combine the lemon juice with the rosemary, thyme, and 2 tablespoons of the oregano. Puree on high to break down the herbs, then gradually pour in the olive oil and the 4 cups (1 L) of canola oil to emulsify. Reserve 1 cup (250 ml) of the vinaigrette and refrigerate; pour the rest into a large shallow baking pan. Arrange the lamb chops in the pan in a single layer and turn to coat. Cover the lamb chops and refrigerate for 3 days.

2. Fill a medium bowl with cold water. Line a baking sheet with parchment paper. Peel the potatoes and slice them crosswise ¼ inch (6 mm) thick. Using a 1½-inch (3.5 cm) round cookie cutter, stamp out a smaller round from each slice and add to the water; save the trimmings in a container of water for another use. In a large pot, heat 3 inches (7.5 cm) of canola oil to 250°F (120°C). Drain the potatoes and pat dry with a thick kitchen towel. Fry the potatoes in batches, stirring often, for 5 minutes per batch. Using a slotted spoon, transfer the potatoes as they're done to the prepared baking sheet. Spread out on the baking sheet and freeze for at least 1 hour. Reserve the oil in the pot for the second frying.

PHOTOGRAPH ON PAGES 2–3

3. Drain the lamb chops and let them come to room temperature. Heat a grill or a grill pan. Toss the lamb chops with 2 tablespoons of the oregano and season with salt and white pepper. Grill the lamb chops over medium-high heat, basting occasionally with ½ cup (125 ml) of the reserved vinaigrette, until charred, about 3 minutes per side for medium-rare. Transfer to a platter and let rest.

4. Heat the reserved oil to 350°F (175°C). Fry the frozen potatoes in batches, stirring often, until golden brown, about 3 minutes per batch. Return them as they're done to the prepared baking sheet and season with the crushed red pepper, salt, and remaining 1 tablespoon of oregano. Transfer to a serving bowl and sprinkle with cheese. Season the lamb chops with salt and white pepper and serve with the fries, Cucumber Yogurt Spread, the remaining vinaigrette, and lemon wedges.

NOTES The lamb chops need to marinate for 3 days, so plan accordingly.

A deep fryer can be used instead of a pot on the stove. Just make sure you're frying in at least 3 inches (7.5 cm) of oil.

The potato trimmings can be used to make Garlicky Potato Spread (page 23).

VARIATIONS
The dried oregano can be replaced with the same amount of fresh. Try this recipe also with thin pork chops.

MAKE AHEAD The fries can be prepared through Step 2 and frozen in a resealable plastic bag for up to 1 week.

SERVE WITH For a first course, set out a meze spread of Braised Giant White Beans with Tomato Sauce (page 34), Classic Greek Salad (page 49), and Stuffed Grape Leaves with Cumin Yogurt (pages 30–31).

WINE Earthy Xinomavro from Naoussa, Cabernet Franc from central Greece, or dry Mavrodaphne from the Peloponnese or Cephalonia.

Braised Leg of Lamb with Sour Pasta Pearls

Before opening Kyma, I went to visit my aunt Rena in Athens. She pinched my cheeks, gave me a kiss, and sent me into the kitchen to pull a heavy casserole from the oven. Next, she had me lift out the leg of lamb that had been cooking for hours, and I got a lesson in the uses of braising liquid: Thea Rena poured in slightly tart trahana, a pebbly kind of pasta the size of couscous, which swelled in the aromatic liquid, absorbing the tomato, garlic, and onion flavors. Then she added the bright tastes of olive oil, lemon juice, and fresh herbs. Her lamb became a signature recipe at the restaurant; my customers won't let me take it off the menu. • **8 SERVINGS**

LAMB

One 4½- to 5-pound (2 to 2.25 kg) semi-boneless leg of lamb (aitchbone removed)

Kosher salt and freshly ground white pepper

1 tablespoon dried oregano

3 tablespoons canola oil

3 large Vidalia (sweet) onions (2 pounds/ 1 kg total), thinly sliced

2 heads of garlic (4 ounces/125 g total), cloves peeled and chopped

6 cups (1.5 L) chicken stock

10 thyme sprigs (15 g)

PASTA AND ASSEMBLY

2 cups (250 g) sour trahana pasta (see Notes, page 66)

2 cups (500 ml) Tomato Compote (page 221)

¾ cup (25 g) chopped mixed herbs, such as chives, dill, and parsley

¾ cup (185 ml) extra virgin olive oil

½ cup (125 ml) fresh lemon juice

Kosher salt and freshly ground white pepper

Finely grated mizithra cheese (see page 163) or ricotta salata cheese, for sprinkling

1. LAMB Heat the oven to 325°F (165°C). Season the lamb with salt, pepper, and the oregano. In a very large skillet, heat the canola oil until shimmering. Add the lamb and cook over medium-high heat until browned on all sides, about 10 minutes. Transfer the lamb to a large enameled cast-iron casserole. Add the onions and garlic to the pot and cook over medium heat, stirring occasionally, until softened, about 10 minutes.

2. Add the vegetables to the lamb along with the stock and thyme. Press a parchment paper lid on top, cover, and bring to a simmer. Transfer the pot to the oven and cook the lamb, turning it once, until a cake tester slides easily into the meat, 3½ to 4½ hours. Remove the pot from the oven and let cool slightly. Reduce the oven temperature to 275°F (135°C).

3. Transfer the lamb to a large ovenproof platter, cover with foil, and keep warm in the oven. Strain the braising liquid through a fine sieve into a medium bowl, pressing on the solids, and skim off the fat; discard the solids in the sieve.

(CONTINUED)

4. PASTA In a large saucepan, bring 4 cups (1 L) of the braising liquid to a simmer. Add the pasta and cook over medium-low heat, whisking occasionally, until tender, about 10 minutes. If needed, add more braising liquid a splash at a time until the pasta is cooked and saucy. Remove the pan from the heat and stir in the Tomato Compote, herbs, olive oil, and lemon juice. Season with salt and pepper.

5. ASSEMBLY Spoon some of the pasta into a deep serving platter and sprinkle with the cheese. Set the lamb on top and serve. Pass the remaining braising liquid and pasta separately.

NOTES Braising liquid should simmer but never boil, so aim for tiny bubbles; you may need to reduce the oven temperature. Save any leftover liquid for your next braise.

If you're not rushed, let the lamb cool completely in the liquid before continuing; the extra time makes the meat very juicy.

I like to cook the lamb until the meat is falling-off-the-bone tender; it's served with a spoon.

The pasta will continue to absorb liquid, so just before serving add more of the braising liquid to make it saucy if needed.

VARIATIONS
Try this recipe with bone-in lamb shoulder or eight 1-pound (500 g) lamb shanks. It can also be prepared with 4 pounds (1.75 kg) of boneless lamb shoulder.

MAKE AHEAD The lamb can be prepared through Step 2 and refrigerated in the braising liquid for up to 3 days. Warm through before continuing.

SERVE WITH To continue the homey theme, try Wilted Greens (page 114) or Eggplant Stew with Onions and Tomato Sauce (pages 36–37). And Classic Greek Salad (page 49) brings a refreshing contrast to the meal.

WINE Aged Xinomavro from Naoussa or full-bodied Goumenissa.

Cheese-Stuffed Rack of Lamb with Eggplant Stew

I enjoy connecting with my heritage by researching traditional Greek recipes and modernizing them. For instance, this recipe draws inspiration from the experience of eating at my uncle Tykie's table. We'd snack on graviera cheese while garlic-stuffed leg of lamb roasted in the oven. In my own kitchen, I stuff an elegant rack of lamb with the cheese and baste it with garlic butter. • **4 SERVINGS**

Two 1¼-pound (625 g) frenched racks of lamb

4 to 6 ounces (125 to 180 g) graviera cheese (see page 163) or Pecorino Romano cheese, cut into ¼-inch (6 mm) bars

Kosher salt and freshly ground white pepper

2 tablespoons canola oil

2 garlic cloves, crushed with skin on

3 thyme sprigs

3 tablespoons (45 g) unsalted butter

Fleur de sel and chopped parsley, for sprinkling

Eggplant Stew with Onions and Tomato Sauce (pages 36–37)

1. Heat the oven to 400°F (200°C). Set the lamb racks fat side up on a carving board. For each rack, push a sharp, thin knife horizontally into the center of the meat. Turn the rack and repeat on the other side. Insert a clean sharpening steel into the slit, wiggling and pushing it through to the other side to create a pocket for stuffing. Push 2 or 3 of the cheese bars into the pocket, filling it completely. Using kitchen twine and starting in the middle of the rack, tie a loop around the meat and knot it between each bone, including the very ends of the meat (see Note).

2. Set a large cast-iron or other heavy ovenproof skillet over high heat until very hot.

Season the lamb racks with kosher salt and pepper. Reduce the heat to medium-high and add the oil. Add the lamb, fat side down, and cook until richly browned, about 3 minutes. Turn the lamb fat side up and cook for 2 minutes. Transfer the skillet to the oven and roast the lamb until an instant-read thermometer inserted into the thickest part of the meat registers 125°F (50°C) for rare, about 15 minutes.

3. Set the skillet over medium heat. Add the garlic, thyme, and butter and cook until the butter is foamy. Carefully tip the skillet and, using a large spoon, baste the meat repeatedly until the butter is browned and smells nutty, 2 to 3 minutes.

4. Transfer the lamb to a carving board and let stand for 5 minutes. Remove and discard the strings. Slice between the lamb ribs to make four 3-rib servings and transfer to plates. Spoon the browned butter over the lamb, sprinkle with fleur de sel and parsley, and serve with the eggplant stew.

NOTE Tying the lamb between the ribs keeps the meat in a nice round shape as it cooks.

WINE FULL-BODIED Xinomavro blends from Naoussa or Amynteo, or Greek Syrah.

Braised Lamb and Roasted Tomatoes in Thieves' Purses

Food served in a tied paper or plastic pouch or a crepe is called a "beggar's purse" in English. In Greece, however, it's kleftiko, which means "thief's purse." In this recipe, the components—braised lamb shanks, roasted plum tomatoes, fried fingerling potatoes, and confit garlic cloves—are first cooked separately, then united in transparent Fata paper, which makes for a dramatic presentation. • **4 SERVINGS**

Four 1-pound (500 g) lamb shanks, trimmed (see Notes)

Kosher salt and freshly ground white pepper

½ cup (125 ml) canola oil

1 pound (500 g) Vidalia (sweet) onions, thinly sliced

2 garlic cloves, thinly sliced

5 thyme sprigs

6 cups (1.5 L) chicken stock

4 small plum tomatoes (1 pound/500 g total), quartered lengthwise

3 tablespoons extra virgin olive oil, plus more for drizzling

1 teaspoon dried oregano

4 fingerling potatoes, each about 2.5 inches (5 cm) long

1 teaspoon black peppercorns

1 bay leaf

8 cloves of Garlic Confit (page 219)

4 sheets Fata paper (see Notes)

Chopped parsley, for sprinkling

Fleur de sel and micro herbs, for garnish

1. Heat the oven to 325°F (165°C). Season the lamb with kosher salt and pepper. In a large skillet, heat ¼ cup (60 ml) of the canola oil until shimmering. Add the lamb, in batches if needed, and cook over medium-high heat until browned on all sides, about 15 minutes. Transfer the lamb to a large enameled cast-iron casserole.

2. Add 3 cups (300 g) of the onions, the sliced garlic, and 4 thyme sprigs to the skillet and cook, stirring occasionally, until softened, about 5 minutes. Using a slotted spoon, transfer the aromatics to the lamb along with the stock. Press a parchment paper lid on top, cover, and bring to a simmer. Transfer the pot to the oven and cook the lamb, turning it once, until a cake tester slides easily into the meat, 1½ to 3½ hours. Remove the pot from the oven and let cool. Increase the oven temperature to 350°F (175°C).

3. Transfer the lamb to a carving board and pull the meat off the bones; discard the bones. Strain the braising liquid through a fine sieve into a medium bowl, pressing on the solids, and skim off the fat; discard the solids in the sieve.

4. Set a rack on a rimmed baking sheet. Arrange the tomatoes on the rack cut side up. Drizzle with 1 tablespoon of the olive oil, season with kosher salt, pepper, and the oregano, and roast until the tomatoes are tender but still hold their shape, 20 to 30 minutes. Remove from the oven and let cool. Keep the oven on.

5. In a small saucepan, cover the potatoes, peppercorns, bay leaf, and remaining 1 thyme sprig with cold water and bring to a boil. Cook over medium-high heat until tender, 15 to

20 minutes. Drain and let cool slightly, then halve the potatoes lengthwise. Discard the aromatics.

6. In a medium skillet, heat the remaining ¼ cup (60 ml) of canola oil until shimmering. Add the potatoes cut side down and cook over medium-high heat until golden brown on the bottom, 3 to 5 minutes. Turn the potatoes over, add the Garlic Confit, and cook until the garlic cloves are lightly browned, 2 to 3 minutes. Using a slotted spoon, transfer the potatoes and garlic cloves to a paper towel–lined plate. Wipe out the skillet.

7. Warm the remaining 2 tablespoons of olive oil in the same skillet. Add the remaining 2 cups (200 g) of onions. Season with kosher salt and pepper and cook over low heat, stirring occasionally, until caramelized, 20 to 25 minutes. Using a slotted spoon, transfer to a paper towel–lined plate.

8. Cut the Fata paper (see Notes) into four 20-inch (50 cm) squares. Working with 1 square at a time, push the paper into a small glass measuring cup to make it easy to fill. Add ½ cup (90 g) of the lamb, then layer 2 tomato quarters, 1 potato half, 1 confit garlic clove, and one-fourth of the caramelized onions on top. Repeat layering the lamb, tomatoes, potato, and garlic (no onions). Sprinkle with parsley and pour in ¼ cup (60 ml) of the braising liquid. Using kitchen string, tie the paper into a pouch.

9. Set the pouches in a large shallow baking pan and fill with ¼ inch (6 mm) of hot water. Transfer to the oven and bake until hot,

about 20 minutes. Transfer each pouch to a plate or a serving bowl. Cut the pouches open just below the string. Drizzle with olive oil, garnish with fleur de sel and micro herbs, and serve.

NOTES This is a fun recipe to eat right out of the bag. Cut the pouches open in front of your guests or pass around the scissors so they can cut their own. Alternatively, if you tie the bags like you do your shoes, your guests can open them easily with the pull of a string.

Don't have lamb shanks for this recipe? Substitute 2 pounds (1 kg) boneless lamb shoulder or lamb leg, cut into 1½-inch (4 cm) pieces. The meat cooks until it's completely tender.

Fata paper is a clear film you can heat to up to 400°F. It is sold in rolls and sheets and can be purchased online.

VARIATIONS
The lamb shanks can be replaced with pork shanks, pork butt, or a braising cut of beef, such as chuck or short ribs. Or try a whole chicken or chicken parts, but reduce the cooking time to about 1 hour.

MAKE AHEAD The lamb can be prepared through Step 2 and refrigerated in the braising liquid for up to 5 days. The roasted tomatoes can be refrigerated for up to 3 days.

SERVE WITH As appetizers, I like Lemony Quinoa Salad (page 35), Cucumber Yogurt Spread (page 20), and Cheese and Wild Mushroom Shredded Phyllo Pies (page 83).

WINE Full-bodied Xinomavro, Rapsani Reserve, or Mavrotragano from Santorini.

PHOTOGRAPH ON PRECEDING SPREAD

VEGETARIAN

Melted Leeks with Bell Pepper Stew

I wanted to create a leek that's as texturally satisfying as steak. This one requires a knife and fork to slice yet is silky in the mouth. Hang on to the recipe for the pepper stew, spetzofai; it's incredibly versatile. I serve it with everything from grilled cuttlefish and sautéed grouper or halibut to grilled lamb chops. • **4 SERVINGS**

BELL PEPPER STEW

1 cup (250 ml) canola oil

1½ bell peppers, red, yellow, and/or green, cut into ¼-inch (6 mm) dice (1½ cups)

1 small Vidalia (sweet) onion, sliced ½ inch (1.25 cm) thick

1 teaspoon minced oil-packed Calabrian chile (see Notes), or ½ teaspoon crushed red pepper

Kosher salt and freshly ground white pepper

¾ cup (185 ml) Tomato Compote (page 221)

2 tablespoons ouzo

2 teaspoons fresh lemon juice

3 tablespoons (27 g) drained capers

3 tablespoons (25 g) cracked green olive julienne

3 tablespoons (25 g) Kalamata olive julienne

2 teaspoons thinly sliced chives

LEEKS AND ASSEMBLY

Kosher salt

4 large leeks, white and light green parts only, each top tied with string (see Notes)

Fleur de sel and extra virgin olive oil, for garnish

1. BELL PEPPER STEW In a medium saucepan, warm the canola oil. Add the bell peppers and cook over low heat, stirring occasionally, until completely soft, about 15 minutes. Drain the peppers, reserving the oil.

2. In the same saucepan, heat 1 tablespoon of the reserved pepper oil. Add the onion and Calabrian chile and season with kosher salt and white pepper. Cover and cook over low heat until completely soft, about 15 minutes. Add the bell peppers and Tomato Compote and bring to a simmer. Remove the pan from the heat and stir in the ouzo, lemon juice, capers, both olives, and the chives. Season lightly with kosher salt and white pepper.

3. LEEKS In a large skillet of salted boiling water, cook the leeks until a cake tester slides in easily, 20 to 30 minutes. Drain and pat dry with a kitchen towel. Remove the strings.

4. ASSEMBLY Spoon the stew into wide serving bowls and arrange 1 leek in the center of each bowl. Garnish with fleur de sel and olive oil and serve.

NOTES The remaining reserved pepper oil can be used to sauté vegetables.

Spicy Calabrian chiles come whole in jars. You'll need to drain one and finely chop it.

Tying the leek tops prevents them from coming apart in the water.

If the leeks don't fit in your serving bowls, halve them crosswise on the diagonal and arrange them overlapping on the pepper stew.

VARIATIONS

If you omit the capers and olives and add a little cumin instead, you have another traditional Greek stew that pairs beautifully with sausage and fish, especially swordfish.

You can also swap in peeled salsify for the leeks.

MAKE AHEAD The pepper stew can be refrigerated for up to 3 days. Add the ouzo and lemon juice just before serving. The cooked leeks can be refrigerated for 4 hours. Reheat them before continuing.

SERVE WITH To keep the meal vegetarian, serve Zucchini and Feta Fritters (pages 44–45) and Classic Greek Salad (page 49) as appetizers.

WINE Floral, crisp Moschofilero from the Peloponnese or Sauvignon Blanc from northern Greece.

Caramelized Fennel
with Sour Pasta Pearls

When I was cooking at the French Laundry in Napa Valley, chef Thomas Keller taught me to braise whole bulbs of fennel until soft, then cut them in half and sear the cut side to a rich brown. Incorporating a nearly charred vegetable in a vegetarian dish adds meatlike depth of flavor. To give it a Greek accent, I recycle the fennel braising liquid to cook trahana, the tangy, pebble-shaped pasta, as an accompaniment. • **4 SERVINGS**

FENNEL

¼ cup (60 ml) canola oil

2 fennel bulbs, stalks trimmed and reserved, fronds used below

1 small onion, thinly sliced (1 cup)

2 garlic cloves, sliced

2 quarts (2 L) water

6 thyme sprigs

3 tablespoons chopped fennel fronds

1 tablespoon fennel seeds

2 teaspoons coriander seeds

2 bay leaves

1 teaspoon black peppercorns

1 star anise pod

PASTA AND ASSEMBLY

¼ cup (20 g) sliced almonds

1 cup (125 g) sour trahana pasta (see Notes, page 66)

3 tablespoons fresh lemon juice

2 tablespoons extra virgin olive oil, plus more for drizzling

2 tablespoons chopped fennel fronds

1 tablespoon chopped parsley

Kosher salt and freshly ground white pepper

Thinly sliced chives and finely grated mizithra cheese (see page 163) or ricotta salata, for sprinkling

1. FENNEL In a large saucepan, heat 2 tablespoons of the canola oil until shimmering. Add the fennel bulbs and stalks, onion, and garlic and cook over medium-high heat, stirring occasionally, until lightly browned, 5 to 8 minutes. Add the water, herbs, and spices and bring to a boil. Press a parchment paper lid on top, cover, and cook over low heat until a cake tester slides easily into the thickest part of a fennel bulb, 45 minutes to 1 hour. Remove the pan from the heat and let the fennel cool in the braising liquid to room temperature. Using a slotted spoon, transfer the fennel bulb to a carving board and pat dry with paper towels. Strain the braising liquid through a fine sieve into a large glass measuring cup, pressing on the solids; discard the solids in the sieve.

2. In a medium skillet, heat the remaining 2 tablespoons of canola oil until shimmering. Slice the fennel bulbs in half through the core, add to the skillet cut side down, and cook over medium-high heat until richly browned, about 5 minutes.

3. PASTA AND ASSEMBLY Meanwhile, heat the oven to 350°F (175°C). Spread the almonds in a pie plate and toast in the oven, stirring occasionally, until lightly browned, 8 to 10 minutes.

(CONTINUED)

4. In a medium saucepan, bring 2 cups (500 ml) of the braising liquid to a simmer. Add the pasta and cook over medium-low heat, whisking occasionally, until tender, about 10 minutes. If needed, add more braising liquid a splash at a time until the pasta is cooked and saucy. Remove the pan from the heat and stir in the lemon juice, olive oil, fennel fronds, and parsley. Season with salt and pepper.

5. Spoon the pasta into shallow serving bowls and sprinkle with chives and the toasted almonds. Arrange 1 fennel half cut side up in each bowl. Season with salt and pepper. Drizzle with olive oil, sprinkle with cheese, and serve.

NOTE The pasta will continue to absorb liquid, so add more of the braising liquid just before serving to make it saucy if needed.

VARIATIONS

You can use orzo, couscous, or a grain such as bulgur instead of the trahana. Cook it in boiling water instead of the braising liquid and flavor it with the same ingredients.

MAKE AHEAD The braised fennel can be refrigerated in the braising liquid for up to 3 days. Reheat in the liquid before continuing.

SERVE WITH Before the fennel, serve Roasted Beet Salad with Manouri Cream and Buttered Walnuts (page 38) and Lamb Phyllo Spirals (pages 84–85).

WINE Citrusy, minerally Robola from Cephalonia or green apple–tinged Debina from Epirus.

Zucchini-and-Eggplant-Stuffed Tomatoes

Stuffing whole foods—tomatoes, peppers, eggplant, fish, meats—is a Greek obsession. My grandmother Athanasia's tomatoes yemista were filled with herbed vegetable pilaf, and she cooked them for hours until they were practically falling apart. These are hard to beat. • **4 SERVINGS**

8 firm, ripe medium tomatoes (about 2½ pounds/1.25 kg)

3 tablespoons extra virgin olive oil, plus more for drizzling

¼ small Vidalia (sweet) onion, finely chopped

1 small green zucchini, skin and a little flesh only, cut into ¼-inch (6 mm) dice

1 small yellow squash, skin and a little flesh only, cut into ¼-inch (6 mm) dice

1 small Japanese eggplant, skin and a little flesh only, cut into ¼-inch (6 mm) dice

1 tablespoon Garlic Puree (page 219)

⅓ cup (65 g) short-grain rice

Kosher salt and freshly ground white pepper

¼ cup (8 g) chopped mint

¼ cup (8 g) chopped parsley

1. Heat the oven to 350°F (175°C). Slice ¼ inch (6 mm) off the top of the tomatoes and reserve. Using a melon baller, scoop out the insides of the tomatoes, leaving a thin but sturdy shell, and transfer to a fine sieve set over a medium bowl to collect the juices. Finely chop the insides and add to the bowl.

2. In a large skillet, warm the oil. Add the onion and cook over medium heat, stirring occasionally, for 2 minutes. Add the zucchini, yellow squash, eggplant, and Garlic Puree and cook, stirring occasionally, until crisp-tender, 3 to 4 minutes. Add the rice and cook, stirring to coat, about 1 minute. Add the tomato insides and juice and season with salt and pepper. Bring to a simmer and cook over medium-high heat, stirring occasionally, until the liquid is mostly evaporated, 3 to 4 minutes. Remove the skillet from the heat and stir in the mint and parsley. Let cool slightly.

3. Arrange the tomato shells in a medium baking pan and season with salt and pepper. Spoon the vegetable rice into the tomatoes and drizzle with oil. Set the reserved tops on the tomatoes, add just enough water to coat the bottom of the pan, and drizzle the tomato tops with oil. Cover with foil and bake until the tomatoes are tender but still hold their shape, and the rice is tender, about 45 minutes. Remove the foil and bake for 10 minutes. Using a slotted spoon, transfer the tomatoes to a platter or plates. Let stand for at least 5 minutes and serve hot, warm, or at room temperature.

VARIATION

These stuffed tomatoes are based on my grandmother's vegetarian recipe, but she also prepared a version adding sautéed ground beef or lamb to the mix.

MAKE AHEAD The baked tomatoes can be refrigerated for up to 3 days.

WINE Fresh, aromatic Agiorgitiko rosé from Nemea, Xinomavro from northern Greece, spicy rosé from Crete, or Limniona from Thessaly.

PHOTOGRAPH ON PAGES 182–183

Pan-Roasted Eggplant with Bulgur and Tomato Compote

Eggplant is one of Greece's most loved vegetables. I call it "vegan foie gras," because you can score the cut side of a halved eggplant like a lobe of foie gras, then sear it, and the surface becomes a golden craquelure, crisp giving way to a velvety interior. • **4 SERVINGS**

BULGUR

2 teaspoons canola oil

1 small shallot, finely chopped

¾ cup (130 g) medium bulgur

¾ cup (185 ml) water

1½ cups (375 ml) Tomato Compote (page 221)

½ cup (125 ml) vegetable stock

2 teaspoons Garlic Puree (page 219)

2 tablespoons fresh lemon juice

2 tablespoons ouzo

2 tablespoons extra virgin olive oil, plus more for drizzling

Kosher salt and freshly ground white pepper

2 tablespoons chopped parsley

2 tablespoons chopped mint

EGGPLANTS AND ASSEMBLY

Two 6-ounce (180 g) Japanese eggplants, each about 8 inches (20 cm) long

Kosher salt and freshly ground white pepper

¼ cup (60 ml) canola oil

2 garlic cloves, crushed

3 thyme sprigs

Fleur de sel, for sprinkling

1. BULGUR In a small saucepan, heat the canola oil. Add the shallot and cook over medium heat, stirring occasionally, until softened, about 2 minutes. Add the bulgur and stir to coat with oil. Add the water and bring to a simmer. Cover and cook over low heat until the water is absorbed, 12 to 15 minutes. Fluff the bulgur with a fork. Stir in the Tomato Compote, stock, Garlic Puree, lemon juice, ouzo, and olive oil, season with kosher salt and pepper, and bring to a simmer. Cook over medium heat, stirring occasionally, to blend the flavors, 3 to 5 minutes. Stir in the parsley and mint just before serving.

2. EGGPLANTS AND ASSEMBLY Heat the oven to 350°F (175°C). Line a baking sheet with paper towels. Trim the eggplant ends and halve each eggplant lengthwise. Cut a shallow ¼-inch (6 mm) crosshatch pattern on the cut sides. Quarter each eggplant half crosswise to make a total of 16 pieces. Season with kosher salt and pepper. In a large skillet, warm the canola oil. Add the eggplants cut side down and cook over medium heat until golden brown on the bottom, 5 to 8 minutes. Add the garlic and thyme and turn the eggplant over. Transfer the skillet to the oven and roast until a cake tester slides easily into the eggplants, 10 to 20 minutes, depending on size. Remove from the oven and transfer the eggplants cut side down to the prepared baking sheet to drain.

(CONTINUED)

3. Arrange 4 pieces of eggplant side by side on each plate and sprinkle with fleur de sel. Spoon the bulgur alongside, drizzle the plate with olive oil, and serve.

NOTES The bulgur will continue to absorb liquid, so add more stock to make it saucy if needed.

To prepare the eggplants without turning on the oven, reduce the heat to low after browning them, cover, and cook slowly for 5 minutes. Turn them over and cook the other side until tender, 5 to 7 minutes.

VARIATION
Swap in green zucchini or yellow squash for the eggplant.

MAKE AHEAD The cooked bulgur can be refrigerated overnight. Add the Tomato Compote, stock, Garlic Puree, lemon juice, ouzo, and olive oil, season with salt and pepper, and reheat. Add the herbs just before serving.

SERVE WITH For a completely vegetarian meal, I like to start with Spinach-and-Feta Phyllo Triangles (pages 80–81) and Classic Greek Salad (49).

WINE Fresh Agiorgitiko from Nemea, spicy Mavro Kalavrytino from the Peloponnese, or crisp Greek rosé.

Softly Scrambled Eggs with Tomato and Feta

The French technique of scrambling eggs with butter and stirring them on and off the heat produces a mixture with the consistency of soft polenta. While touring the Domaine Spiropoulos winery in the Peloponnese, I enjoyed a bowlful finished with tomato and feta. In my version, I use homemade tomato sauce, and extra virgin olive oil replaces the butter. • **4 SERVINGS**

4 large eggs

2 tablespoons extra virgin olive oil, plus more for drizzling

Kosher salt and freshly ground white pepper

1 cup (250 ml) Greek Tomato Sauce (page 220), warmed

Crumbled feta cheese (see page 163) and thinly sliced scallions, for garnish

1. In a medium saucepan, combine the eggs (not whisked) and the 2 tablespoons of oil. Using a wooden spoon, stir constantly over medium-high heat for 30 seconds, then 15 seconds off the heat, until the curds are no larger than small couscous grains, 3 to 4 minutes. Season with salt and pepper halfway through and stir in the Greek Tomato Sauce three-fourths of the way through.

2. Scrape the eggs into a serving bowl and garnish with feta and scallions. Drizzle with oil and serve.

NOTES Stirring both in the middle of the saucepan and around the bottom outer edge ensures that the eggs are evenly cooked.

Using a pan with curved sides works best, because nothing gets missed in a corner.

VARIATION

I like to garnish the eggs with butter-poached shrimp.

SERVE WITH In Greece, eggs are eaten throughout the day, and these are excellent for brunch, lunch, as part of a meze spread with Lemony Quinoa Salad (page 35), or as a first course before Grilled Fish with Wilted Greens and Lemon Potatoes (pages 114–115) or Grilled Lamb Chops with Greek Fries (pages 172–173).

WINE Sparkling Moschofilero from the Peloponnese, Debina from Crete, sparkling Xinomavro rosé from Crete, or Limniona from Thessaly.

DESSERTS

Yogurt with Honey and Candied Kumquats

Yogurt with honey is utterly delicious and easily prepared at the last minute—if you have excellent Greek yogurt on hand. I am going to insist: Homemade is the best, and key to bragging rights. And I'm not asking you to take up beekeeping, but it is important to use the highest-quality honey. I prefer imported organic honey from Greece.

• **4 SERVINGS**

CANDIED KUMQUATS

24 kumquats, halved crosswise

¾ cup (150 g) sugar

¼ cup (60 ml) light corn syrup

¼ cup (60 ml) water

1 teaspoon fresh lemon juice

1 small clove

YOGURT AND ASSEMBLY

1½ cups (375 ml) Greek yogurt, preferably homemade (page 223)

Greek honey, for drizzling (see Notes)

1. CANDIED KUMQUATS Prepare a medium bowl of half ice, half water. In a medium saucepan, cover the kumquats with water and bring to a boil. Simmer over medium-high heat for 10 minutes, then drain. Transfer to the ice water for 1 minute; drain. Repeat simmering, draining, and chilling the kumquats. Squeeze out the seeds and insides of the kumquats and discard, leaving only the peels. Return the kumquat peels to the pan, cover with water, and bring to a simmer. Cook for 5 minutes and drain.

2. In a small saucepan, bring the sugar, corn syrup, water, lemon juice, and clove to a simmer, stirring to dissolve the sugar. Add the kumquat peels and cook over medium-low heat, stirring occasionally, until translucent,
10 to 15 minutes. Remove the pan from the heat and let cool. Cover and refrigerate for 24 hours.

3. Using a slotted spoon, transfer the kumquat peels to a 1-cup (250 ml) heatproof jar. Bring the syrup to a simmer and cook over medium-high heat until reduced to ½ cup (125 ml), about 8 minutes. Pour the hot syrup over the kumquat peels, let cool, and seal the jar.

4. YOGURT AND ASSEMBLY Spoon the yogurt into serving bowls, drizzle with honey, and serve. Pass the Candied Kumquats separately.

NOTES The Candied Kumquats need to be prepared 1 day ahead, the homemade yogurt 2 days ahead, so plan accordingly.

The kumquats are boiled three times to remove the fruit's bitterness. If you're going to the trouble of making Candied Kumquats—and you should—go ahead and triple the batch.

Infused honeys from Greece are outstanding, notably a pine-and-thyme version from Crete made by Meligyris, available at yolenis.com.

Yogurt-with-honey makes a great breakfast, light lunch, or pre-bed snack.

MAKE AHEAD The candied fruit can be refrigerated for up to 6 months.

WINE Chilled tsipouro or other fresh eau-de-vie from Thessaly.

Creamy Rice Pudding with Candied Figs

I'm nuts for homemade rizogalo. This warm variation enriched with butter is from my Savannah, Georgia, friend Sophia Drakulas. I serve it with luscious candied figs, a kind of whole-fruit preserve. Everything about this rice pudding is oh-so-delicious. • **8 SERVINGS**

CANDIED FIGS

1 cup (200 g) sugar

⅓ cup (100 ml) light corn syrup

⅓ cup (100 ml) water

2 teaspoons fresh lemon juice

1 whole clove

8 firm, ripe black or green figs, each scored with an X in the bottom

RICE PUDDING

1 cup (200 g) Valencia or another medium-grain rice

6 cups (1.5 L) whole milk

¾ cup (150 g) sugar

2 cinnamon sticks, plus ground cinnamon for dusting

2 vanilla beans, split lengthwise and seeds scraped, or 2 teaspoons pure vanilla extract

1 long strip of lemon zest, cut with a vegetable peeler

Pinch of kosher salt

2 large egg yolks

1 tablespoon (15 g) unsalted butter

1. CANDIED FIGS In a small saucepan, bring the sugar, corn syrup, water, lemon juice, and clove to a simmer, stirring to dissolve the sugar. Add the figs and cook over medium-low heat, stirring occasionally, until tender but still intact, 10 to 15 minutes. Remove the pan from the heat and let cool slightly. Cover and refrigerate for 24 hours.

2. Using a slotted spoon, transfer the figs to a 2-cup (500 ml) heatproof jar. Bring the syrup to a simmer and cook over medium-high heat until reduced to ⅔ cup (160 ml), about 10 minutes. Pour the hot syrup over the figs, let cool, and seal the jar until ready to use.

3. RICE PUDDING In a large saucepan, combine the rice with the milk, sugar, cinnamon sticks, vanilla beans and seeds, lemon zest, and salt. Bring to a simmer, stirring to dissolve the sugar. Cook over medium-low heat, stirring occasionally and scraping all the way down to the bottom of the pan to make sure the mixture doesn't stick, until the rice is tender and the liquid thickens, about 30 minutes. Remove the pan from heat and let stand for 5 minutes. Remove the cinnamon sticks, vanilla beans, and lemon zest. Quickly and thoroughly stir in the egg yolks until smooth. Stir in the butter. Keep the pudding warm, covered, or let cool, then cover and transfer to the refrigerator to chill completely. Spoon the rice pudding into bowls, dust with ground cinnamon, and serve warm or chilled. Pass the Candied Figs separately.

NOTES The figs need to be refrigerated for 24 hours, so plan accordingly.

You don't want to cook the rice so long that it completely absorbs the milk. The pudding should be runny, because the rice will continue to soak up the liquid as it cools.

WINE Fresh, floral Muscat from Samos, Patras, or Rio Patras.

Manouri Cheese Panna Cotta with Candied Quince

This is a Greek take on Italian panna cotta. The eggless custard gets its velvety texture from manouri, a slightly crumbly, almost sweet cheese. The Candied Quince garnish is a winner here—and with many pudding-like desserts. • **4 SERVINGS**

CANDIED QUINCE

1 cup (200 g) granulated sugar

⅓ cup (100 ml) light corn syrup

⅓ cup (100 ml) water

2 teaspoons fresh lemon juice

1 whole clove

1 quince, peeled, cored, and cut into julienne strips

PANNA COTTA

1 cup (250 ml) heavy cream

⅔ cup (160 ml) whole milk

1½ cups (180 g) crumbled manouri cheese (see page 163) or shredded fresh mozzarella cheese

½ cup (65 g) confectioners' sugar

2 gelatin sheets (see Notes)

1. CANDIED QUINCE In a small saucepan, bring the granulated sugar, corn syrup, water, lemon juice, and clove to a simmer, stirring to dissolve the sugar. Add the quince and cook over medium-low heat, stirring occasionally, until translucent and tender, about 15 minutes. Remove the pan from the heat and let cool. Cover and refrigerate for 24 hours.

2. Using a slotted spoon, transfer the quince to a 2-cup (500 ml) heatproof jar. Bring the syrup to a simmer and cook over medium-high heat until reduced to ⅔ cup (160 ml), about 10 minutes. Pour the hot syrup over the quince, let cool, and seal the jar until ready to use.

3. PANNA COTTA In a medium saucepan, combine the cream with the milk, cheese, and confectioners' sugar. Using an immersion blender, puree the mixture. Bring to a simmer over medium heat, stirring constantly. Remove the pan from the heat.

4. In a medium bowl of cold water, soak the gelatin until softened, 2 to 3 minutes. Drain the gelatin and squeeze dry. Add the gelatin to the warm cream mixture and stir until dissolved. Strain through a fine sieve into a medium glass measuring cup, pressing on the solids. Pour into four 8-ounce (250 ml) glasses and cover with plastic wrap. Refrigerate until set, at least 3 hours.

5. Remove the plastic from the glasses, spoon the Candied Quince on the Panna Cotta. Serve.

NOTES The Candied Quince needs to be refrigerated overnight, so plan accordingly.

Though a notoriously hard fruit, quince cooks quickly when cut into julienne strips.

Sheet gelatin is available at specialty markets. However, powdered gelatin can be used instead: In a small bowl, sprinkle 1½ teaspoons of powdered gelatin over ¼ cup (60 ml) of the cream and let stand until softened, about 5 minutes. Add to the warm cream mixture in Step 4.

MAKE AHEAD The Panna Cotta can be refrigerated overnight.

WINE Fresh, floral Muscat from the islands of Samos or Limnos.

TIPS FOR MAKING GREEK PIES

WORKING WITH PHYLLO

1. As thin as it is, store-bought phyllo dough actually comes in different thicknesses, numbered one through ten. Still, I use only two readily available sizes. I like the suppleness of thin phyllo (No. 4) for fashioning spirals. Also, it's wispy enough that it melts on the inside of the shaped pastry while the outside stays crisp. And I use country phyllo (No. 10) to roll "cigars" and triangles, because it's just a little bit stronger.

2. Thaw unopened frozen phyllo in the refrigerator for 8 hours or overnight. Then let it stand at room temperature for about 2 hours before removing from the box, so the brittle dough doesn't crack.

3. While the dough comes to room temperature, make your clarified butter. The individual sheets of phyllo need to be brushed with melted butter to keep them separate so they bake into flaky layers. I clarify the melted butter—that is, remove the milk solids—so the butter doesn't burn when the pastry is baked. You lose some of the butter when clarifying it, so start with about 25 percent more solid butter than the amount of clarified butter listed in the recipe. For instance, to make ¼ cup (60 ml) of clarified butter, melt 6 tablespoons (100 g) of diced unsalted butter in a small saucepan over medium-high heat, swirling the pan occasionally; take care not to brown or burn it. Remove the pan from the heat and skim off the foam. Pour the remaining butter into a bowl, leaving behind the whitish milk solids at the bottom (which is what burns); discard the solids. Clarified butter can be refrigerated for up to 1 month, so you can make extra to have on hand; melt it gently to use.

4. Phyllo dries out quickly. Carefully unroll the sheets on a dry work surface. (While phyllo needs humidity, the sheets will stick when wet.) The moment it's removed from the box and unrolled, cover it with the plastic that comes with it (or a piece of wax paper or plastic wrap) and then with a damp towel. Keep the unused phyllo covered as you work.

5. Find a big brush to paint the butter on the phyllo sheets so the job goes quickly.

6. Once you've shaped the pastry, you want to protect it with a layer of melted butter. This ensures that the phyllo dough and fillings don't dry out.

7. My phyllo-wrapped pies can be assembled ahead and refrigerated for up to 2 days before baking. They can also be frozen for up to 1 month. There's no need to thaw them; just add a few minutes to the baking time.

8. Even though phyllo pastries do not spread, space them slightly apart on the baking sheet so they don't stick together and tear when you pull them apart.

9. I like the beautiful golden exterior I get from cooking individual pies first in a little clarified butter in a skillet, before sliding them into the oven to heat through. But there's nothing wrong with baking them straight away without browning them. You won't get the same coppery color, but they'll still taste great. To approximate what you'd get from browning them in butter, broil them for a minute or two once they're heated through. One caveat: they'll be spotted with color rather than evenly browned on top.

VARIATIONS

1. To make a large pie instead of individual pastries, line a glass baking pan or a pie pan with five sheets of thin phyllo (No. 10), brushing each sheet with clarified butter. Spread the filling in the pan and layer five more sheets of buttered phyllo on top. Tuck in the phyllo and bake the pie at 350°F (175°C) until golden brown and heated through, about 1 hour.

2. Or, line a pie pan with pie dough, spread the filling in the pan, and cover with more pie dough. Trim and crimp the edges. Brush the crust with beaten egg and make a few slits in the top before baking at 350°F (175°C) until golden brown, about 1 hour.

Phyllo-Wrapped Banana
with Flourless Chocolate Cake

Kataifi is the Greek word for shredded phyllo dough and for a light shredded-phyllo pastry that's rolled in nuts, baked, and finished with sugar syrup. This version is both new and reverential of the classic dessert. I roll the dough around a banana sprinkled with pistachios, then roast it until crispy and drizzle it with honey. It's paired with a decadent chocolate cake and yogurt sorbet. • **4 SERVINGS**

CHOCOLATE CAKES

3½ ounces (100 g) bittersweet chocolate (60 to 70 percent cacao), preferably Valrhona Manjari, chopped, plus more for shaving

3 tablespoons (45 g) unsalted butter, diced, plus melted butter for brushing

2 large egg yolks

3 large egg whites

BANANA KATAIFI AND ASSEMBLY

4 ounces (125 g) frozen shredded-phyllo dough, thawed

¼ cup (60 ml) clarified butter (see Step 3, page 199)

2 firm, ripe bananas

2 teaspoons finely chopped pistachios

¼ cup plus 2 tablespoons (120 g) Greek honey

4 scoops Yogurt Sorbet (page 216)

1. CHOCOLATE CAKES In a medium saucepan, bring 2 inches (5 cm) of water to a simmer. In a medium bowl, combine the chopped chocolate with the diced butter. Set over the simmering water and heat, stirring occasionally, until melted and smooth. Remove the bowl from the heat and whisk in the egg yolks. In another medium bowl, whip the egg whites until they hold a stiff peak. Whisk one-fourth of the egg whites into the chocolate mixture until smooth. Add the remaining egg whites and whisk well to eliminate any bubbles. Brush 4 cups of a muffin pan with melted butter, line with plastic wrap, and brush with melted butter. Pour in the batter and freeze until firm, at least 3 hours.

2. Heat the oven to 325°F (165°C). Remove the muffin pan from the freezer. Bake the cakes for 9 minutes, turning the muffin pan halfway through. Remove from the oven and freeze the cakes until firm enough to remove from the ramekins, about 2 hours. Before serving, bring the cakes to room temperature, remove them from the ramekins, and discard the plastic.

3. BANANA KATAIFI Increase the oven temperature to 375°F (190°C). Line a rimmed baking sheet with parchment paper. On a work surface, spread half of the phyllo in a rectangle the length of a banana with a short side in front of you. Brush the phyllo with 2 tablespoons of the clarified butter. Set the banana crosswise on the near end of the phyllo and sprinkle with 1 teaspoon of the pistachios. Tightly roll up the banana in the phyllo and transfer to the prepared baking sheet. Repeat with the remaining phyllo, clarified butter, banana, and pistachios. Transfer to the oven and bake until the phyllo is crisp, about 20 minutes. Remove from the oven and immediately drizzle with the honey.

4. ASSEMBLY Cut each banana crosswise into 4 equal pieces. For each dessert, arrange 1 piece of banana in the center of a dinner plate and another perpendicular to it. Set a cake on the opposite side and top with a scoop of sorbet. Shave chocolate over the banana and serve.

VARIATION
Hazelnuts or walnuts can replace the pistachios.

MAKE AHEAD The Chocolate Cakes can be prepared through Step 2 and frozen for up to 1 week; bring them to room temperature before serving.

WINE Mavrodaphne from Patras or Cephalonia or aged Malvasia from Monemvasia.

Baklava

This spice syrup–soaked nut dessert with brittle phyllo layers can take two forms: layered in a large baking pan, then baked and cut into squares or diamonds, or rolled into individual pastries. I grew up on the baking pan recipe and find it too dense and filling. Pastry chef Frank Kaltsounis's rolled version is light and airy yet flavor-packed.

• **4 SERVINGS PLUS LEFTOVERS**

⅔ cup (160 ml) water

⅔ cup (130 g) plus 3 tablespoons sugar

¼ cup (60 ml) light corn syrup

½ lemon

1 cinnamon stick, plus 1¼ teaspoons ground cinnamon

1 whole clove, plus ½ teaspoon ground cloves

2 cups (240 g) shelled walnuts, finely chopped

½ cup fine dry breadcrumbs

6 frozen phyllo sheets (no. 4), thawed

1 cup (250 ml) clarified butter (see Step 3, page 199)

¼ cup (30 g) shelled pistachios

4 scoops Pistachio Ice Cream (page 216)

1. In a medium saucepan, combine the water with ⅔ cup (130 g) of the sugar, the corn syrup, lemon, cinnamon stick, and whole clove. Bring to a simmer over medium heat, stirring to dissolve the sugar, and cook until reduced to 1¼ cups (310 ml), about 6 minutes. Remove from the heat and let cool completely. Strain the syrup through a fine sieve into a glass measuring cup; discard the solids in the sieve.

2. In a medium bowl, toss the walnuts with the breadcrumbs, ground cinnamon, ground cloves, and remaining 3 tablespoons of sugar.

3. Heat the oven to 400°F (200°C). Lay 1 phyllo sheet on a work surface with a short side in front of you. Set a 16-by-¼-inch (40-by-6 mm) dowel crosswise on the phyllo, leaving a 4-inch (10 cm) border. Fold the border over the dowel and brush with clarified butter. Spread ½ cup (60 g) of the filling in an even layer across the bottom edge of the folded phyllo and up 4 inches (10 cm). Using the dowel, roll the phyllo tightly around the filling into a log. Gently scrunch both ends of the phyllo toward the center, then slide lengthwise off the dowel into an 8-by-10-inch (20-by-25 cm) shallow baking pan; brush with clarified butter. Repeat with the remaining phyllo sheets, filling, and clarified butter. When all of the baklava logs are in the pan, cut each one crosswise into 3 equal pieces. Bake until the baklava is golden brown, about 15 minutes. Remove from the oven and immediately pour 1 cup (250 ml) of the syrup evenly over the top. Let stand for 1 hour to absorb all of the syrup.

4. Meanwhile, reduce the oven temperature to 350°F (175°C). In a small bowl, toss the pistachios with the remaining ¼ cup (60 ml) of syrup, then strain, reserving the syrup. Spread the pistachios on a baking sheet and bake until they no longer stick to each other and a thin layer of sugar forms, about 7 minutes.

5. Arrange 4 pieces of baklava on each plate and drizzle the reserved syrup around them. Garnish with a scoop of ice cream and the candied pistachios. Serve immediately.

NOTE The filling stores well; double or triple the recipe to have extra on hand for the next batch of baklava.

VARIATIONS
The baklava can also be stacked on a platter and served with a bowl of ice cream.

Swap hazelnuts for the walnuts. For an even more decadent version, drizzle melted chocolate over the baklava before serving.

MAKE AHEAD The filling can be packed in an airtight container and frozen for up to 3 months. The finished pastries can stand, covered, at room temperature for up to 4 days.

WINE Rich Muscat from Samos, Limnos, or the Peloponnese; Vinsanto from Santorini; or Mavrodaphne from Patras or Cephalonia.

Orange Sponge Cakes with Shaved White Chocolate

Pastry chef Frank Kaltsounis rejuvenates ravani, an old-school citrus-soaked orange cake, by baking it in individual pans instead of one large one. This recipe, developed for the home cook, combines both techniques, baking the batter in a single large pan, but using a ring mold to stamp it into mini cakes for serving. • **4 SERVINGS**

1 cup (250 ml) water

1½ cups (300 g) plus 1 tablespoon and 2 teaspoons sugar

1 vanilla bean, split lengthwise and scraped, or 1 teaspoon pure vanilla extract

Finely grated zest of 2 oranges, plus ½ orange and ½ cup (125 ml) fresh orange juice

2 teaspoons cornstarch

8 tablespoons (125 g) unsalted butter, softened, plus more for brushing

3 large eggs, separated

⅓ cup (40 g) cake flour

3 tablespoons (25 g) all-purpose flour

½ cup (70 g) semolina flour

½ teaspoon baking powder

½ cup (125 ml) heavy cream

White chocolate, for shaving

1. In a small saucepan, combine the water with 1 cup (200 g) of the sugar, the vanilla bean and seeds, and the orange half and bring to a simmer over medium heat, stirring to dissolve the sugar. Remove from the heat and let cool to room temperature. Strain the orange syrup through a fine sieve into a small glass measuring cup. Discard the orange; rinse the vanilla bean and save for another use. Wipe out the saucepan.

2. In the same saucepan, combine ¼ cup (60 ml) plus 2 tablespoons of the orange juice with 2 teaspoons of the sugar and bring to a simmer over medium heat, stirring to dissolve the sugar. In a small bowl, whisk the remaining 2 tablespoons of orange juice with the cornstarch. Whisk this mixture into the simmering orange juice and cook until thickened, about 1 minute. Remove from the heat, let cool, and transfer the orange cream to a plastic bag.

3. Heat the oven to 350ºF (175ºC). Brush an 8-inch (20 cm) square baking pan with butter. In a large bowl, using a hand mixer, cream the 8 tablespoons (125 g) of butter with ¼ cup (50 g) of the sugar and half of the orange zest until light and fluffy, about 3 minutes. Beat in the egg yolks one at a time. Sift the three flours with the baking powder into the butter mixture and fold together until just combined. In a medium bowl, using clean beaters, whip the egg whites with ¼ cup (50 g) of the sugar until they hold a medium peak. Using a rubber spatula, gently fold the egg whites into the butter mixture in three additions until smooth.

4. Scrape the batter into the prepared pan, smooth the top, and bake until a toothpick comes out clean and the top is golden brown, about 45 minutes. Remove the cake from the oven and immediately pour the orange syrup evenly over the top. Let cool to room temperature. Using a 2½-inch (6 cm) ring mold or ramekin, cut out 4 cakes from the pan. Save the remaining cake for snacking.

5. In a medium bowl, combine the heavy cream with the remaining 1 tablespoon of sugar and orange zest and whip until it holds a stiff peak. For each dessert, place a cake in the center of a plate. Cut a ¼-inch (6 mm) corner off the plastic bag with the orange cream and pipe sixteen ¼-inch (6 mm) dots around the cake. Dollop the whipped cream on the cake, shave white chocolate on top, and serve.

NOTE Instead of stamping out cake rounds, you can cut the cake into 2-inch (5 cm) squares for serving.

VARIATION
Lemons can be swapped in for the oranges.

MAKE AHEAD The cake can be wrapped in the pan and refrigerated for up to 3 days.

SERVE WITH These orange cakes are especially good with vanilla ice cream or raspberry sorbet.

WINE Fresh Muscat from the islands or the Peloponnese.

Little Greek Doughnuts

These warm, fluffy, deep-fried balls come covered in Greek honey, chopped walnuts, and cinnamon and melt in the mouth. My father still talks about impatiently waiting for loukoumades as his mother popped them out of the simmering oil. The recipe is easy; if your doughnuts aren't perfectly round the first time, they'll still taste great, so keep practicing! • **4 SERVINGS**

1 cup (250 ml) warm whole milk

½ cup (125 ml) warm water

3 tablespoons extra virgin olive oil

1½ cups (180 g) cake flour

1 cup (130 g) all-purpose flour

Three ¼-ounce packets (20 g total) active dry yeast

2 teaspoons sugar

2 teaspoons salt

¼ cup (30 g) shelled walnuts

Canola oil, for deep-frying

Greek honey, for drizzling (see Notes)

Ground cinnamon, for dusting

1. In a large bowl, combine the milk with the water and olive oil. In a medium bowl, whisk 1¼ cups (150 g) of the cake flour with the all-purpose flour, yeast, sugar, and salt. Add the dry ingredients to the wet ingredients and whisk until smooth. Cover the bowl with plastic wrap and let the batter rise in a warm place until it triples in size, about 1½ hours.

2. In a small dry skillet, toast the walnuts over medium-high heat, stirring occasionally, until fragrant, about 4 minutes. Finely chop the walnuts.

3. In a large saucepan, heat 2 inches (5 cm) of canola oil to 350°F (175°C). Gently press down the batter. Add the remaining ¼ cup (30 g) of cake flour and hand mix to incorporate.

4. Line a baking sheet with paper towels. In a small glass of water, dip a 1-tablespoon measure. Working in batches, drop the dough by the tablespoon into the oil and fry, turning occasionally, until golden brown, 3 to 5 minutes. Using a slotted spoon, transfer to the prepared baking sheet as they're cooked. Skim the oil with the slotted spoon to remove any bits of dough. Transfer the doughnuts to a large bowl, generously drizzle with honey, and turn to coat. Transfer to plates and dust with cinnamon. Sprinkle with the chopped walnuts and serve immediately.

NOTES Go for excellent honey here; with so few ingredients (dough, honey, nuts, cinnamon), the quality of each makes a huge difference.
  Be careful not to overmix the batter.

MAKE AHEAD The batter can be prepared through Step 1, pressed down, and refrigerated overnight.

WINE Sweet, aromatic Greek Muscat; eau-de-vie from Thessaly; or aromatic Malvasia from Monemvasia, Paros, or Crete.

Almond Cake
with Greek Coffee Frosting

When my former pastry chef Frank Kaltsounis told me he baked a killer almond cake, I scratched my head. It's not the first thing you think of when it comes to Greek desserts. Then I tasted the extremely moist (syrup-soaked), nutty (tons of ground almonds) cake and decided I could eat it anytime, anywhere, every day. The trick was to add a Hellenic twist. Since almond cake is excellent with an espresso and a piece of bittersweet chocolate, I asked my current pastry chef, Daniela Ascencio, to develop a coffee frosting and to shower it with chocolate shavings. The result feels right at home in the Greek repertoire. • **12 SERVINGS**

ALMOND CAKE

1 pound (500 g) unsalted butter, diced, softened

1½ cups (300 g) granulated sugar

10 large eggs

1 pound (500 g) almond meal

½ cup (60 g) all-purpose flour

1 teaspoon baking powder

1 cup (250 ml) whole milk

1 tablespoon pure vanilla extract

SUGAR SYRUP

3 cups (600 g) granulated sugar

2 cups (500 ml) water

1 whole clove

Juice of ½ lemon

FROSTING AND ASSEMBLY

2 ounces (60 g) vegetable shortening

8 tablespoons (125 g) unsalted butter, diced, softened

1¼ cups (160 g) confectioners' sugar, sifted

1 teaspoon pure coffee extract

Bittersweet chocolate, for shaving

1. ALMOND CAKE Heat the oven to 375°F (190°C). Coat a 9-by-13-inch (23-by-33 cm) baking pan with vegetable oil spray. In a stand mixer fitted with the whisk, whip the butter at medium-low speed, scraping the bowl occasionally, until smooth, 3 to 4 minutes. Gradually add the granulated sugar, whipping and scraping the bowl occasionally, until fluffy, 2 to 3 minutes. Beat in the eggs one at a time.

2. In a large bowl, whisk together the almond meal, flour, and baking powder. Add to the egg mixture and beat at medium-low speed, scraping the bowl occasionally, until incorporated. Beat in the milk and vanilla until smooth. Spread the batter in the prepared pan and bake until golden brown, about 1½ hours. Let the cake cool in the pan for 10 minutes.

3. SUGAR SYRUP Meanwhile, in a medium saucepan, bring the sugar, water, and clove to a boil, stirring, until the sugar dissolves. Simmer over medium-low heat until slightly thickened, 10 to 15 minutes. Stir in the lemon juice. Strain through a fine sieve into a large glass measuring cup. Pour the syrup, 1 cup (250 ml) at a time, over the cake, waiting until one batch of syrup is absorbed before adding the next. Let cool completely.

4. FROSTING AND ASSEMBLY In a stand mixer fitted with the whisk, whip the shortening with the butter at medium-low speed, scraping the bowl occasionally, until smooth, 3 to 4 minutes. Add the confectioners' sugar and whip, scraping the bowl occasionally, until fluffy. Add the coffee extract and whip until smooth. Spread the frosting evenly over the cake and refrigerate for at least 24 hours and up to 3 days. Cut the cake into 3-inch (7.5 cm) squares and transfer to plates. Using a vegetable peeler, shave the chocolate over the cake and serve.

NOTE The cake is best served at room temperature but needs to be refrigerated overnight, so plan accordingly.

SERVE WITH The cake on its own is all you need, but it's also nice with sliced strawberries or other fresh fruit, or a scoop of vanilla, chocolate, or coffee ice cream.

WINE Rich, aged, aromatic Muscat from Samos, Rio Patras, or Cephalonia. Or aged Malvasia from Crete or the Peloponnese.

Semolina Custard and Blueberry Phyllo Pies

The traditional Greek milk pie galaktoboureko, a layered combo of lush custard and phyllo pastry prepared in a large shallow baking pan and served in squares, never gets old. Pastry chef Frank Kaltsounis simply gave this old-fashioned dessert a makeover by crafting individual pies with outsides that crackle, and I added blueberries. Eating one is a sequence of crunch then sink as you bite into crispy pastry and soft vanilla custard and berry compote. • **MAKES 4 PIES/4 SERVINGS**

BLUEBERRY COMPOTE

8 ounces (250 g) blueberries (1½ cups)

¼ cup (50 g) sugar

2 tablespoons water

1 teaspoon fresh lemon juice

SEMOLINA CUSTARD AND ASSEMBLY

½ cup (125 ml) whole milk

Finely grated zest of ¼ lemon

½ inch (1 cm) vanilla bean, split lengthwise and seeds scraped, or ⅛ teaspoon pure vanilla extract

Kosher salt

¼ cup (50 g) sugar

1 large egg yolk

2 tablespoons (15 g) fine semolina flour

4 frozen phyllo sheets (no. 4), thawed

¼ cup plus 2 tablespoons (100 ml) clarified butter (see Step 3, page 199)

4 scoops store-bought blueberry sorbet, Yogurt Sorbet (page 216), Mahlepi Ice Cream (page 215), or vanilla ice cream

1. BLUEBERRY COMPOTE In a small saucepan, combine ¾ cup (125 g) of the blueberries with the sugar, water, and lemon juice. Bring to a simmer and cook over medium heat, stirring often, until the blueberries release their liquid, about 2 minutes. Add the remaining ¾ cup (125 g) of blueberries and cook, stirring often, until syrupy, about 2 minutes. Remove the pan from the heat and let cool.

2. SEMOLINA CUSTARD In another small saucepan, combine the milk with the lemon zest, vanilla seeds, and a pinch of salt and bring to a simmer. In a medium bowl, using a hand mixer, beat the sugar with the egg yolk until the mixture is pale and falls in a slowly dissolving ribbon when the beaters are lifted, 2 to 3 minutes. Gradually pour ¼ cup (60 ml) of the hot milk mixture into the sugar-egg mixture, beating constantly, then whisk this mixture back into the remaining milk. Gradually add the semolina and cook over medium heat, whisking constantly, until the custard is thick, about 5 minutes. In a stand mixer fitted with the whisk, whip the custard at low speed until completely cool, about 20 minutes.

3. Line a baking sheet with parchment paper. Lay 1 phyllo sheet on the prepared baking sheet with a long side in front of you. Brush with clarified butter. Cover with a second phyllo sheet and brush with clarified butter. Continue layering and buttering with the remaining 2 phyllo sheets. Transfer to the refrigerator and chill until the butter is firm, at least 30 minutes.

(CONTINUED)

4. ASSEMBLY Heat the oven to 375°F (190°C). Brush four 4-ounce (125 ml) ramekins with clarified butter. Using a pizza cutter or a sharp knife, cut the stacked phyllo into six 5-inch (13 cm) squares. Using a spatula, carefully separate a phyllo square from the parchment paper. Set it on a prepared ramekin and gently push in the phyllo, making sure it gets into the corners. Repeat with the remaining ramekins. Spoon 2 tablespoons of the custard into each ramekin and top with 2 tablespoons of the compote. Tear the 2 remaining phyllo squares into pieces. Arrange over the compote until completely covered. Set the ramekins on a baking sheet and transfer to the oven. Bake until golden brown, about 12 minutes.

5. Remove the ramekins from the oven and let cool slightly. Using a small spoon, transfer each pie to a dessert plate. Set a scoop of sorbet on top, swipe the plates with blueberry compote, and serve.

VARIATIONS

You can omit the blueberries from the compote, if you wish. Or sub in another fruit, such as diced strawberries or peaches. Pair the ice cream or sorbet flavor accordingly, or top with Mahlepi Ice Cream (page 215).

MAKE AHEAD The Blueberry Compote and the Semolina Custard can be refrigerated separately for up to 3 days.

WINE Fresh Vinsanto from Santorini or Malvasia from Monemvasia, Crete, or Paros.

Hazelnut Baklava Sundaes with Brownie "Croutons"

My kitchen's ice cream–and–sorbet drawer (packed with eight or nine flavors) is right next to where the baklava and chocolate sauce are made, so this particular sundae was inevitable. To make a crunchy topping, sheets of phyllo are layered with chopped nuts and chocolate and baked until crisp. It's a simple alternative to elaborate rolled baklava. • **4 SERVINGS**

BROWNIE

8 tablespoons (125 g) unsalted butter, sliced, plus softened butter for brushing

8 ounces (250 g) bittersweet chocolate chips (50 to 60 percent cacao)

4 large eggs

2 cups (400 g) granulated sugar

1 tablespoon pure vanilla extract

1 cup (130 g) all-purpose flour

½ cup (65 g) cake flour

2 tablespoons (10 g) unsweetened cocoa powder

¼ teaspoon baking powder

¼ teaspoon kosher salt

BAKLAVA AND ASSEMBLY

3 tablespoons (25 g) finely chopped blanched hazelnuts

2 teaspoons plain dry breadcrumbs, such as panko

1 teaspoon raw organic sugar

⅛ teaspoon ground cinnamon

⅛ teaspoon ground cloves

2 ounces (60 g) bittersweet chocolate chips (50 to 60 percent cacao)

1 frozen phyllo sheet (no. 4), thawed

2 tablespoons clarified butter (see Step 3, page 199)

1 tablespoon Greek honey

4 scoops Mahlepi Ice Cream (page 215) or store-bought vanilla ice cream

1. BROWNIE Heat the oven to 350°F (175°C). Line an 8-inch (20 cm) square baking pan with foil, pressing it firmly into the pan and leaving a 2-inch (5 cm) overhang. Brush the foil with the softened butter. In a medium microwave-safe bowl, combine the sliced butter and the 8 ounces (250 g) of chocolate. Microwave on medium-high for about 1 minute. Stir and microwave in 15- to 20-second bursts, stirring in between, until the mixture is melted and smooth.

2. In a large bowl, combine the eggs with the granulated sugar and vanilla. Using a hand mixer, beat at medium speed until pale and fluffy, 2 to 3 minutes. Beat in the chocolate mixture at low speed until smooth. Sift both flours with the cocoa, baking powder, and salt into the batter and fold together just until smooth. Scrape the batter into the prepared pan, smooth the top, and bake until a toothpick inserted into the center comes out with a few moist crumbs attached, 40 to 45 minutes. Transfer the pan to a rack; let the brownie cool completely in the pan. Using the foil overhang, lift the brownie out of the pan and transfer to a carving board. Cut one-fourth of the brownie into 1-inch (2.5 cm) squares; save the rest for snacking. Keep the oven on.

3. BAKLAVA In a small bowl, combine the hazelnuts with the breadcrumbs, raw sugar,

cinnamon, and cloves. In a small micro-wave-safe bowl, microwave the 2 ounces (60 g) of chocolate on medium-high for about 1 minute. Stir and microwave in 15- to 20-second bursts, stirring in between, until the chocolate is melted and smooth.

4. Line a baking sheet with parchment paper. Lay the phyllo sheet on a work surface with a long side in front of you. Brush with the clarified butter. Using a pizza cutter or a sharp knife, cut the phyllo lengthwise into 3 rectangles. Sprinkle half of the nut mixture evenly on a rectangle. Using a spoon, drizzle one-third of the melted chocolate over the nuts. Set a plain rectangle on top, sprinkle with the remaining nut mixture, and drizzle with one-third of the melted chocolate. Top with the remaining plain phyllo rectangle.

5. Carefully transfer the stacked phyllo to the prepared baking sheet. Cover with parchment paper, set another baking sheet on top, and bake until the baklava is golden brown, 10 to 15 minutes. Remove from the oven and remove the top baking sheet and parchment. Drizzle the baklava with the honey and let cool.

6. ASSEMBLY Scoop the ice cream into serving bowls. Add 1 or 2 brownies and drizzle with the remaining melted chocolate. Break some of the baklava into shards over the top and serve immediately.

NOTE The brownie recipe makes more than you need for the sundaes, but who ever complained about leftover brownies? I call them croutons because they're cut into small cubes for garnishing.

MAKE AHEAD The baklava and brownies can be stored separately in airtight containers for up to 3 days.

WINE Vinsanto from Santorini.

Mahlepi Ice Cream

Mahlepi seeds are similar to coriander seeds in shape and size but much more floral. Pastry chef Frank Kaltsounis infuses them in half-and-half to make Greek-scented ice cream. • **MAKES ABOUT 2 CUPS (500 ML)**

2 cups (500 ml) half-and-half

4 ounces (125 g) pouring (pâtissier) fondant (see Notes)

1½ tablespoons mahlepi seeds, crushed (see Notes)

⅓ cup (65 g) sugar

1. In a small saucepan, combine the half-and-half with the fondant and mahlepi seeds and bring to a simmer over medium heat, stirring occasionally. Add the sugar and cook, stirring, until dissolved. Remove the pan from the heat and let cool to room temperature. Scrape the mahlepi cream into a bowl, cover, and refrigerate for 24 hours.

2. Pour the mahlepi cream through a fine strainer into an ice cream maker and spin according to the manufacturer's directions. Transfer to an airtight container, cover, and freeze until firm, at least 2 hours.

NOTES The mahlepi cream needs to steep for 24 hours, so plan accordingly.

Mahlepi seeds are available at Greek markets and online.

Fondant, which is cooled sugar syrup that's whipped into a white sugar glaze, is available at specialty food and baking supply shops and lepicerie.com.

MAKE AHEAD The ice cream can be frozen for up to 1 month.

Pistachio Ice Cream

Pastry chef Frank Kaltsounis developed this delicious ice cream to go with baklava, but it would also make for an awesome dessert with sweet cherries, peaches, or plums sautéed in butter. • **MAKES ABOUT 2 CUPS (500 ML)**

1⅓ cups (330 ml) whole milk
2 tablespoons heavy cream
½ cup (100 g) sugar
6 large egg yolks
2 tablespoons pistachio paste (see Notes)

1. In a small saucepan, bring the milk and cream to a simmer. In a medium bowl, whisk the sugar with the egg yolks until smooth. Gradually pour ½ cup (125 ml) of the hot milk into the yolk mixture, whisking constantly, then whisk this mixture back into the remaining milk. Cook over medium heat, whisking constantly, until slightly thickened, 2 to 3 minutes. Remove the pan from the heat, add the pistachio paste, and, using an immersion blender, mix until smooth. Strain through a fine sieve into a medium glass measuring cup. Cover and refrigerate until cold.

2. Pour the mixture into an ice cream maker and spin according to the manufacturer's instructions. Transfer to an airtight container, cover, and freeze until firm, at least 2 hours.

NOTES Pistachio paste is available at specialty food and baking supply shops and nuts.com.

To speed up the chilling in Step 1, pour the mixture into a medium stainless steel bowl, set it in a bowl of half ice, half water, and let cool completely, whisking often.

Yogurt Sorbet

Pastry chef Daniela Ascencio's three-ingredient recipe has pure, tangy yogurt flavor. And it's super easy: Melt sugar in water and let it cool, then stir in yogurt and freeze. Serve this sorbet drizzled with honey or melted chocolate. Or sprinkle it with crushed walnuts or just about any fruit you can think of. • **MAKES ABOUT 2 CUPS (500 ML)**

¾ cup (200 ml) water
¾ cup (150 g) sugar
1¾ cups (400 ml) thick Greek yogurt, preferably homemade (page 223)

1. In a small saucepan, bring the water and sugar to a simmer, stirring to dissolve the sugar. Remove the pan from the heat and let cool completely. Whisk in the yogurt until smooth. Strain through a fine sieve into a medium glass measuring cup. Cover and refrigerate until cold.

2. Pour the mixture into an ice cream maker and spin according to the manufacturer's instructions. Transfer to an airtight container, cover, and freeze until firm, at least 2 hours.

NOTE To speed up the chilling in Step 1, pour the sugar syrup into a medium stainless steel bowl, set it in a bowl of half ice, half water, and let cool completely, whisking often.

MAKE AHEAD The sorbet can be frozen for up to 1 month.

WINE Fresh tsipouro, Greek eau-de-vie, or aromatic Muscat from Samos, Limnos, Patras, Rio Patras, or Cephalonia.

Watermelon Sorbet

I created this sorbet to accompany Watermelon and Feta Salad (page 47), but it's also refreshing on hot summer days with just a slice of feta.

• **MAKES ABOUT 2 CUPS (500 ML)**

12 ounces (350 g) seedless watermelon flesh (no rind), cubed
¾ cup (150 g) sugar
¼ cup (60 ml) water

1. In a food processor, puree the watermelon until very smooth. Strain the puree through a fine sieve into a medium glass measuring cup, pressing on the solids; discard the solids in the sieve.

2. In a small saucepan, bring the sugar and water to a simmer, stirring to dissolve the sugar. Remove the pan from the heat and let cool completely. Whisk the sugar syrup into the watermelon puree until smooth. Cover and refrigerate until cold.

3. Pour the mixture into an ice cream maker and spin according to the manufacturer's instructions. Transfer to an airtight container, cover, and freeze until firm, at least 2 hours.

NOTE To speed up the chilling in Step 2, pour the sugar syrup into a medium stainless steel bowl, set it in a bowl of half ice, half water, and let cool completely, whisking often.

MAKE AHEAD The sorbet can be frozen for up to 1 month.

WINE Fresh tsipouro, Greek eau-de-vie, or aromatic Muscat from Samos, Limnos, Patras, Rio Patras, or Cephalonia.

Beet Sorbet

While cooking at the French Laundry in Napa Valley, I learned chef Thomas Keller's repertoire of savory sorbets.

• **MAKES ABOUT 2 CUPS (500 ML)**

2 medium beets (about 1 pound/500 g total), scrubbed
4½ cups (1.125 L) water
½ tablespoon Greek honey
½ cup plus 2 tablespoons (125 g) sugar

1. Heat the oven to 375°F (190°C). In a small deep baking pan, combine the beets with 4 cups (1 L) of the water. Cover with foil and bake until a cake tester slides easily into the beets, about 2 hours. Remove the pan from the oven and drain the beets, reserving ½ cup (125 ml) of the cooking liquid. Let the beets cool slightly, then peel them. Cut the beets into 1-inch (2.5 cm) pieces. In a blender, puree the beets with the honey and reserved cooking liquid until smooth.

2. In a small saucepan, bring the sugar and remaining ½ cup (125 ml) of water to a simmer, stirring to dissolve the sugar. Stir in the beet puree. Remove the pan from the heat and let cool. Cover and refrigerate until cold.

3. Pour the mixture into an ice cream maker and spin according to the manufacturer's instructions. Transfer to an airtight container, cover, and freeze until firm, at least 2 hours.

WINE FRESH tsipouro, Greek eau-de-vie, or aromatic Muscat from Samos, Limnos, Patras, Rio Patras, or Cephalonia.

BASICS

Garlic Puree

Instead of peeling and chopping garlic cloves as I go, I prepare massive batches of this raw puree. The addition of olive oil and salt makes it slightly less pungent for adding to spreads (when there's no further cooking) and helps it keep in the refrigerator.

- **MAKES ABOUT 1 CUP (250 G)**

2 heads of garlic (4 ounces/125 g total), cloves peeled
½ cup (125 ml) extra virgin olive oil
½ teaspoon kosher salt

In a food processor or blender, puree the garlic with the oil and salt until fairly smooth. Scrape the puree into a 1-cup (250 ml) jar with a lid and seal.

NOTE: This foundation recipe makes enough for several recipes and can easily be scaled up or down.

MAKE AHEAD: The Garlic Puree can be refrigerated for up to 1 week.

Garlic Confit

Cloves of garlic turn pillowy and sweet when cooked slowly in olive oil without browning. This building-block confit makes enough for several recipes and can easily be scaled up or down.

- **MAKES ABOUT 1 CUP (250 G)**

2 heads of garlic (4 ounces/125 g total), cloves peeled and root ends trimmed
½ cup (125 ml) extra virgin olive oil
3 thyme sprigs
3 oregano sprigs
½ teaspoon kosher salt

In a small saucepan, combine the garlic with the oil, thyme, oregano, and salt and cook at 140°F (60°C) until a cake tester slides easily into a clove, about 30 minutes. Remove from the heat and let cool. Transfer the garlic and oil to a 1-cup (250 ml) jar with a lid and seal.

VARIATION
Add ¼ teaspoon of crushed red pepper to give the garlic, and especially the olive oil, a spicy kick.

MAKE AHEAD The Garlic Confit can be refrigerated for up to 2 weeks.

SERVE WITH The mellow garlic cloves are especially good stirred into soups, pastas, vegetables, and salads— particularly recipes with eggplant, mushrooms, and peppers. The garlic-flavored oil is excellent drizzled on fish, chicken, lamb, or beef right before serving.

Greek Tomato Sauce

It's the dried oregano that defines this foundational tomato sauce as Hellenic. The recipe can easily be scaled up or down. • **MAKES ABOUT 3 CUPS (750 ML)**

2 tablespoons canola oil

1 small onion, halved and thinly sliced

4 garlic cloves, chopped

2 pounds (1 kg) plum tomatoes, chopped

1 bay leaf

¼ cup (60 ml) extra virgin olive oil

1 teaspoon dried oregano

Kosher salt and freshly ground white pepper

1. In a large saucepan, heat the canola oil until shimmering. Add the onion and cook over medium-high heat, stirring occasionally, until lightly browned, 5 to 8 minutes. Add the garlic and cook, stirring, until fragrant, about 30 seconds. Add the tomatoes and bay leaf and bring to a simmer, then cook over medium heat, stirring occasionally, until the sauce thickens, 20 to 30 minutes. Discard the bay leaf.

2. Pass the sauce through a food mill into a medium bowl. Stir in the olive oil and oregano. Season with salt and pepper. Scrape the tomato sauce into a jar with a lid and seal.

NOTE I pass the tomatoes through a food mill in Step 2 to remove the skins for a super-silky sauce. If you don't mind a coarser sauce, you can puree the sauce directly in the pan using an immersion blender.

VARIATION

Dried oregano is the Greek go-to herb for basic tomato sauce, but ½ teaspoon each of chopped thyme and rosemary could be subbed in.

MAKE AHEAD The tomato sauce can be refrigerated for up to 3 days.

Tomato Compote

This sauce right out of chef Auguste Escoffier's classic repertoire shows my French training. Peeled, seeded, and chopped tomatoes are simmered until the juices evaporate, then minced shallots that have been softened in thyme-flavored olive oil are folded in. The result is fresher and chunkier than Greek Tomato Sauce (page 220).

• **MAKES ABOUT 3½ CUPS (875 ML)**

3¼ pounds (1.75 kg) ripe red tomatoes

¼ cup (60 ml) plus 2 tablespoons extra virgin olive oil

6 shallots (4 ounces/125 g total), finely chopped

3 thyme sprigs

Kosher salt and freshly ground white pepper

1. Bring a large saucepan of water to a boil. Prepare a large bowl of half ice, half water. Core the tomatoes and cut a shallow X in the bottom of each. Working in batches, blanch the tomatoes in the boiling water until the skin begins to peel, about 5 seconds. Using a slotted spoon, transfer the tomatoes as they're done to the ice bath to stop the cooking, about 1 minute; drain. Peel the tomatoes, halve them horizontally, and squeeze out the seeds.

2. In a food processor, pulse the tomatoes to a coarse puree. In a medium saucepan, cook the tomato puree over medium heat, stirring occasionally, until the water mostly evaporates, 30 to 40 minutes.

3. Meanwhile, in a small saucepan, warm 2 tablespoons of the oil. Add the shallots and thyme and cook over medium-low heat, stirring occasionally, until the shallots are softened but not browned, about 5 minutes. Remove and discard the thyme. Stir the shallots and remaining ¼ cup (60 ml) of oil into the tomatoes. Season with salt and pepper. Scrape the compote into a 4-cup (1 L) jar with a lid and seal.

VARIATION

I often add 1 cinnamon stick and 1 teaspoon of ground cumin to the tomato puree in Step 2 for a warmly spicy flavor. Remove and discard the cinnamon before adding the shallots.

MAKE AHEAD The compote can be refrigerated for up to 5 days.

Béchamel Sauce

Thick, decadently rich béchamel is the standard topper for moussaka and the layered baked pasta pastichio. Since I lighten traditional Greek dishes, my sauce uses far less flour and gains airiness from whipped egg whites folded in at the end. I also stir in cheese for extra flavor. • **MAKES 10 CUPS (2.5 L)**

3 sticks (400 g) unsalted butter, sliced

2½ cups (300 g) all-purpose flour

6 cups (1.5 L) whole milk

3½ ounces (100 g) graviera cheese (see page 163) or Pecorino Romano cheese, shredded

Kosher salt and freshly ground white pepper

Freshly grated nutmeg, for seasoning

5 large egg whites (150 g total)

1. In a large saucepan, melt the butter. Add the flour and cook over low heat, stirring often with a wooden spoon, until the flour is cooked but still white, about 30 minutes. Gradually pour in the milk, stirring until smooth after each addition, and cook over medium heat until the sauce is as thick as a puree, about 20 minutes total. Add the cheese, season with salt, pepper, and nutmeg, and stir until smooth. Remove the pan from the heat and let cool completely, stirring occasionally to prevent a skin from forming.

2. In a medium bowl, whip the egg whites until they hold a stiff peak, then fold them into the béchamel.

NOTES Once the egg whites have been folded into the béchamel, use the sauce within 1 hour.

To make 1 cup (250 ml) of sauce, melt 2 tablespoons (30 g) of unsalted butter. Add ¼ cup (30 g) of all-purpose flour and cook over low heat, stirring often, for 10 minutes. Gradually pour in 1 cup (250 ml) of whole milk and cook over medium heat, stirring often, for 5 minutes. Stir in 2 tablespoons (15 g) of grated cheese. Fold in 1 large whipped egg white.

MAKE AHEAD The sauce can be prepared through Step 1 and refrigerated for up to 2 days. Let it come to room temperature before continuing.

Homemade Greek Yogurt

Yogurt is so important in a Greek household that my father tells stories of his mother's fierce rivalry with her Savannah, Georgia, friends. The contest begins with the starter—preferably homemade yogurt saved from an earlier batch. In my family, this starter is as sacred as the sourdough starter is for an artisan baker. Imagine my grandmother Theone's frustration when my dad carelessly ate the last bite of yogurt! My yia yia was forced to go to one of her competitors for a replacement starter, but today you can use a high-quality organic yogurt from the store. • **MAKES ABOUT 4 CUPS (1 L)**

4 cups (1 L) organic whole milk

4 cups (1 L) organic half-and-half

½ cup (125 ml) organic Greek yogurt, preferably homemade

1. In a large saucepan, bring the milk and half-and-half to a boil over medium heat, stirring occasionally. Remove the pan from the heat and let cool to 100°F (40°C). Add the yogurt and whisk until smooth. Strain the mixture through a fine sieve into a large glass bowl; discard the solids in the sieve. Cover with plastic wrap and let stand in a warm place for 2 days.

2. Transfer the bowl to the refrigerator and chill until cold, about 3 hours. Line a colander with 2 layers of cheesecloth and set over a large bowl. Pour in the yogurt. Cover the colander and transfer it with the bowl to the refrigerator; let the yogurt drain until thick, about 12 hours. Discard the whey that drains or reserve it for another use.

NOTES In a hot Southern kitchen, it takes about 2 days for the yogurt mixture to incubate. It may take longer in a cool Northern kitchen, so plan accordingly.

My yia yia always covered her yogurt mixture with a blanket while it was incubating to keep it warm.

Once the yogurt has set in the refrigerator, I let it thicken by hanging it in cheesecloth on a hook over a bowl.

For looser yogurt, drain it for less than 12 hours.

This recipe can be doubled or tripled.

VARIATIONS

The options for flavoring yogurt are endless. I vary it with coriander (page 104), cumin (pages 36–37), preserved lemon (pages 101–102), and saffron (page 44).

MAKE AHEAD Homemade yogurt can be refrigerated for up to 1 week.

SERVE WITH Yogurt is great with Greek honey or layered in a parfait glass with granola and fresh fruit or spoon sweets, such as Candied Figs (page 196), Candied Quince (page 199), or Candied Kumquats (page 195).

Homemade Pita Bread

I'll never forget coming home from school to the sound of dough being pounded by my grandmother Athanasia. The great thing about this version is that all the ingredients—including the yeast—go into one bowl at the same time for mixing. I pinch the raised dough into pieces and roll them into rounds, then brush them with oil and pop them on a hot grill to cook. The result: slightly charred, yeasty pita. • **MAKES ABOUT 1 DOZEN PITA BREADS**

5½ cups (735 g) bread flour, plus more for dusting

Three ¼-ounce packets (20 g total) active dry yeast

1 tablespoon (20 g) Greek honey

1 tablespoon (15 g) kosher salt, plus more for sprinkling

1⅓ cups (330 ml) room temperature water

½ cup (125 ml) room temperature whole milk

¼ cup (60 ml) extra virgin olive oil, plus more for brushing

1. In a stand mixer fitted with the dough hook, combine all the ingredients. Beat at low speed, scraping down the side of the bowl occasionally, until a soft, smooth dough forms, 6 to 7 minutes.

2. Shape the dough into a ball. Brush the same bowl with oil. Return the dough to the bowl and turn it in the oil to coat. Cover the bowl with plastic wrap and let the dough rise in a warm place until doubled in size, about 45 minutes.

3. Brush a baking sheet with oil. Gently press down the dough. Pinch it into twelve 3 ½-ounce (100 g) pieces. Using oiled cupped hands, shape the dough pieces into balls and transfer them to the prepared baking sheet. Cover the sheet loosely with plastic wrap and let the dough balls rise in a warm place until doubled in size, about 45 minutes.

4. On a lightly floured work surface, roll 1 ball into a 7- to 8-inch (18 to 20 cm) round, lifting the dough and giving it a quarter turn between each pass. Using a fork, prick the pita all over to prevent a pocket from forming. Transfer the pita to a floured baking sheet and cover with wax paper. Repeat with the remaining dough balls, making two stacks.

5. Have ready a clean kitchen towel. Heat a grill or a grill pan. Working in batches, lightly brush the tops of the pitas with oil and sprinkle with salt. Grill the pitas oiled side down over medium to medium-high heat until charred on the bottoms, 45 seconds to 1 minute. Brush the tops with oil and sprinkle with salt. Turn over the pitas and grill until cooked through, 45 seconds to 1 minute. Transfer to the towel as they're done and wrap. Serve warm or at room temperature.

NOTES In a hot Southern kitchen, it takes about 45 minutes for the dough to double in bulk. It may take longer in a cool Northern kitchen, so plan accordingly.

To make rolling out the dough balls super easy (no flour, no turning, no sticking), roll each one between 2 silicone mats or sheets of parchment paper.

It doesn't really matter whether the pitas are perfectly round after they're rolled out, but you can reshape them gently with your hands before grilling.

VARIATION

It doesn't always work, but if you want to try making pita bread with a pocket, do not prick holes in the dough. If you succeed, try stuffing the pitas with Classic Greek Salad (page 49) for a great vegetarian sandwich.

MAKE AHEAD In Step 2, the dough can be refrigerated overnight to double in size before shaping it and giving it a second rise. The grilled pitas can be stored in a resealable plastic bag and refrigerated for up to 3 days. Brush them with oil and reheat on the grill or in a 325°F (165°C) before serving.

SERVE WITH Bendy pita makes an ideal scoop for spreads (see pages 20–27) or an edible plate for Classic Greek Salad (page 49) or grain salads like Lemony Quinoa Salad (page 35).

GREEK WINE GUIDE

BY SOFIA PERPERA

I had big plans for North America's wine-drinking future. As a Greek enologist recently married to an American and living in Atlanta, Georgia, I wanted to bring my country's stellar wines to my new home. But my first year promoting them was frustrating. In 2002, the sum total of Greek wine presence seemed to appear in the "other" category, if at all. Local importers weren't aware that in the past few decades radical quality improvements had completely transformed this ancient wine culture. Greece's vast number of unfamiliar native grapes and their tongue-twisting names didn't help my crusade. Greek wine got no respect.

To spread the word of our superb-but-unsung wines, I took a step back. In 2003, I returned to Greece and, with some of the pivotal producers, launched the campaign All About Greek Wine, which morphed three years later into the Wines of Greece. We cracked the door open, and Greek wines are finally starting to get the critical acclaim they deserve. Today Greece is one of the fastest-growing viticultural regions worldwide. From 2010 to 2016, exports jumped by 65 percent in value, and now you can find these exciting bottles in almost any good wine store and on carefully curated wine lists—especially at non-Greek restaurants.

To complement my pairing suggestions, which accompany each of Pano's recipes, here's a starter guide to one of the world's great wine regions. I include Greece's main and up-and-coming indigenous grapes, from Assyrtiko to Xinomavro. Bonus: Pano and I each contributed a personal list of recommended wineries that have adequate distribution in the United States. Mine is organized by region, and Pano's favorites are arranged by grape. I hope you'll feel empowered to pour these outstanding wines at your own table.

Remaking an Ancient Wine Culture

Greece's winemaking history stretches back more than 4,000 years. In fact, the world's oldest known winepress, which dates from about 1600 BC, was discovered on the island of Crete. Classical Greeks also created the first culture of wine. More than an easygoing thirst quencher, wine was worshipped, alongside its god, Dionysus. Artisans fabricated elaborate ceremonial cups and gloriously illustrated vessels for drinking the divine elixir at intellectual symposiums and dinner parties.

The Greeks quickly realized wine's commercial and propaganda potential, trading it throughout the ancient world and using it to spread their civilization. They also understood the importance of terroir—the distinctive character of the land on which grapes are grown—and special cuvées were shipped in earthenware amphoras inscribed with the producer's name, essentially an appellation system existing millenniums before France's Appellation d'Origine Contrôlée (AOC), or "controlled region of origin." Fraudsters faced stiff penalties.

Paradoxically, this ancient wine region has come of age only in the last 35 years. At the turn of the 20th century, production had been interrupted by the phylloxera devastation. Decades of stagnation followed—the result of world wars; forced population exchanges between Greece and Turkey; emigration to Europe, the United States, and beyond; and a military dictatorship.

There things stood until 1981, when Greece joined the European Union and attracted massive investment. Wineries were finally rebuilt using the most modern technology available. And a new generation of energetic winemakers traveled abroad to study at the best schools, notably in France, Italy, and the United States. When they returned home, they applied up-to-date farming and winemaking practices to Greece's indigenous grapes, along with international varieties, spurring an industry renaissance.

Next-Wave Winemaking

In this new era, young producers are injecting the business with fresh optimism and ideas. I'm thrilled to watch them dive deeper into the possibilities of our four major grapes, Assyrtiko, Moschofilero, Agiorgitiko, and Xinomavro. They're excited by more native varieties, too, such as Malagousia and Roditis, and regional grapes like Vidiano from Crete and Robola from Cephalonia. These pioneers are also crafting new styles of wines from lesser-known grapes. With Savatiano, for example, mostly familiar as the base grape in traditional retsina, they're making terroir-driven wines with the capacity to evolve and improve. And their experiments are upending the image of Mavrodaphne as a fortified, sweet wine by producing distinctive, dry reds with great aging potential.

Even cheap, pine-flavored retsina is being reconsidered in biodynamic, natural, orange, and late-release forms. And while Greece is not yet known for its sparkling wines, multiple projects—including a *pét-nat* (from the French *pétillant-naturel*) retsina—are already in the works all over Greece. Another emerging trend is producing wines from a single vineyard with specific, individual, and occasionally quirky characteristics, instead of blending grapes from different plots or areas.

Since the world is just beginning to discover and appreciate the quality of our wines, they're still excellent values, especially in the medium-to-upper price ranges. They outperform their modest prices and can easily compete with much more expensive wines.

As producers pay tighter attention to soils, grapes, and techniques, with some boundary pushers working outside time-honored styles,

wine drinkers can expect quality-minded, small-production wines that express the nuances of our unique terroir and prized indigenous grapes, as well as the international varieties grown here. One thing will not change: the food friendliness of these wines. Wine has always been an integral part of our gastronomy, and these are serious wines for the table. No self-respecting Greek would be caught drinking any wine without food.

The Greek Vineyard

Our landscape combines just the right elements for crafting world-class wines, including favorable soil, terrain, and weather conditions. With consistent Mediterranean sunshine, mild winters, dry summers, and cool evenings, quality doesn't fluctuate here from year to year, unlike many other wine-growing regions. The soils vary from sandy and rock to clay and limestone, with most everything else in between—including volcanic soils.

INDIGENOUS VARIETIES

Hundreds of native grape varieties (300 plus) give Greece's vineyards their fantastic diversity. This unique collection frequently earns our wine its own category on lists at wine-centric restaurants, instead of being lumped into that "other" category with assorted, under-the-radar bottles.

The citrusy whites display an array of floral and fruity aromas with crisp, clean, mineral-driven flavors. And since they have wonderful acidity and are not overly oaky (new oak would obscure the purity of the fruit), they pair well with all kinds of cuisines.

Our native red varieties have a fruity and earthy nose, combined with fresh acidity, and lend themselves to many different wine styles, ranging from fresh, pleasing reds and rosés to extraordinarily complex, full-bodied wines with long-aging potential.

In the dessert-wine category, Greece's offerings rival the best from around the world.

White Grapes

Assyrtiko is one of Europe's finest "noble" white grapes. Originating on the breathtaking island of Santorini, where it's the premier variety, it's now planted throughout Greece. But it is in Santorini's unique volcanic ecosystem that this grape is truly distinctive, producing dry, full-bodied, mineral-rich whites with refreshing acidity and a delicate citrusy nose. Outside of Santorini, the wines are more aromatic and less flinty. Wherever they're made, they drink beautifully when fresh or oak-aged and can be enjoyed young or cellared for years. (Combining high levels of both alcohol and acidity, Assyrtiko is one of the few white Mediterranean varieties with serious aging potential.) When produced in Santorini, in blends with other grapes such as Aidani and Athiri, Assyrtiko also makes excellent dessert wines called Vinsantos. At the table, Assyrtiko pairs beautifully with a surprising range of food. It matches all kinds of seafood, yet its strong character also makes it a good partner for poultry and even red meats, such as lamb. Fried vegetables or seafood is a favorite go-with, too, because Assyrtiko's tanginess cuts against the delicious fat.

In the 1970s, **Malagousia** was on the verge of extinction. Fortunately, it was rediscovered and planted at Domaine Porto Carras under the supervision of Stavroula Kourakou, where enologist Evangelos Gerovassiliou demonstrated its enormous potential. Ever since, it's been planted throughout Greece and is now one of the country's most promising white grapes. Malagousia yields medium-bodied, dry whites with expressive peach and apricot aromas, and bell pepper and floral notes. It can age five years or more and also makes excellent dessert wines. When dry, it's a wonderful match for salads, seafood, and light chicken dishes.

Moschofilero is a highly aromatic grayish (light-pink to dark-purple) variety. Its finest wines come from the high-altitude Mantinia plateau in the Peloponnese. The grape produces mostly still dry whites, as well as some serious bubbly; both styles have a wild floral intensity with citrus notes and fresh acidity. Some wineries are also using the grape to make rosés. White, sparkling, or rosé, the wines complement a wide array of cuisines, in particular spicy Middle Eastern and Asian dishes, sushi, and seafood; by itself, it's the perfect aperitif.

Up-and-Coming White Grapes

Debina hails from the northwestern Epirus region, where it's still grown, mainly around the capital Ioannina, in the PDO (Protected Designation of Origin) Zitsa area. Debina produces crisp dry wines, as well as very good sparkling and semi-sparkling wines. The dry whites are steely with green apple and citrus flavors, and hints of flowers. The sparkling and semi-sparkling Zitsa wines, which can be sweet, semisweet, or brut, are showing amazing potential.

Kydonitsa, a very promising grape from Lakonia, in the southern part of the Peloponnese, was a component of sweet medieval Malvasia wines. It produces food-friendly whites with medium acidity, pleasant minerality, and a characteristic aroma of quince, which explains its name, since Kydoni is "quince" in Greek.

Robola, which originated on Cephalonia in the Ionian Islands, today produces PDO Robola of Cephalonia wines. A demanding grape, Robola makes exceptional wines when cultivated with low yields in mountainous vineyards—for instance, the limestone-rich slopes of Mount Aenos. These terroir-driven wines have a citrusy nose with vivid minerality, bright acidity, and good structure.

Widely planted **Roditis** is especially popular in Attica, Macedonia, Thessaly, and the Peloponnese, where it's grown to make PDO Patras wines. It's at its best when cultivated with low yields in mountainous zones, producing elegant, light white wines with citrus flavors and a long finish.

WINES OF GREECE

WINE MAP
PROTECTED DESIGNATIONS OF ORIGIN

THRACE
MACEDONIA
Florina — Edessa — Serres — Drama — Xanthi — Komotini
Amynteo — Naoussa — Kavala — Alexandroupoli
Kastoria — Veria — Thessaloniki
Kozani — Katerini — Polygyros — Mt Athos
Grevena — Goumenissa
Kerkyra — Zitsa — Meteora — Rapsani — Larissa
Ioannina — Trikala — THESSALY
EPIRUS — Karditsa — Volos — Nea Anchialos
IONIAN ISLANDS — Mesenikolas — Mt Meliton
Arta — Mytilini
Preveza — Karpenisi — Lamia
Mesolongi — Amfissa — Delfi
STEREA ELLADA — Thebes — AEGEAN SEA — Chios
Patra — Korinthos
Zakynthos — Nemea — ATTICA — Athina
Pyrgos — Mantinia — Nafplio — Epidavros
Cephalonia — Tripoli — Samos
PELOPONNESE — Paros
Kalamata — Sparti — CYCLADES
Monemvassia — Santorini — DODECANESE — Rhodes
Chania — Rethymno — Heraklion — Archanes — Agios Nikolaos — Sitia
CRETE — Dafnes — Peza

PDO ZITSA
PDO MAVRODAPHNE OF CEPHALONIA
PDO ROBOLA OF CEPHALONIA
PDO MUSCAT OF CEPHALONIA
PDO MAVRODAPHNE OF PATRA
PDO MUSCAT OF PATRA
PDO MUSCAT OF RIO PATRA
PDO PATRA
PDO MANTINIA
PDO NEMEA
PDO MONEMVASIA - MALVASIA

PDO GOUMENISSA
PDO NAOUSSA
PDO AMYNTEO
PDO SLOPES OF MELITON
PDO LIMNOS
PDO MUSCAT OF LIMNOS
PDO RAPSANI
PDO MESENIKOLA
PDO ANCHIALOS

PDO SAMOS
PDO PAROS
PDO MALVASIA PAROS
PDO SANTORINI
PDO VINSANTO
PDO RHODES
PDO MUSCAT OF RHODES

PDO MALVASIA - CANDIA
PDO CANDIA
PDO DAPHNES
PDO ARCHANES
PDO PEZA
PDO SITIA
PDO MALVASIA SITIA

PROTECTED DESIGNATIONS OF ORIGIN

MACEDONIA
- PDO GOUMENISSA **R**
- PDO NAOUSSA **R**
- PDO AMYNTEO **R**
- PDO SLOPES OF MELITON **R, W**

AEGEAN ISLANDS
- PDO SAMOS **W**
- PDO PAROS **R, W**
- PDO MALVASIA PAROS **W**
- PDO SANTORINI **W**
- PDO SANTORINI VINSANTO **W**
- PDO RHODES **R, W**
- PDO MUSCAT OF RHODES **W**
- PDO LIMNOS **R, W**
- PDO MUSCAT OF LIMNOS **W**

PELOPONNESE
- PDO MAVRODAPHNE OF PATRA **R**
- PDO MUSCAT OF PATRA **W**
- PDO MUSCAT OF RIO PATRA **W**
- PDO PATRA **W**
- PDO MANTINIA **W**
- PDO NEMEA **R**
- PDO MONEMVASIA - MALVASIA **W**

IONIAN ISLANDS
- PDO MAVRODAPHNE OF CEPHALONIA **R**
- PDO ROBOLA OF CEPHALONIA **W**
- PDO MUSCAT OF CEPHALONIA **W**

EPIRUS
- PDO ZITSA **W**

THESSALY
- PDO RAPSANI **R**
- PDO MESENIKOLA **R**
- PDO ANCHIALOS **W**

CRETE
- PDO MALVASIA - CANDIA **W**
- PDO CANDIA **R, W**
- PDO DAPHNES **R**
- PDO ARCHANES **R**
- PDO PEZA **R, W**
- PDO SITIA **R, W**
- PDO MALVASIA SITIA **W**

R: RED   **W**: WHITE

PDO Wines: "PDO products" bear a "Protected Designation of Origin" indication.
This wine category comprises Greek wines bearing a Designation of Origin (VQPRD),
in other words, all AOQS and AOC wines.

 WINES OF GREECE

ENTERPRISE GREECE
INVEST & TRADE

EDOAO
NATIONAL INTER-PROFESSIONAL
ORGANIZATION OF VINE AND WINE

One of the world's most underrated vins de terroir, **Savatiano** is the number one grape of Attica, the area surrounding Athens. Despite its chief use as the base grape in retsina, in Attica's dry summers, Savatiano also yields graceful, well-balanced, and food-driven whites with the aromas of citrus and flowers and amazing aging potential.

Vidiano, the leading white grape on Crete, makes dry, medium- to full-bodied wines with vivid acidity and aromas of peach, apricot, and mountain herbs. It's available both as a fresh single-varietal wine aged in stainless steel tanks and in barrel. Vidiano also blends well with other grapes, such as Vilana, and shows very interesting potential to evolve.

White Muscat is grown in many areas around Greece, but the most noteworthy vineyards are on the Aegean islands of Samos and Rhodes, in the region surrounding Patras in the northwestern Peloponnese, and on the Ionian island of Cephalonia. Greece's sweet Muscats were once the obsession of antiquity's wine world and, today, the highly aromatic grape yields some of the best value-for-money dessert wines anywhere. They are intensely floral with citrus flavors and, when aged in oak, develop a textured bouquet of dried fruits, honey, and nuts. The dry versions are also aromatic, but light and delicate, with moderate acidity.

Red Grapes

The ancient **Agiorgitiko** variety is found primarily in Nemea, in the northeastern Peloponnese. It yields plush wines that stand out for their deep red color and remarkable complexity. The grape's soft tannins, together with its balanced acidity, can create many different styles: richly layered reds for the cellar as well as deliciously aromatic dry rosés and light, easy-drinking reds redolent of fresh red fruit. Agiorgitiko's exceptionally food-friendly wines go with a range of cuisines.

Xinomavro is one of Greece's most noble grapes. The backbone of Macedonia's wines, it's grown in four different appellations, including the PDO single-appellation regions of Naoussa

and Amynteo, and in Rapsani and Goumenissa, where it's blended. This grape makes some of the world's most layered terroir-driven wines with superb aging potential. They vary from earthy and spicy to more fruit forward, offering a bouquet of olives, dried tomatoes, and sweet spice together with fresh red fruits, such as gooseberry and raspberry. Bolstered by firm tannins, good structure, and vivid acidity, they pair best with lamb, game, aged rich yellow cheeses, and charcuterie.

Up-and-Coming Red Grapes

Kotsifali is one of Crete's most popular red grapes. It's planted largely around Heraklion and is a part of the Peza and Archanes appellations, where it's blended with Mandilaria, another local red. Kotsifali yields food-friendly, medium-bodied wines with a lovely profile of spice, dried red fruit, and even flowers. With good acidity and medium tannins, it's an ideal partner for many different Mediterranean dishes, including casseroles, grilled lamb, sausages, and other meat dishes.

Liatiko, or **Iouliatico,** was named for the month of July (*Ioulios* in Greek), when it ripens. Another Crete native, the grape is cultivated around Heraklion, where it makes a single-variety wine in the PDO region of Daphnes, and is the predominant variety in the PDO region of Sitia. Liatiko is primarily used to make sweet wines but is now showing much promise in dry reds. Both are pale with ample acidity and tannins, and they deliver an added depth of red fruit and sweet spice.

An ancient variety mentioned by Homer, **Limnio** is moderate in color and alcohol with elegant tannins and an herb-spice-red fruit profile of uncommon depth. Limnos is its home, but the grape is extensively planted in northern Greece, particularly in the Halkidiki region, where it's a part of the PDO Slopes of Mount Meliton and Thrace. It makes interesting blends with international grapes such as Cabernet Sauvignon.

Limniona is Greece's most up-and-coming red grape. It hails from Thessaly, but recently winemakers in multiple regions have been cultivating it. The variety produces crisp, deep purple—red wines with rather high alcohol and an aromatic blend of botanics and ripe red fruit. Its bottlings are ready to be drunk fresh or, with its great affinity for oak, after several years of aging.

The Aegean islands are home to **Mandilaria,** also one of the principal red grapes in Rhodes and in Crete, where it's known as Mandilari. The variety makes intensely dark reds with strong tannins and medium acidity that are redolent of raisins, fresh red fruit, and leather with botanical notes. The grape's intense color has earned it the alternate name, **Vaftra,** meaning "painter," since it's often used to boost the color of paler varieties. In Crete it's a part of the appellations Peza and Archanes; in Paros it's blended with the white Monemvasia grape to make the PDO Paros; and in Rhodes it's the sole grape used for the PDO Rhodes.

Dense, dark **Mavrodaphne,** meaning "black laurel," is chiefly found in the northwestern Peloponnese regions of Achaia and Ilia as well as the Ionian island of Cephalonia. It's blended with the Korinthiaki grape to create the delicious fortified dessert wines Mavrodaphne of Patras and Mavrodaphne of Cephalonia—Greece's answers to Port. In the last few years, wineries have begun producing some delicious dry reds from Mavrodaphne, too. Sweet or dry, it displays high levels of alcohol and medium acidity with aromas of dried fruit, sweet spice, and flowers.

One of Greece's rising-star red grapes, "black crunchy" Mavrotragano—its literal meaning—comes from Santorini. This crisp, deep red, richly bodied varietal has great structure with ripe red fruit-sweet spice-botanical aromas. It ages well for several years.

Spirits

If you're at a Greek table laden with plates of olives, feta cheese, stuffed grape leaves, and silky dips, there's probably also an open bottle of licorice-y ouzo or tsipouro. Unlike some other brandies, such as grappa and Armagnac, which are after-dinner drinks, ouzo and tsipouro are enjoyed either as an aperitif or while munching on food, usually vibrant meze. Both are clear and colorless, although ouzo becomes cloudy once ice or water is added to dilute its strength. What makes them different? It's the origin of the alcohol that's distilled. Tsipouro is made from grape skins, while ouzo is produced from molasses (mainly), grains, or, in rare cases, grapes.

For a spirit to be called **ouzo,** it must be produced in Greece by distilling pure alcohol (96 percent) from agricultural products. Ouzo is made from a double-distillation process—like Cognac—but during the second distillation, various aromatics are added according to the producer's recipe. The flavoring possibilities include anise, fennel seeds, coriander, mastic of Chios, cardamom, ginger, cinnamon, clove, and orange or lemon peel. Ouzo can be either a pure alcohol, in which case the label specifies 100 percent ouzo, or simple ouzo, which contains at least 20 percent alcohol, plus a blend of alcohol, water, and flavorings. By law, ouzo must have an alcoholic strength of at least 37.5 percent.

Tsipouro is an eau-de-vie made by distilling grape skins laced or not with anise seeds. It's crafted throughout Greece, but noteworthy zones of production are Thessaly, Epirus, Macedonia, and Crete, where it's known as tsikoudia or raki. After grapes are pressed for wine, a small part of the grape must, including the grape skins and seeds, is left to ferment. During fermentation, the sugars turn into alcohol, which is distilled to produce tsipouro. This spirit normally has an alcoholic strength of between 38 and 45 percent.

SOFIA'S RECOMMENDED WINERIES BY REGION

THRACE
Kikones Estate
Tsantali-Maronia SA
Vourvoukeli Estate

MACEDONIA

Eastern Macedonia
Drama
Domaine Costa Lazaridi
Nico Lazaridi
Oinogenesis
Pavlidis Estate
Wine Art

Kavala
Domaine Biblia Chora

Central Macedonia
Goumenissa
Aidarinis Estate
Chatzivaritis Estate
Tatsis Estate

Halkidiki
Domaine Porto Carras
Tsantali-Agios Pavlos
Tsantali-Mount Athos

Naoussa
Argatia Winery
Boutari
Dalamaras Winery
Diamantakos Estate
Fountis Estate
Karydas Estate
Kir Yianni Estate
Kokkinos Estate
Thymiopoulos
   Vineyards
Tsantali

Pella
Ligas Estate

Thessaloniki
Domaine Gerovassiliou
Kechris Winery

Western Macedonia
Amynteo
Alpha Estate
Karanikas Estate
Kir-Yianni Estate

Kozani
Dio Filoi Estate
Voyatzis Estate

THESSALY
Dougos Winery
Katsaros Estate
Tsantali-Rapsani
   Vineyards
Tsililis-Theopetra Estate
Zafeirakis Estate

EPIRUS
Glinavos Estate
Katogi-Strofilia
Zoinos Winery

STEREA ELLADA-EVIA

Attica
Boutari-Roxani Matsa
   Estate
Greek Wine Cellars
Harlaftis Winery
Mylonas Winery
Papagiannakos Winery
Strofilia Winery
Vassiliou Estate

Evia
Avantis Estate
Lykos Winery

Veotia
Domaine Hatzimichali
Sokos Wines

PELOPONNESE

Achaia
Achaia Clauss
Achaion Estate
Antonopoulos
   Vineyards
Cavino
Oenoforos Winery
Parparoussis Winery
Rouvalis
Tetramythos

Ilia
Brintziki Estate
Mercouri Estate
Sant'Or Wines

Laconia
Monemvasia Winery

Mantinia
Bosinakis Winery
Boutari
Domaine Spiropoulos
Domaine Tselepos
Nassiakos Winery
Troupis Winery

Nemea
Bairaktaris Wines
Boutari
Driopi Estate
Domaine Skouras
Domaine Spiropoulos
Gaia Wines
Gioulis Estate
Greek Wine Cellars
Harlaftis Winery
Lantides Estate
Palivou Estate
Papaioannou Estate
Semeli Wines
Strofilia Winery
Vassiliou-Nemeion
   Estate

IONIAN ISLANDS

Cephalonia
Gentilini Wines
Foivos Wines
Robola Cooperative
Sclavos Wines

CRETE

Chania
Karavitakis Wines
Manoussakis Winery

Heraklion
Alexakis Winery
Boutari-Scalani Estate
Douloufakis Winery
Economou Winery
Lyrarakis Wines
Mediterra Wines
Rhous Winery
Silva Daskalaki

AEGEAN ISLANDS

Paros
Moraitis Winery

Samos
Union of Vinicultural
   Cooperatives of
   Samos

Santorini
Artemis Karamolegos
   Winery
Boutari
Canava-
   Chryssou-Tselepos
Canava Roussos
Domaine Sigalas
Estate Argyros
Gaia Wines
Gavalas Estate
Hatzidakis Winery
Koutsoyannopoulos
   Winery
Santo Wines
Vasaltis Winery
Venetsanos Winery

PANO'S RECOMMENDED WINERIES BY GRAPE

WHITE

Assyrtiko
Alpha Estate
Domaine Biblia Chora
Domaine Sigalas
Estate Argyros
Gaia Wines
Lyrarakis Wines
Pavlidis Estate

Debina
Domaine Glinavos

Malagousia
Alpha Estate
Domaine Gerovassiliou
Domaine Porto Carras
Papagiannakos Winery
Thymiopoulos Vineyards

Moschofilero
Boutari
Domaine Skouras
Domaine Spiropoulos
Domaine Tselepos
Semeli Wines

Robola
Gentilini Wines
Robola Cooperative
Sclavos Wines

Roditis
Oenoforos
Papantonis Winery
Vassiliou Estate

Savatiano
Mylonas Winery
Papagiannakos Winery
Vassiliou Estate

Vidiano
Douloufakis Winery
Lyrarakis Wines
Karavitakis Wines
Manoussakis Winery
Rhous Winery

RED

Agiorgitiko
Domaine Skouras
Driopi Estate
Mitravelas Estate
Palivou Estate
Papaioannou Estate

Kotsifali
Alexakis Winery
Karavitakis Wines
Lyrarakis Wines
Manoussakis Winery
Rhous Winery

Kydonitsa
Domaine Biblia Chora
Monemvasia Winery

Liatiko
Douloufakis Winery
Lyrarakis Wines

Limnio
Domaine Gerovassiliou
Domaine Porto Carras

Limniona
Tsilili

Mandilaria
Domaine Sigalas

Mavrodaphne
Achaia Clauss
Gentilini Wines
Mercouri Estate

Mavrotragano
Domaine Gerovassiliou
Domaine Sigalas
Estate Argyros

Xinomavro
Alpha Estate
Dalamaras Winery
Katsaros Estate
Kir-Yianni Estate
Thymiopoulos Vineyards

SPIRITS

Ouzo
Babatzim
Barbayianni
Metaxa
Ouzo 12
Plomari

Tsipouro
Idonkio
Katsaros Estate
Mavrakis
Tsilili

INDEX

ACKNOWLEDGMENTS

I want to thank my Yia Yia Athanasia for her passion for cooking and for her ability to teach me the wonderful enjoyment of cooking at an age when most kids would rather be out playing with their friends.

I want to thank my father, Ignatius Pano, and my mother, Georgia, for guiding me as a young man and chef, supporting me on my adventures, and giving me the opportunity to learn what it is to be a successful restaurateur and entrepreneur. You have always been extremely generous and I appreciate all that you have done for me.

I want to thank my brother, Niko, and my sister, Anne, for having my back and for being my biggest fans. I could not be more proud and honored to have such awesome siblings and professionals with whom to work side by side.

I want to thank BLRG chef Piero Premoli for supporting and assisting me throughout the years from opening Kyma, cooking together all over the country, opening six restaurants for the company, putting up with my intensity, and always finding a way to point out the positive in a world that is sometimes not.

I want to thank Kyma chefs Eric Cutillo, Will Smith, and Charideen Spencer for working with me all these years. Your assistance on this book was tremendous and I will never forget the early morning meetings, the recipe writing, and our over-the-top photo shoot.

I want to thank Francesco Tonelli for working with me on this book, for your amazing talent, and for our friendship. The photos in this book are beyond my expectations and, in my opinion, some of your greatest work.

I want to thank Jane Sigal for co-authoring this book with me and for capturing the essence of what we do. Your enthusiasm while testing the recipes and excitement for the flavors are a testament to your passion for cooking and writing.

I want to thank Christo Makrides for putting up with our crazy family and for truly having our best interests in mind. You are a brother to all of us and I am truly grateful for your insight, compassion, and drive.

I want to thank Nicholas Sousounis and Nicholas Brown for all of your hard work and dedication to making Kyma one of the best Greek restaurants in the country and for having the strength to stand up for what we believe makes Kyma great.

I want to thank Frank Kaltsounis and Daniela Ascencio for all the great pastry over the years, and Stratos Lambos for your help and brotherhood.

I want to thank the BLRG family and Kyma staff, past and present, who I have had the pleasure of working with. We share a special place in the Atlanta dining scene as culinary elites who cook first, rest last, and run the best restaurants in town.

I want to thank Jacque Hamilton for the amazing love you have for me and for never letting anything bring me down. Thank you for being there for me and for all of your many blessings.

I want to thank my mentors Eric Ripert, Jean-Georges Vongerichten, and Thomas Keller for the life-lasting lessons and memories of cooking in the best kitchens in the world and for your friendships over the years—I could not be more blessed than to have worked for all three of you.

Last but not least, Sofia Perpera—thank you for being my other greatest fan! Your expertise and knowledge of Greek wines is unsurpassed by any other. Thank you for your wine guidance at Kyma and selections in this book. Guess what? We finally did it! A modern Greek cookbook full of great Greek recipes and wine pairings that explore the amazing foods and wines of Greece! Sagapo Poli!